Teacher Education Policy and Practice in Europe

Teacher Education Policy and Practice in Europe provides a critical overview of the current challenges facing teacher education policy and practice in Europe. Drawing on a wide range of contributions, the book demonstrates that in order for teachers to reassume their role as agents of change, it is crucial to create a vision of a future European teacher and promote active engagement in preparing children to live and act in a multicultural and increasingly changing world.

The book suggests ways in which teachers could be prepared to meet and overcome the struggles they will encounter in the classroom, including recommendations for teacher education, which open up new possibilities for policy, practice, and research. Considering their own experiences as teachers, contributors also cover topics such as teacher education for the 21st century, the profile of the European teacher, citizenship and identity, social inclusion, linguistic and cultural diversity, and comparative education.

Teacher Education Policy and Practice in Europe is essential reading for academics, researchers, and postgraduate students engaged in the study of teacher education, educational policy and educational theory. It should also be of great interest to research-active teacher educators and practising teachers.

Ana Raquel Simões is an Assistant Professor at the Department of Education and Psychology of the University of Aveiro, Portugal.

Mónica Lourenço is a Postdoctoral Research Fellow at the Research Centre 'Didactics and Technology in Education of Trainers' (CIDTFF) of the University of Aveiro, Portugal.

Nilza Costa is a Full Professor in Education at the Department of Education and Psychology of the University of Aveiro, Portugal.

Routledge Research in Teacher Education

The Routledge Research in Teacher Education series presents the latest research on Teacher Education and also provides a forum to discuss the latest practices and challenges in the field.

Community Fieldwork in Teacher Education
Theory and Practice
Heidi L. Hallman and Melanie N. Burdick

Lessons from the Teachers for a New Era Project
Evidence and Accountability in Teacher Education
G. Williamson McDiarmid and Kathryn Caprino

Teacher Education in England
A Critical Interrogation of School-led Training
Tony Brown

Critical Feminism and Critical Education
An Interdisciplinary Approach to Teacher Education
Jennifer Gale de Saxe

Learning to Teach in England and the United States
The Evolution of Policy and Practice
Maria Teresa Tatto, Katharine Burn, Ian Menter, Trevor Mutton and Ian Thompson

Learning from Latino English Language Learners
Critical Teacher Education
Edited by Pablo Ramirez, Christian Faltis, and Ester De Jong

Teaching Towards Freedom
Supporting Voices and Silence in the English Classroom
Geraldine DeLuca

Teacher Education Policy and Practice in Europe
Challenges and Opportunities for the Future
Edited by Ana Raquel Simões, Mónica Lourenço, and Nilza Costa

For more information about this series, please visit: www.routledge.com/Routledge-Research-in-Teacher-Education/book-series/RRTE

Teacher Education Policy and Practice in Europe

Challenges and Opportunities for the Future

Edited by Ana Raquel Simões, Mónica Lourenço, and Nilza Costa

LONDON AND NEW YORK

First published 2018
by Routledge
2 Park Square, Milton Park, Abingdon, Oxon OX14 4RN

and by Routledge
711 Third Avenue, New York, NY 10017

Routledge is an imprint of the Taylor & Francis Group, an informa business

© 2018 selection and editorial matter, Ana Raquel Simões, Mónica Lourenço, Nilza Costa; individual chapters, the contributors

The right of the editor to be identified as the author of the editorial material, and of the authors for their individual chapters, has been asserted in accordance with sections 77 and 78 of the Copyright, Designs and Patents Act 1988.

All rights reserved. No part of this book may be reprinted or reproduced or utilised in any form or by any electronic, mechanical, or other means, now known or hereafter invented, including photocopying and recording, or in any information storage or retrieval system, without permission in writing from the publishers.

Trademark notice: Product or corporate names may be trademarks or registered trademarks, and are used only for identification and explanation without intent to infringe.

British Library Cataloguing-in-Publication Data
A catalogue record for this book is available from the British Library

Library of Congress Cataloging-in-Publication Data
A catalog record for this book has been requested

ISBN: 978-1-138-30643-1 (hbk)
ISBN: 978-1-315-14176-3 (ebk)

Typeset in Galliard
by Apex CoVantage, LLC

Contents

List of figures   vii
List of tables   viii
Foreword   ix
List of abbreviations   xi
List of contributors   xiii

PART 1
Painting the picture of teacher education in Europe   1

1 Introduction: How to become a European teacher? Exploring the (need for a) concept   3
ANA RAQUEL SIMÕES, MÓNICA LOURENÇO, AND NILZA COSTA

2 Teacher education and the profile of European teachers   11
JOANNA MADALIŃSKA-MICHALAK

PART 2
Tackling challenges and opportunities in teacher education   27

3 Developing teachers' competences to work in a European context: The HOWBET experience   29
NILZA COSTA

4 Future needs of learners in a European context   40
ILZE IVANOVA AND ILZE KANGRO

5 Linguistic diversity: How to deal with it in a classroom   57
SEIJA JESKANEN

Contents

6 European teachers and inclusive education   71
JUDITH 'T GILDE

7 Teaching and learning for citizenship education   88
ANA RAQUEL SIMÕES

8 Comparative studies and teacher education   104
WILFRIED HARTMANN

9 The European dimension in practice: Ideas for the classroom   123
MÓNICA LOURENÇO (ORG.), EGLĖ ABECIŪNAITĖ, KARIN BERGER, GABRIELA DOBIŃSKA, TAMARA GOBBO, FILIPE MOREIRA, AND ANNA TAZBIR

PART 3
Envisioning the future of teacher education   141

10 Restructuring teacher education in the UK: Insights into the future   143
JOANNA MCINTYRE

11 Teacher education in Europe in the midst of anti-Europeanism: Implications and recommendations for policy, practice, and research   161
MÓNICA LOURENÇO AND ANA RAQUEL SIMÕES

Index   175

Figures

4.1	The 21st century word cloud: expectations from education	51
7.1	Dimensions of citizenship education	89
7.2	Word cloud created by HOWBET students on citizenship education	100
8.1	Foci of research	112
8.2	Method and approach of research	112
9.1	Game card with the map of Europe	127
9.2	Example of a crossword puzzle	131
9.3	Example of cards with themed questions	136

Tables

3.1	Data concerning students enrolled in the HOWBET Summer School	32
3.2	Main goals, competences, and learning outcomes of the HOWBET Summer School	33
3.3	Topics of the HOWBET Summer School and teacher educators responsible	34
3.4	Criteria for assessment	35
3.5	Grading system to assess students' individual e-portfolios (adapted from Costa, 2014)	35
3.6	Questionnaires used to evaluate the HOWBET Summer School (adapted from Costa, 2014)	36
4.1	Overview of the workshop entitled 'Future needs of learners in a European context'	50
5.1	The Multicultural Policy Index for some European countries (adapted from Tolley, 2016, p. 6)	59
7.1	Overview of the workshop entitled 'Citizenship education in Europe'	98
8.1	Hilker's four-step procedure for comparison	109
8.2	Dimensions of comparative research	111
8.3	Scales used in various countries to measure achievement in secondary schools	115
8.4	The Portuguese school system as described by students	116
8.5	Summing up of answers by national groups	118
9.1	Lesson plan entitled 'Where are you from?'	128
9.2	Lesson plan entitled 'Discover Europe'	132
9.3	Lesson plan entitled 'Backpacking through Central Europe'	137

Foreword

In some countries, school teachers are employees of their state – *Beamte* in Germany, *fonctionnaires* in France, for example – and allegiance to the state may be exacted formally with an oath or remain implicit. In most, if not all countries, teachers are expected and assumed to have responsibilities to their state, to teach a curriculum which is 'national' in name or intention, and to prepare young people to live and work – with a strong leaning to the second – in 'our' country. Schools and teachers have served the monism of the mythologised 'nation state' since the inception of state-funded and state-organised education, in Europe and the Americas since the 19th century. They have all and always educated 'good (i.e., loyal) citizens' and 'good (i.e., efficient) workers'.

The authors and editors of this book challenge the nationalist tradition present in all education systems, albeit more strongly in some than in others. Their vision of a 'European teacher' has the characteristics of pluralism: an identification with 'unity in diversity', a knowledge of multiple education systems, of policies, of European histories, of contemporary multiculturalism and intercultural dialogue, and a plural linguistic competence. The project and summer school on which this book is based created a space in which 'mono-' could become 'pluri-'.

The success of the project shows that such opportunities need to be multiplied. They need to be offered to the individual teacher, and replicated in teacher education systems. Teachers themselves need a constant counter-balance to what they experienced in their own nationalist education, over many formative years, from primary school onwards. This powerful influence is not easily countered; it needs challenging, critical analysis. The HOWBET (How to Become a European Teacher) Summer School experience and others similar need to be multiplied in a career-long 'European' professional education and training.

As for teacher education systems, as is pointed out in this book, they are relatively new and constantly mutating. If a teacher career lasts 30–40 years, then the previous generation, and ones before it, often had no education and little training; the training was, moreover, based on the inadequate notion of 'apprenticeship'. The transfer of teacher education to universities, and the consequent move to professionalisation, lagged behind that of medicine and the law. The recognition that schools – and particularly primary schools – are, at least as much and probably more than universities, crucial for the individual and the communities to which they belong, is even now but a slow and incomplete process. That the quality of school teachers is a *sine qua non* in assuring quality education is also slowly being recognised, symbolised for example in France by the change of title from *institutrice/instituteur* to *professeur des écoles*.

The authors of this book rightly argue for a professional education and identity for teachers which is lifelong, and which, in the notion of the 'European teacher', breaks away from traditional nationalism, and is founded on an interpretation of society appropriate to the 21st century in Europe. This is the first step, conceptually and in practice. The European project, difficult though it is and despite current challenges, can serve as an indicator of how states and citizens can cooperate not only economically – a perspective which dominates current affairs – but also culturally, intellectually, and, indeed, emotionally. A teacher who identifies as 'European' becomes aware of the significance of this identity by comparative study, as the participants in the HOWBET Summer School discovered. This will be strongly reinforced when they encounter contrasting 'others', for example Asians, with their own educational systems and traditions. At the same moment, a process of comparison will replicate the shift to a European identity, to create a global teacher identity. They will find comparable and enriching purposes in the ambitions of the Association of Southeast Asian Nations, for example, not unlike those of the European Union. This will be the second step.

These are longer-term ambitions. The steps from nationalist, to Europeanist, to internationalist thinking and practices for teachers are complex and likely to take another generation. This book reveals the complexity but it also provides strong theory and illustrations of theoretically well-founded practices which can be transferred and emulated in many other locations and forms of teacher education. The editors and authors are to be congratulated on a book which is an embodiment of many years of innovation, a signpost for their readers and colleagues.

Michael Byram
Emeritus Professor at Durham University
December 2017

Abbreviations

AHS	*Allgemeinbildende Höhere Schule* (academic secondary schools for academically gifted children)
BERA	British Educational Research Association
CEFR	Common European Framework of Reference for Languages
CIES	Comparative and International Education Society
CLIL	Content and Language Integrated Learning
CPD	Continuing Professional Development
EACEA	Education, Audiovisual, and Culture Executive Agency
EDC	Education for Democratic Citizenship
ELP	European Language Portfolio
ENTEP	European Network on Teacher Education Policies
ERASMUS	EuRopean community Action Scheme for the Mobility of University Students
ETUCE	European Trade Union Committee for Education
EU	European Union
FREPA	Framework of Reference for Pluralistic Approaches
GCSE	General Certificate of Education
GTCS	General Teaching Council for Scotland
HOWBET	How to Become a European Teacher
HRE	Human Rights Education
ICT	Information and Communication Technology
ILD	Index of Language Diversity
IP	Intensive Programmes
ITE	Initial Teacher Education
ITT	Initial Teacher Training
LDI	Linguistic Diversity Index
NATO	North Atlantic Treaty Organization
OECD	Organisation for Economic Co-operation and Development
Ofsted	Office for Standards in Education, Children's Services and Skills (UK)
PGCE	Postgraduate Certificate in Education
PGDE	Postgraduate Diploma in Education
PISA	Programme for International Student Assessment

QTS	Qualified Teacher Status
RSA	Royal Society for the Encouragement of Arts, Manufactures and Commerce
SCITT	School Centred Initial Teacher Training
SEED	Scottish Executive Education Department
SEN	Special Education Needs
UNESCO	United Nations Educational, Scientific and Cultural Organisation

Contributors

Eglė Abeciūnaitė is a finance consultant for Scandinavian enterprises with a solid working practice in multicultural projects. She did her Bachelor's degree at Vytautas Magnus University, Lithuania, focusing on an analysis of the mobility challenges encountered by ERASMUS students during their preparation for a future career. She has a study background in career and professional consulting and a teacher qualification. She is conducting further studies at Vilnius University in the field of Economics.

Karin Berger is a language teacher for the subjects of Italian and Spanish at a secondary school in Austria. In addition to a teacher training programme, she also completed Romance Studies combined with Journalism and Communication at the University of Vienna, Austria. Throughout her academic studies, she participated in several international exchange programmes and took a semester abroad at the Ca' Foscari University in Venice, Italy. At her home institution, she organised and participated in extracurricular tutorials designed to support undergraduate students. In 2016, she worked as a scientific assistant in the research project entitled 'War of Pictures 1945–1955' at the Department of Communication of the University of Vienna. Her main interests include language teaching, language development, and multilingualism in society, to which she has also dedicated her thesis.

Nilza Costa is a Full Professor in Education at the Department of Education and Psychology of the University of Aveiro, Portugal, with nearly 40 years of experience. She has a Bachelor's degree in Physics Education from Oporto University, and a Doctoral degree in Education from the Institute of Education of the University of London. She was a founding member of the Research Centre titled 'Didactics and Technology in Education of Trainers' (CIDTFF), and coordinator of this Centre from 2012 to 2016. One of the focus of her teaching and research interests is teacher education. She has been involved in teaching, research and development activities in several European countries and also in Brazil and Africa (Angola, Cape Verde, and Mozambique).

Gabriela Dobińska has a Master's degree in resocialisation pedagogy and special education from the University of Łódź, Poland. She is the author of elaborations on the functioning of resocialisation institutions for minors. Her scientific interests include social maladjustment of youth and conditioning of the resocialisation process.

Judith 't Gilde currently works at the University of Utrecht, the Netherlands, as an educational advisor and trainer. She is finishing her Doctoral degree at the University of Vienna, Austria, where she previously worked as a university assistant. She has a Master's degree in Educational Sciences and International Development. She worked on educational topics for international organisations such as UNICEF, Voluntary Service Overseas (VSO), and the International Atomic Energy Agency (IAEA) in India, Pakistan, Nigeria, Bosnia-Herzegovina, Austria, and the Netherlands. She has lectured and researched about inclusive education and participated and coordinated the European 'TEMPUS IV Project: training for teachers & education managers in diversity'. Her Doctoral degree is about inclusive education and teacher's professional development. She is interested in topics such as intercultural education, diversity and the development of inclusive education in different countries.

Tamara Gobbo is an accredited teacher for the subjects of English, Philosophy, and Psychology from the University of Vienna, Austria. She holds a Bachelor's degree in Cultural and Social Anthropology and was a member of the student study and research Model Curriculum group, to which she contributed with various papers. During her studies, she attended several international working internships and study abroad trainings, including a one-year high school exchange in Maryland, USA, and a one-year ERASMUS study abroad programme in Valencia, Spain. Presently, she works as a researcher at the University of Milano Bicocca, Italy, in the project titled 'MIME – Mobility and Inclusion in Multilingual Europe', which is funded by the European Commission. Her main research interests include language education, plurilingualism, and diversity education.

Wilfried Hartmann is a university professor and renowned researcher in the areas of comparative and international education, and language didactics. He taught for nearly 40 years at the University of Hamburg, Germany, where he was also vice president of the university and dean of the faculty of education. For many years he served as vice chair of the governing board of the UNESCO Institute for Education and as a director of the European University Foundation – *Campus Europae*. Currently he works as an academic advisor for international educational institutions. He has published more than 110 monographs and articles in 12 countries.

Ilze Ivanova is *Doctor paedagogiae* and Professor in Education. She has been working for Doctoral, Master's, Bachelor's, and Professional Programmes in the Faculty of Education, Psychology and Art of the University of Latvia for more than 30 years. She lectures in the field of the development of educational tendencies, lifelong learning, andragogy, development of educational environment, and inclusive education. She is the head of the Department of Education Sciences, as well as a programme director of the Master's degree in Education Sciences. She acts as a scientific guide for Doctoral and Master's theses. She has experience as an expert in the accreditation of programmes in higher education; as a coordinator and participant in TEMPUS, PHARE and SOCRATES projects; and organiser of distance education courses. Her research interests include development of educational tendencies, teacher education, educational environment, and lifelong learning.

Seija Jeskanen is a Senior Lecturer at the school of Applied Educational Science and Teacher Education of the University of Eastern Finland. She has expertise in the areas of educational science, especially pedagogic theory, teacher education, language education, and intercultural education. She has taught for nearly 20 years in different teacher education programmes (class teacher education, subject teacher in foreign language education, and international Master's degree programme in early language education). At the moment, her main research interest is in linguistic awareness.

Ilze Kangro is *Doctor philosophiae* and Professor at the Faculty of Education, Psychology and Art, Teacher Education Department, of the University of Latvia. She delivers courses in German Literature, Information and Communication Technology (ICT) in Foreign Language Education, and German Academic Language for Research. From 2004 to 2012 she was head of the Teacher Education Department, implementing, together with the faculty, several innovations in teacher education in Latvia. She has experience as an expert in the accreditation of programmes in higher education and as a coordinator and participant in TEMPUS and SOCRATES projects. Her research interests include teacher education, German language and literature, ICT in education, interpreting, and translation.

Mónica Lourenço is a Postdoctoral Research Fellow at the CIDTFF of the University of Aveiro, Portugal, where she is developing a project on the internationalisation of teacher education. She has a Doctoral degree in Didactics and Teacher Education, a Master's degree in Linguistics and Teaching, and a Bachelor's degree in Modern Languages and Literature (English and German). Her main research interests are plurilingualism, teacher education, internationalisation of the curriculum, and global citizenship education. She is co-author of the book *Early Years Second Language Education: International Perspectives on Theory and Practice* (Routledge, 2015).

Joanna Madalińska-Michalak is Professor of Social Sciences (Field Educational Research) at the University of Warsaw, Poland, and chair of Didactics and Teacher Education of the Faculty of Education at the University of Warsaw. Her research work has focused on educational leadership, teacher education, teachers' and school principals' development, and research ethics. She serves for global, international, and national scientific organisations. She serves as a member of the Board of Directors of the International Council of Education for Teaching, a representative of the Polish Educational Research Association in the World Education Research Association, a member of the Council Board of the European Educational Research Association, chair of Teacher Education Policy in Europe Scientific Network, president of the Polish Educational Research Association, and a member of the Board of Scientific Associations at the Polish Academy of Science.

Joanna McIntyre is an Associate Professor in English Education and has leadership responsibility for Initial Teacher Education (ITE) at the University of Nottingham, England. Jo has taught in a range of ITE and Master's programmes. Previously, as a teacher of English, a head of department, and an Advanced Skills Teacher, she developed a strong philosophy about the importance of English to students as a means of personal expression, developing cultural values, critical enquiry, and fostering creativity. This has led to an interest in research which focuses on narrative and on creativity. Jo has worked on a range of funded research projects and is particularly interested in young people's arts and creative practices and learning in and out of school, as well as research on the discourses surrounding schools and the teachers that work in them, the lives of both long-serving and beginner teachers, and approaches to mentoring.

Filipe Moreira is a Primary Teacher with extensive experience in developing national and international ICT projects related with the introduction to programming. Among these projects are the Principe Project, which focused on the development of programming classes in public schools from Sao Tome and Principe, and the Mi-Go Project, which consisted of the development of a tangible programmed robot. At the moment, he is a research fellow and Doctoral student in Multimedia and Education at the University of Aveiro, Portugal. He is also a member of the Center for Research in Communication, Information and Digital Culture (CIC·DIGITAL) and of the Center of ICT Competences in the same university.

Ana Raquel Simões is an Assistant Professor at the Department of Education and Psychology of the University of Aveiro, Portugal. She holds a Doctoral degree in Language Education and has published book chapters and papers in scientific international and national journals. She has also taken part and coordinated national and international research projects. Since January 2000, she has been a member of the Open Laboratory for the Learning of Foreign Languages (LALE), based at the CIDTFF, where she is responsible for activities within the fields of research, dissemination and cooperation with society. She is supervisor of several Doctoral and Master's theses.

Anna Tazbir graduated from the Faculty of Mathematics and Computer Science of the University of Łódź, Poland, in 2015, and from the Faculty of Management of the same university in 2016. She has a Master's of Arts in Mathematics and a Bachelor's degree in Accounting. Since April 2016, Anna has been teaching Mathematics and English at a primary school in Radomsko (in central Poland).

Part 1
Painting the picture of teacher education in Europe

1 Introduction

How to become a European teacher? Exploring the (need for a) concept

Ana Raquel Simões, Mónica Lourenço, and Nilza Costa

Contextualisation and motivations for the book

Teacher education in a global world

The complexity of today's world, characterised by unprecedented technological (r)evolution, increased mobility and migration, and as rapid and profound societal change, presents new challenges to teaching and teacher education. In the past, teachers were simply mediators of knowledge, the students were taught in similar ways, and the goal was standardisation and conformity (Schleicher, 2012). Today, teachers are being asked to keep pace with rapidly developing knowledge areas and approaches to students' learning and assessment, to use new technologies, to personalise learning experiences to ensure that every learner has the chance to succeed, to embrace diversity with differentiated pedagogies, and to promote students' creativity (Darling-Hammond & Lieberman, 2013; Townsend, 2016).

All of these demands imply the need to rethink teacher education programmes to help in-service and prospective teachers develop confidence in their ability, as well as the knowledge, skills, and attitudes to meet and overcome the challenges they will encounter in their classrooms. For this matter, many nations around the world have undertaken wide-ranging reforms of curriculum, instruction, and assessment, describing how and where teachers should be prepared for their work, and identifying (sometimes prescribing) what they should know and be able to do to meet the demands of the 21st century (see Loughran & Hamilton, 2016 for a review).

At European level, the education of teachers has long been considered a priority, given the vital role teachers play in advancing human potential, shaping future generations and influencing society as a whole. The need for a well-qualified profession, within a lifelong learning perspective, and the idea of a mobile profession based upon partnerships, have been understood as key principles that policymakers should follow to impact the quality of education across Europe (European Commission, 2005, 2007, 2013; Hudson & Zgaga, 2008; Madalińska-Michalak, Niemi, & Chong, 2012).

The Bologna Declaration (1999) has been particularly important in setting forth this agenda, mainly through the following measures: the adoption of a system of easily readable and comparable degrees to ensure compatibility between European qualifications and transparency of graduate achievement; the encouragement of student and staff mobility, via the Lifelong Learning Programmes; co-operation in quality assurance; and the promotion of a 'European dimension' in higher education, considering that teacher education programmes should not only have national educational perspectives in mind, but also develop teachers' competences to educate students to live in a European area and to face challenges arising from this setting.

In this respect, the concept of 'European teacher' has been gaining attention across Europe in the last decades, not without controversy and doubt (Schratz, 2010, 2014; Valenčič Zuljan & Vogrinc, 2011).

The 'European teacher': concept and relevance

The first discussions around the concept of 'European teacher' started during a meeting of the European Network on Teacher Education Policies (ENTEP), which was formed at the initiative of the Portuguese Minister of Education in 1999. This group has since then offered a transnational space for intensive debate concerning critical teacher education policy issues that were brought to light by the Bologna Declaration, with a special focus on questions of 'Europeanness' and mobility within the profession. In the ENTEP report entitled *The first ten years after Bologna*, Michael Schratz (2010) defines the 'European teacher' as a teacher working within a European context of professionalism, who not only has the same competences as any other 'good teacher' (i.e., self-awareness and reflection, professionalism in dealing with diversity and uncertainty, collaboration, and personal mastery), but also possesses specific competences in the European dimension concerning:

1 *European identity*: regarding himself/herself as someone with roots in a specific country, but simultaneously belonging to a greater European whole – the idea of 'unity in diversity', which provides a valuable perspective on questions of heterogeneity and an open mind towards the world at large;
2 *European knowledge*: being aware of other educational systems, policy matters at European level, European world affairs, and European history (histories), and their influence on contemporary European society;
3 *European multiculturalism*: being aware of his/her own culture, but still open to other cultures and to intercultural dialogue;
4 *European language competence*: speaking more than one European language with differing levels of competence;
5 *European professionalism*: being able to teach in any European country by linking up cross-curricular themes from a European perspective, exchanging curricular content and methodologies with colleagues from other European countries, or paying attention to and learning from different teaching and learning traditions; and

6 *European citizenship*: showing solidarity with citizens in other European countries and sharing values such as respect for human rights, democracy and freedom; and fostering autonomous, responsible and active citizens for a Europe of tomorrow.

These facets of the European dimension seem to be particularly important for in-service and prospective teachers working in the European context today. Indeed, the recent arrival of migrant children to European countries amid the refugee crisis; the rise of xenophobic groups and right wing extremist parties across Europe; the European Union (EU) referendum in the UK and growth of anti-European sentiments; the financial crisis and huge unemployment rates in the teaching profession; and the intensification of a neoliberal 'culture of accountability', with standardised performance measures and global large-scale assessment surveys, such as the Programme for International Student Assessment (PISA), taking the lead (Beckett, 2013; Meyer & Benavot, 2013), have all contributed to increased fragmentation and tensions in European societies, and to low self-esteem and dissatisfaction in the teaching profession, and have undermined the educational responses teachers should be giving to issues of inclusion and social justice (The Teacher Education Group, 2016; Townsend, 2016).

Therefore, in order for teachers to assume their role as agents of change in the 'old' continent, it is crucial to create a vision of a future European teacher and promote teachers' active engagement in preparing children to live and act in a multicultural and increasingly changing world. This can be carried out through cross-national collaboration and mobility, working together, joining ideas and efforts to help prospective teachers become critical and engaged citizens who understand the difficulties and obstacles of the current era, and taking action to create a more equitable, peaceful and sustainable Europe. By bringing together teacher educators and students from various countries, ERASMUS (EuRopean community Action Scheme for the Mobility of University Students) Mobility Intensive Programmes (IPs) may embody these efforts.

'How to become a European teacher': a mobility intensive programme for prospective teachers

ERASMUS Mobility IPs create an international learning environment favourable for developing rich and far-reaching visions and reflecting about possible solutions to face unknown future challenges. IPs promote participants' communication, argumentation, and foreign language skills, develop critical thinking, foster openness to and respect for diversity, and support mutual understanding, all crucial competences for the teaching profession.

This edited book is the result of an IP, the first Campus Europae summer school in the field of teacher education, dedicated to discussing and advancing ideas on the European dimension of teacher education. This 10-day summer school, entitled 'HOWBET – How to become a European teacher: Challenges for the present and the future', took place in Portugal in 2014, and brought together 36 student teachers and 11 teacher educators from 8 European universities that were part of the Campus Europae network: the University of Vienna (Austria), the University of Eastern Finland (Finland), the University of Hamburg (Germany), the University of Latvia (Latvia), Vytautas Magnus University (Lithuania), the University of Łódź (Poland), the University of Novi Sad (Serbia), and the host institution, the University of Aveiro (Portugal).

The main aims of the HOWBET Summer School were to promote an understanding of 'Europeanness' in prospective teachers' profile and to develop competences that enabled them to learn how to teach and behave as a European teacher. More particularly, the student teachers were expected to be able to characterise the main European trends in education and teacher education policies; to identify similarities and differences across education systems in the participating countries; to develop teaching and learning skills under conditions of diversity (cultural, social, and economic); to strengthen Information and Communication Technology (ICT) skills in teaching and learning; to enhance foreign language skills (English, but also other languages as a result of mobility); to develop sensitivity towards differences in a multicultural environment; and to work together with students and teachers from the participating countries.

Drawing on the experience of the HOWBET Summer School, the main purposes of this book are not only to share and discuss the results of the IP, but also to construct a critical overview of the current challenges and opportunities facing teacher education policy and practice in Europe, in order to propose sustained guidelines for teacher education with a European dimension.

Themes, structure, and contents of the book

Along with the general topic of the book – the preparation of qualified teachers to face Europe's challenges and the improvement of teacher education – chapters cover other relevant topics in the field of teacher education, particularly in the current political, social, and economic context. Covered themes are: teacher education for the 21st century, the profile of the European teacher, European citizenship and identity, social inclusion, linguistic and cultural diversity, and comparative education. These themes are addressed in 11 chapters written by a wide range of European contributors who participated in the IP (both teacher educators and student teachers), and by renowned experts in the field, bringing together their real-life experiences and unique viewpoints.

The book is divided into three main parts, which cover distinct but intertwined dimensions of the opportunities and challenges related to the education of European teachers. Part 1, 'Painting the picture of teacher education in Europe', which includes two chapters, presents an overview of the most pressing issues challenging teacher education across Europe and impacting the profile of European teachers. Chapter 1, this introduction, which was written by the editors, contextualises the book, provides a clarification of the concept of 'European teacher', and justifies its relevance in the current era as a possibility to contribute to the promotion of social cohesion, social justice, and inclusion. The editors make the case for International Mobility IPs as vehicles to infuse 'Europeanness' in prospective teachers' profile and prepare them to deal with the challenges of the globalised world.

Chapter 2, 'Teacher education and the profile of European teachers', written by Joanna Madalińska-Michalak, from Poland, remains within the same theme, addressing the changing role of teachers in contemporary societies in Europe and the characteristics of European teachers. Special attention is given to European guidelines for teacher education, namely related to the induction phase of teacher development, and to teacher quality. According to the author, teacher education perceived as a continuum within a lifelong learning perspective and commitment to develop teacher professionalism can make a difference in quality teachers and quality teaching.

Part 2, 'Tackling challenges and opportunities in teacher education', focuses on the experience of the HOWBET Summer School, using it as a core to construct a more critical overview of some of the challenges and opportunities drawn by the social, political, and professional changes taking place in the field of teacher education. This section begins with Chapter 3, 'Developing teachers' competences to work in a European context: The HOWBET experience', written by Nilza Costa, the Portuguese coordinator of the IP. The chapter describes and discusses the rationale behind the HOWBET Summer School, the participating students and teachers, the contents and themes of the sessions, the working methodology, and the assessment methods. The effects of the programme on the participants' personal and professional development are also analysed, drawing on the results from two sets of questionnaires. The chapter ends with a plea, highlighting the benefits of cross-collaboration and the need for shared responsibility in teacher education.

Chapters 4 and 5 address the competences required by teachers to support learning in a world driven by globalisation, urbanisation, digitalisation, and diversity. In Chapter 4, Ilze Ivanova and Ilze Kangro, from Latvia, discuss the 'Future needs of learners in a European context', which have become increasingly complex and diverse. The authors examine how teachers and teacher educators can support learning, develop students' potential, and help them gain a better understanding of the problems of the 21st century. They conclude that new tools and processes, characterised by sociability, collaboration, simplicity, and connections should be used in order to make students' learning more active and connected to real life.

A similar take is shared by Seija Jeskanen, from Finland, who writes in Chapter 5 about 'Linguistic diversity: How to deal with it in a classroom'. The chapter draws attention to the increasing linguistic diversity in European societies, in particular as a result of migration, and to the demands this diversity is placing on education systems, schools, teachers, and teacher education programmes. In this regard, it considers the skills and competences required by European teachers working in linguistically and culturally diverse schools, presenting some tools put together by European organisations for this matter.

Chapters 6 to 9 discuss possibilities related to overcoming some of the challenges identified in the two previous chapters. In Chapter 6, Judith 't Gilde from the Netherlands writes about 'European teachers and inclusive education', advocating a broader understanding of inclusion as a human right. According to the author, it is imperative for European teachers not only to know about inclusion (including students with special needs in the general-education classroom) and its current developments, but also—and most importantly—to experience opportunities to discuss and learn about how to deal with it in the classroom. Drawing on research conducted in Austria, Pakistan and Nigeria, the author reviews the current preparedness of teachers for inclusion, looking at the notions of fixed ability and transformability. The chapter ends with a discussion of the main challenges and opportunities for the present and the future of teacher education in relation to inclusive education.

Another possibility to promote inclusion and overcome divisiveness and prejudice in Europe is put forward by Ana Raquel Simões, from Portugal, who writes in Chapter 7 about 'Teaching and learning for citizenship education'. The chapter starts with a discussion of the notion, aims, and history of citizenship education in Europe and moves on to a comparative analysis of European school curricula and teacher education programmes regarding citizenship education, as well as of the results from the most recent Eurobarometer survey on this subject. Pointing to a new type of citizenship education for the global world, where individuals are asked to be responsible and actively engaged, the author presents some suggestions for practical activities to promote teaching through and for European democratic citizenship and human rights. The chapter ends with student reflections from the workshop on the theme.

The focus on comparison is even more noticeable in Chapter 8, 'Comparative studies and teacher education', written by Wilfried Hartmann, from Germany. In this chapter, the author discusses the usefulness of comparative approaches in all academic fields, defines the place of comparison in education and pedagogy, and highlights the importance of raising awareness of this method among those students who want to become European teachers. The chapter also presents some comparative tools that were used in the HOWBET Summer School, as well as some of the results obtained.

Chapter 9, 'The European dimension in practice: Ideas for the classroom', offers a more practical take on the issue of 'Europeanness'. The chapter, organised by Mónica Lourenço, from Portugal, and resulting from the international collaboration of groups of students who participated in the HOWBET Summer School, sheds more light into the possibilities of integrating the European dimension in education. This is carried out through the proposal of three lesson ideas addressing different aspects of this dimension: language learning by children with a migration background, knowledge of European geography and history through the discovery of European monuments, and encouragement of mobility in a virtual backpacking journey through Central Europe. Each section includes a lesson plan and sample resources designed to provide teachers with tools that can be used and adapted in their own contexts.

Part 3, 'Envisioning the future of teacher education', includes two chapters that present a more critical perspective of the field, regarding the major tensions created by the reshaping of teacher education curricula in many countries and growing anti-European sentiments. Chapter 10, 'Restructuring teacher education in the UK: Insights into the future', written by Joanna McIntyre, from the UK, offers a case study of the ways in which teacher education is being reshaped within this country through an exploration of the impact of the different national reviews of teacher education in England, Scotland, and Wales. The chapter illustrates the different emphases within policy expectations of teacher education across these three regions, with the most extreme being the unique emphasis within England on school-led teacher preparation. The chapter closes with a reflection on what these unique characteristics mean for the future of UK-based teacher education in a post-Brexit European context.

Finally, in Chapter 11, 'Teacher education in Europe in the midst of anti-Europeanism: Implications and recommendations for policy, practice and research', Mónica Lourenço and Ana Raquel Simões bring together the main issues developed along the book; present guidelines to be introduced in teacher education, namely concerning the preparation of teachers to work and act in a European area; and propose educational policy recommendations supporting transnational networks of teacher education practitioners to share experiences and best practices. Furthermore, they put forward some ideas for educational research around teacher education that were approached in the book.

Final note

We would like to take this opportunity to thank all the people who made this publication possible. First of all, to our contributors for their perseverance during the editing procedures and their hard work in redrafting chapters according to our feedback. Your forbearance and determination have been heart-warming, and we are eternally grateful to you for contributing in such a decisive manner to this unique collection. We would also like to thank the reviewers for carefully reading our initial proposal and for giving such constructive comments that substantially helped improving the quality of the book. We extend our sincere gratitude to the editorial team at Routledge for taking this project on, believing in us, and for taking time out of their days to making sure our writings were well prepared. Finally, a word to our readers: we hope that the work of all of those involved in the preparation of this edited volume and the originality of this experience is both inspiring and motivating.

References

Beckett, L. (Ed.). (2013). *Teacher education through active engagement: Raising the professional voice*. Abingdon: Routledge.
Bologna declaration – The European higher education area. (1999). Retrieved from www.aic.lv/ace/ace_disk/Bologna/maindoc/bologna_declaration.pdf (accessed 21 September 2017).

Darling-Hammond, L., & Lieberman, A. (2013). *Teacher education around the world: Changing policies and practices*. Abingdon: Routledge.

European Commission. (2005). *Common European principles for teacher competences and qualifications*. Brussels: European Commission.

European Commission. (2007). *Improving the quality of teacher education*. Brussels: European Commission.

European Commission. (2013). *Supporting teacher competence development for better learning outcomes*. Strasbourg: European Commission.

Hudson, B., & Zgaga, P. (2008). *Teacher education policy in Europe: A voice of higher education institutions*. Umeå: Faculty of Teacher Education, University of Umeå and Centre for Educational Policy Studies, Faculty of Education, University of Ljubljana.

Loughran, J., & Hamilton, M. L. (Eds.). (2016). *International handbook of teacher education* (Vol. 1). Singapore: Springer.

Madalińska-Michalak, J., Niemi, H., & Chong, S. (2012). *Research, policy, and practice in teacher education in Europe*. Łódź: University of Łódź Publishing House.

Meyer, H-D., & Benavot, A. (2013). *PISA, power, and policy: The emergence of global educational governance*. Oxford: Symposium Books.

Schleicher, A. (2012). *Preparing teachers and developing school leaders for the 21st century: Lessons from around the world*. Paris: Organisation for Economic Co-operation and Development.

Schratz, M. (2010). What is a 'European Teacher'? In O. Gassner, L. Kerger, & M. Schratz (Eds.), *The first ten years after Bologna* (pp. 97–102). Bucureşti: Editura Universităţii din Bucureşti.

Schratz, M. (2014). The European teacher: Transnational perspectives in teacher education policy and practice. *CEPS Journal, 4*, 11–27.

The Teacher Education Group. (2016). *Teacher education in times of change: Responding to challenges across the UK and Ireland*. Bristol: Policy Press.

Townsend, T. (Ed.). (2016). *International perspectives on teacher education*. Abingdon: Routledge.

Valenčič Zuljan, M., & Vogrinc, J. (Eds.). (2011). *European dimensions of teacher education: Similarities and differences*. Ljubljana, Kranj: Faculty of Education, The National School of Leadership in Education.

2 Teacher education and the profile of European teachers

Joanna Madalińska-Michalak

Introduction

The present chapter focuses on the issues connected with teacher education in Europe and the profile of European teachers. Teacher education – in an effort to address its complexity – is seen in a wide sense and is not limited to teacher education in higher education institutions in Europe. It is stressed that the quality of teacher education is perceived as one of the most important factors influencing the quality of teachers, and their teaching and learning, with direct implications in student learning and their educational achievements and outcomes. Teacher education is presented as a continuum: from Initial Teacher Education (ITE) through induction phase into profession to Continuing Professional Development (CPD). Special attention is paid to the European guidelines on teacher education and particularly to the induction phase of teacher development. The chapter shows that induction has a pivotal role in the continuum of teacher lifelong learning, as it creates opportunities to relate back to ITE and to prepare teachers for career-long CPD.

The basic premise of this chapter is that teacher education perceived as a continuum within a lifelong perspective can make a difference in quality teachers and quality teaching at school (Cochran-Smith & Zeichner, 2005; European Commission, 2015; Hudson, 2017). At the same time teacher education is more likely to be effective in supporting high-quality teachers who are dedicated to respond to the increasing demands of a changing world when it also plays a powerful, deliberate, and consequential role in developing teacher professionalism with a consideration of the role played by school leaders (Day, 2017; Loughran, 2017; Zhu, Goodwin, & Zhang, 2017). This chapter, therefore, contributes to a long-standing debate on teacher education in Europe and the competences that enable teachers to act as European teachers and to work in the international education environment.

The changing role of teachers in the 21st century

In the changing world of the early 21st century—characterised by increasing social, economic, and cultural interactions; and unprecedented technological evolution, mobility, and migration—school education and teachers' work are also changing. As part of these changes, the role of school education and, more particularly, the role of teachers and the quality of their teaching and learning are seen to be central to student attainment and school improvement efforts. Indeed, teachers, whose role is becoming ever more complex (Darling-Hammond & Lieberman, 2013; Day & Gu, 2010; Schleicher, 2012; Schratz, 2014), are identified as the most important factor influencing the quality of education in schools (Abbott, 1988; Barber & Mourshed, 2007; Darling-Hammond, 1999; European Commission, 2012b, 2012c, 2013a; Hattie, 2003, 2008; OECD, 2005, 2009, 2010, 2011, 2014, 2016).

Recent decades have brought significant shifts in the context of key competences for reforms and transformations taking place in the modern world and the rapidly growing knowledge society. As highlighted in Chapter 4 of this book, young people need a wider range of competences than ever before to flourish in a globalised economy and in increasingly diverse societies. Many will work in jobs that do not yet exist. Technology will continue to change the world in ways we cannot imagine. The European Council has repeatedly stressed the key role of education and training for the future growth, long-term competitiveness and social cohesion of the European Union (EU). To achieve this, it is crucial to fully develop the potential for learning, innovation, and creativity of European citizens. In this increasingly complex world, creativity and the ability to continue to learn and to innovate will count as much as, if not more than, specific areas of knowledge liable to become obsolete. Lifelong learning should be the norm (CEC, 2007).

The new conceptual learning framework of the Organisation for Economic Co-Operation and Development (OECD) – 'Learning Compass 2030' (OECD, 2016) – shows that there are increasing demands on schools to prepare students for more rapid economic and social change, for jobs that have not yet been created, and for technologies that have not yet invented, and to solve social problems that have not been anticipated in the past. Education at school should aim to foster holistic student learning and well-being. The OECD project aims to develop a framework to better understand the competences (i.e., the knowledge, skills, attitudes, and metacognition) that will prepare students for a more volatile, uncertain, complex, and ambiguous world in 2030. The project focuses not only on cognitive dimensions, but it also embraces social and emotional aspects of students' learning as well (i.e., tolerance, respect, fairness, personal and social responsibility, integrity, and self-awareness). For such an education, there is a need to work on teachers and teacher education in order to put a greater emphasis on teachers' knowledge, skills, attitudes, and values. Therefore, there is no more room for teachers who are simply mediators of knowledge and for such main goals of education as standardisation and conformity (Schleicher, 2012).

However, in the light of the contemporary challenges, the demands placed on schools and teachers are becoming more complex. Modern societies expect schools and teachers to deal effectively with different languages and student backgrounds; to be sensitive to culture and gender issues; to promote students' creativity, tolerance, and social cohesion; to respond to disadvantaged students and students with special educational needs; to use new technologies; and to keep pace with rapidly developing fields of knowledge and approaches to students' learning and assessment in order to ensure that every learner has the chance to succeed (Darling-Hammond & Lieberman, 2013; European Commission, 2011a; OECD, 2009, 2011). In the European Commission document entitled *Supporting teacher competence development for better learning outcomes* it is pointed out that:

> When many teachers undertook their initial education, knowledge about learning and teaching was less developed, many teaching tools were not available and the role of education and training was more narrowly conceived. For example, the increased availability of educational resources via the worldwide web, including Open Educational Resources, means that both teaching staff and learners have, potentially, a much wider range of learning materials at their disposal and teachers will increasingly need the competences to find, evaluate and deploy learning materials from a wider range of sources, and to help learners acquire these competences.
> (European Commission, 2013a, p. 7)

Considering such expectations towards schools, the teacher's role is changing, resulting in broaden teacher responsibility at different levels. Some examples of areas of broadened teacher responsibility that are indicated in the OECD (2005) report are as follows:

At the individual student level

- Initiating and managing students' learning processes;
- Responding effectively to the learning needs of the student as an individual learner; and
- Integrating formative and summative student assessment.

At the classroom level

- Teaching in multicultural classrooms;
- New cross-curricular emphases; and
- Integrating students with special needs.

At the school level

- Working and planning in teams;
- Evaluating and systematically improving the school's planning;
- Using ICT in teaching and administration;
- Conducting projects between schools, and international cooperation; and
- Managing and sharing school leadership.

At the level of parents and the wider community

- Providing professional advice and support to parents; and
- Building community partnerships for learning.

The analysis of contemporary challenges shows that there is an ongoing need for such teachers who are capable of preparing students for a society and an economy in which they will be expected to be self-directed learners who are able and motivated to keep learning over a lifetime. Teachers need to help students acquire not only the skills that are the easiest to teach and easiest to test, but also, more importantly, ways of thinking and working (creativity, critical thinking, problem solving, decision making, learning, communication, and collaboration), tools for working (including ICT), and skills around citizenship, life and career, and personal and social responsibility for success in modern democracies (OECD, 2011). There is a need for such teachers who are able and willing to learn and adapt, who possess new subject knowledge and utilise new pedagogical approaches throughout their career. This active learner engagement in learning requires also thinking, questioning, and knowledge-creating teachers who recognise the need to work in collaboration with others, valuing diversity of perspectives, sharing learning and teaching problems, and seeking solutions through ongoing inquiry (OECD, 2009, 2011), and developing their practices of mindful teaching (Shirley & MacDonald, 2016).

According to the OECD's report *Teachers matter* (2005), which is about school teachers and their preparation, recruitment, work, and careers, all countries are seeking to improve their schools and to respond better to higher social and economic expectations. As the most significant and costly resource in schools, teachers are seen as a priority for public policy, and likely to become even more so in future years. Improving the quality of schooling depends, in large measure, on ensuring that competent people want to work as teachers, that their teaching is of high quality, and that all students have access to high-quality teaching, which is the basis for improving student learning.

The conclusions that emerge from research on the factors that influence student learning clearly show that:

- The largest source of variation in student learning is attributable to differences in what students bring to school – their skills, abilities, expectations, motivation, behaviour and attitudes, and family and community background. Such factors are difficult for policymakers to influence, at least in the short run.
- Factors to do with teachers and teaching are the most important influences on student learning. In particular, 'teacher quality' is the single most important school variable influencing student achievement.
- There is a positive relationship between the measures of student performance, most commonly standardised test scores, and readily measurable teacher characteristics such as qualifications, teaching experience, and indicators of

teachers' academic ability or subject-matter knowledge, but perhaps to a lesser extent than may have been expected (see OECD, 2005, pp. 23–27).

In the light of the research findings, teachers and teacher policy, especially teacher education policy, are seen – in contemporary times – as vital in any changes in the school system (see Hargreaves & Shirley, 2017; Zhu et al., 2017). Special attention is paid to teachers and teaching, which are perceived as having the most important influence on student learning. In particular, the broad consensus is that 'teacher quality' and 'quality of teacher teaching and learning' are the most important school variables influencing student achievement.

Teacher education: towards quality and continuity

There is now substantial research indicating that the quality of teachers depends on the quality of their teacher education (Cochran-Smith & Fries, 2005; Flores, 2016; Hudson, 2017; Zhu et al., 2017), and this is also reflected in the European policy documents published by the European Commission (2007) and the Commission of the European Communities (2007). Quality of teacher education is perceived as one of the most important factors influencing the quality of teaching and teachers' qualities, as well as student learning and student educational achievements and outcomes (OECD, 2005, 2011).

However, there is no consensus about what in fact is quality in teacher education (Russel & Martin, 2016). Indeed, the concept of quality of teacher education is complex and elusive. As research shows, quality teachers matter for quality teaching, and at the same time – as Flores (2016) rightly indicates – 'quality teachers, depend to a great extent, on the quality of teacher education programmes. However, it is possible to identify different ways of understanding teacher quality and teacher education quality in diverse contexts' (p. 187). Regarding the issue of quality of ITE, Russel and Martin (2016) propose a focus on quality as it may be perceived by the four major players: teacher candidate, mentor teacher, faculty supervisor, and teacher educator. According to the authors, each of these major players performs a significant and significantly different role in a programme of teacher education. The authors argue that the four different roles lead to four different interpretations of the meaning of quality in ITE.

In the contemporary literature on teacher education it is stressed that teacher education needs to prepare teachers who are continuous learners themselves, able to work in collaboration with others and to engage actively with others in thinking about learners, transforming the learning process, and learning for school development (Madalińska-Michalak, Niemi, & Chong, 2012; OECD, 2009, 2011, 2014). In this context, teachers have an ongoing commitment to maintain their professional expertise and recognise themselves as lifelong learners, as contexts around them and requirements presented to them change across their career. To do this, it is essential that teachers engage in an appropriate balance of professional development that enables them to progress their learning in ways that are relevant to their own individual needs and those of their pupils throughout their career (Madalińska-Michalak, 2017).

The issue of improving the quality of teacher education is one of the key subjects appearing in the current debate on the directions of education policy in the EU (CEC, 2007; European Commission, 2010) and the main goals of the process of reforming education systems in European countries. For policymakers working on improving education systems, it is therefore important to develop policies that support the professional development of teachers.

Teacher professional development is a lifelong process that starts at ITE and ends at retirement (European Commission, 2011b). Generally, teacher education should be conceived of and organised as a unified continuum – as a lifelong process that is divided into three specific stages:

1. ITE (a pre-service course before entering educational institutions as a qualified teacher);
2. induction (the process of providing training and support during the first few years of teaching or the first year[s] in a particular school); and
3. CPD of teachers (an in-service process for practicing teachers).

The European Commission assumes that provision for teacher education and development can be more effective if it is coordinated as a coherent system at national level, and is adequately funded. The best method is to set up a unified continuum of provision embracing ITE, induction into the profession, and career-long CPD that includes formal, informal, and non-formal learning opportunities. In practice, this can provide the opportunities for each teacher to:

- take part in an effective programme of induction during their first three years in post/in the profession;
- have access to structured guidance and mentoring by experienced teachers or other relevant professionals throughout their career;
- take part in regular discussions of their training and development needs, in the context of the wider development plan of the institution where they work.

(CEC, 2007, pp. 13–14)

As we can see from the European policy documents on teachers and their profession, the European Commission assumes – in the light of the issue of lifelong learning and teacher development – that all teachers would benefit if they are encouraged and supported throughout their careers to extend and develop their competences via formal, informal, and non-formal means, and if they are able to have their relevant formal, and non-formal learning recognised. According to the European policy on teacher education, the quality of teachers' development depends on the support that is given to them in each of these phases (European Commission, 2011b). ITE, induction, and CPD of the highest quality, and access to support throughout their careers, are essential for the quality of teachers (European Commission, 2011b, 2012b, 2013a).

Teachers in Europe should also have access to other opportunities for their CPD (such as exchanges and placements, whether or not funded through the Lifelong Learning Programme), and the opportunity and time to study for gaining further qualifications. Teachers should take part in studies and research at a higher-education level. Special attention should also be paid to promoting creative partnerships between the institutions in which teachers work, the world of work, higher education, and research institutions, and other agencies, as they can help to support high-quality training and effective practice, and to develop networks of innovation at local and regional levels (CEC, 2007).

The European guidelines for teacher education: teachers and induction support

The current context for teacher education in Europe is – as it has been shown earlier – partly shaped by the shifting social, economic, and political circumstances, whether local, national, or global in nature. Any considerations on teacher education should be 'nested' within wider education systems.

> Acknowledging its complexity and hybridity, teacher education can be understood by means of a layered, ecological perspective – and described as an activity system whose aims and outcomes are culturally shaped by its contexts, rules, roles and actors. Activity systems are characterized by ongoing contradictions and change, constantly interacting with other activity systems and responding to external pressures.
> (Caena, 2017, p. 179)

In this view, teacher education needs to take stock of situated, context-driven features and needs, and especially it should be perceived in connection with higher education in Europe and its changes and challenges (Zgaga, 2014).

The European Commission works with the EU countries to raise standards of teaching and teacher education. European experts meet regularly to examine specific aspects of teacher education, discuss common challenges, and exchange good practices. European experts have produced guidance for policymakers in such documents as: *Developing coherent and system-wide induction programmes for beginning teachers: A handbook for policymakers* (European Commission, 2010), *Assessment of key competences in initial education and training: Policy guidance* (European Commission, 2012b), *Supporting teacher competence development for better learning outcomes* (European Commission, 2013a), and *Supporting teacher educators for better learning outcomes* (European Commission, 2013b).

Following an informal meeting of Education Ministers in Gothenburg, in September 2009, on the professional development of teachers and school leaders, the Council agreed in the following month, amongst other things, that in view of the increasing demands placed upon teachers and the growing complexity of their roles, teachers need access to effective personal and professional support throughout their careers, and particularly during the time they first enter the profession. Special attention should be paid to sufficient and effective teachers' support and guidance during the first few years of their careers.

In all European countries, in order to become a qualified school teacher, candidates are required to have undertaken academic studies, including a course of study in education which provides them with the theoretical and practical skills (including school placements) needed to join the teaching profession. However, ITE is not enough (OECD, 2014), since it cannot provide teachers with the knowledge and skills necessary for a lifetime of teaching, especially in times when

> teacher education has been unable or unwilling to make connections between the vast amount of in-depth research conducted at the level of the individual teacher, and the world of policy in which education is essentially seen as a systemic, industrial activity.
>
> (Harford & Gray, 2017, p. 27)

Regarding prospective teachers, teacher education is sometimes perceived in reality as a 'phase change' between school-as-pupil and school-as-teacher, rather than as 'entry into a profession' (ibid).

Nowadays, there is a strong call both in the research on teacher education and in European policy documents for the development of coherent and system-wide induction programmes supporting beginning teachers. The induction itself is seen as a unique phase of transition from university to teaching, as a period of socialisation into profession, and as the formal programme of support that is given to newly qualified teachers in the first steps of their teaching career, usually with mentoring at school (see European Commission, 2010; Flores, 2016; Livingston, 2012; Madalińska-Michalak, 2017).

Many new teachers entering the field do not receive the necessary support or feedback they need to develop into effective teachers (Eurydice, 2009; OECD, 2014). Regulations or recommendations on support measures for newly qualified teachers are increasingly widespread. The European Trade Union Committee for Education (ETUCE) states: 'Providing support and systematic guidance to teachers at this stage has critical implications for their subsequent professional commitment and also in preventing newly educated teachers from leaving the teaching profession after only a few years' (European Commission, 2010, p. 13). This statement indicates that formal and non-formal induction programmes can contribute to increasing both the quality and the quantity of teachers. The aim of the formal induction programmes is not only to support beginning teachers, but also to safeguard the quality of those teachers that will gain a full teaching license. The first years are seen as a probation period (in some cases such probation periods end with a formal exam that students need to pass). In countries where such probation periods exist, the state (through the ministry or a national agency) has a strong control over induction programmes. Non-formal induction programmes are not connected with the probation periods or the gaining of full teacher status, but are mainly focused on supporting beginning teachers in the transition from student teacher to experienced teacher. As in formal induction, this support can focus on professional, social, and personal dimensions (see Eisenschmidt, 2006, 2010; European Commission, 2010).

In the professional dimension, the emphasis is on supporting the beginning teacher in gaining more confidence in the use of essential teacher competences, and the use of didactic methods and tools. The induction phase is perceived as a starting point of the process of lifelong learning as a teacher, forming a bridge between ITE and the CPD phase. In the social dimension, attention is paid to the support of the beginning teacher to become a member of the school and professional community, 'understanding and accepting the qualities, norms, manners and organisational structure that exist within the given school' (European Commission, 2010, p. 15). The personal dimension is connected with the process of development of a professional identity as a teacher. This comprises the development of personal norms towards the profession, pupils, and colleagues. In this dimension, the elaboration of the teacher's view on teaching and learning, as well as the development of an attitude of lifelong learning, play an important role (Harford & Gray, 2017).

The profile of European teachers

As highlighted in the introduction to the book (see Chapter 1), the concept of 'European teacher' has been gaining attention in Europe in the last two decades. One of the first discussions on this topic started during a meeting of ENTEP in 1999. During this meeting, a set of very intriguing questions were asked, namely: 'Does something like a European teacher exist?'; 'Do we want to create a standardised teacher model within Europe?'; 'What makes a teacher European?'; and 'Should we give up our sovereignty as individual member states of the European Union?' (Schratz, 2014, p. 13). These and other questions directed attention to anxieties between transnational integration and national disintegration within the European society. Answering these – at that time – rather unusual questions, meant making a not so-clear bridge between, on the one hand, what it means to teach in a particular European country and its circumstances, and, on the other hand, similarities in generic teacher competences that are required throughout Europe and beyond.

In the ENTEP book entitled *The first ten years after Bologna*, Schratz (2010) pointed out that 'whilst European teachers work within a European context, we still know very little about their "Europeanness", in other words what constitutes a teacher within an understanding of European professionalism' (p. 97). In order to answer the question: 'What makes a teacher "European"?', the author looks at general teacher competences required to meet the challenges of the 21st century and presents research findings on future demands on teacher competences in the Education and Training 2010 process. Taking into account teacher competences, Schratz (2010) indicates that a European teacher not only has the same competences as any other 'good teacher', but also possesses specific competences in the European dimension. Regarding the changing role of teachers and the impact of social changes, any good teacher should:

- promote new learning outcomes, i.e., contribute to citizenship education of students/trainees, promote the development of competences of students/trainees for the knowledge and lifelong learning society, and link the development of new curriculum competences with school subjects;
- work in restructured ways in the classroom, dealing with the social, cultural, and ethnic diversity of students; organising learning environments and facilitating learning processes; and working in teams with teachers and other professionals involved in the learning process of the same students; and
- work 'beyond the classroom' in the school/training centre and with social partners.

Considering the European dimension, Schratz (2014) shows that we can compose a list of required European teacher competences by including such attributes as European identity, European knowledge, European multiculturalism, European language competence, European professionalism, and European citizenship. The list by no means is complete, but it points to general (new) competences of the European teacher (see Chapter 1 for a description of those competences).

Schratz's proposition of the profile of the European teacher is echoed in a very important European policy document on teachers and teaching, entitled *Common European principles for teacher competences and qualifications* (European Commission, 2005). In this document, a vision of a European teaching profession is presented. One can learn from the document that the teaching profession in Europe can be characterised by the following qualities:

- Teaching is a *well-qualified* profession: all teachers are graduates from higher education institutions. Teachers who work in the field of initial vocational education are highly qualified in their professional area and have suitable pedagogical qualifications. Every teacher has broad subject knowledge and a good knowledge of pedagogy. Teachers have the skills and competences required to guide and support learners, and an understanding of the social and cultural dimension of education.
- Teaching is a profession of *lifelong learners*: the education and professional development of every teacher needs to be seen as a lifelong task. It should be structured and resourced accordingly. Teachers are supported to continue their professional development throughout their careers. They should recognise the importance of acquiring new knowledge, and they should be able to innovate and use evidence to inform their work.
- Teaching is a *mobile* profession: mobility is perceived as a central component of initial and continuing teacher education programmes (see ERASMUS programmes). Teachers are encouraged to work or study in other European countries for their professional development purposes.

- Teaching is a profession based on *partnership*: teacher education institutions organise their work collaboratively in partnership with schools, local work environments, work-based training providers, and other stakeholders.

These qualities have been mentioned in this chapter in different places, especially when the issues of quality of teacher education and quality of teaching were raised. Regarding the European policies on teaching, they can create the conditions for improving the societal view of teachers in Europe—and this, can be perceived as a major step in developing teacher professionalism.

In Schratz's concept of 'European teacher' the idea of European teacher professionalism is very briefly presented at the beginning of his paper and is defined as 'being able to teach in any European country by linking up cross-curricular themes from a European perspective, exchanging curricular content and methodologies with colleagues from other European countries, or paying attention to and learning from different teaching and learning traditions' (Schratz, 2014, p. 20). Such a definition can be treated as a starting point for the further discussion on the concept of 'European teacher professionalism'. It is hard to accept the stance of the author that such professionalism should be visible mainly through the ability to teach in any European country with reference to different teaching and learning traditions. The real value of teacher professionalism, not only in each European country, but also across Europe, lies in the assurance that 'it brings of higher standards for learners', as Finn (2017, p. 176) rightly pointed out. Finn poses thought-provoking questions in this context:

> Would we risk patients in hospital on surgeons who were unqualified or did not keep their skills up to date? Could a clever, well-informed and educated debater do the job of a lawyer? Could an able bus driver pilot an aircraft?
>
> (Ibid.)

In conclusion, it is worth stressing that the changing role of teachers within a European dimension, and the current challenges and opportunities facing teacher education policy and practice in Europe, imply the need to rethink teacher education programmes to support teachers in developing their professionalism, and along with it confidence in their ability, as well as the knowledge, skills, and attitudes necessary to meet and overcome the challenges they will encounter in their schools and beyond. One can assume that the role played by teachers in Europe will contribute to raising the awareness of a new expectation of what it means to be a 'European teacher' and what makes a teacher 'European' (see Schratz, 2010, 2014). Indeed, any consideration on the profile of the teacher, especially the European profile, should be directly connected with professionalism in teaching. It is not sufficient for teachers to reach an early professional standard; there is also a need to maintain and improve standards throughout a career, so that teachers can become increasingly expert practitioners, 'who take responsibility for their own development and who are developing their capacity both to use and contribute to the collective understanding of the teaching and learning process' (Donaldson, 2011, p. 15).

Conclusions

The new social, economic, and cultural challenges and demands towards education and teachers have impact on the schools and change them into institutions with modern aims and social contracts. As a reflection of these changes, government publications in Europe—at both national and European levels—stress the technological, economic, and social challenges that schools and therefore teachers face. The changing global context of school education has created the need for new and different knowledge, skills, and values and different patterns of personal and professional lives. Therefore, we need teachers who are well-prepared to perform their roles with quality throughout their careers, as well as to design the ways to support and sustain changes in teacher education across different countries in Europe and beyond it, with an emphasis on the preparation, induction, support, and assessment of new teachers, as well as on teachers' professional knowledge and CPD (see Darling-Hammond & Lieberman, 2013).

Teacher education, even though it is still a relatively young field that is closely related to research on teaching and research on organisations and policy implementation (see Grosmann & McDonald, 2008), is increasingly attracting the attention of researchers, teacher educators, practitioners, and policymakers. The importance of high-quality teacher education that enables teachers to take responsibility for their growth and development of their learning in their own classrooms and their schools is addressed and emphasised in numerous European policy documents.

One notable feature of the contemporary theory, research, and practice in the field of teacher education is consensus on its values and aims: teacher education needs to prepare teachers who are continuous learners themselves and who are able to respond to the challenges of the globalised world in which the school functions. The main aims of teacher education are to provide teachers with studies that guide them to considering themselves as accountable professional actors and to make them aware that they have rights and obligations to contribute to the development of education, and their task is to facilitate different learners to learn better. Teachers have a strong societal function, and this perspective should be integrated into the teacher education curricula. Teachers should be able to know what constitutes professionalism in teaching. Teacher education must be forward-looking and facilitate teachers to think continually about the sort of education that is meaningful and relevant to students' needs in a global context. One of the most vital challenges is to improve teaching and learning skills under conditions of diversity (cultural, social, and economic), and to develop the ability to act, work, and communicate in diverse multicultural educational situations.

Indeed, today there is a growing need to explore diversity of international experience and examine in depth and discuss critically the role of teacher and teacher education in Europe and beyond it (Madalińska-Michalak et al., 2012). We have to assess what is known and what needs to be known, especially within the areas of ideas and practices, and challenges and new trends in teacher education. This new knowledge will help us to rethink the meaning of the quality of teacher and teacher education.

References

Abbott, A. (1988). *The system of professions: An essay on the division of expert labor.* Chicago: University of Chicago Press.

Barber, M., & Mourshed, M. (2007). *How the world's best-performing schools come out on top.* New York, NY: McKinsey & Company.

Caena, F. (2017). Weaving the fabric: Teaching and teacher education ecosystem. In B. Hudson (Ed.), *Overcoming the fragmentation in teacher education policy and practice* (pp. 179–200). Cambridge: Cambridge University Press.

CEC (Commission of the European Communities). (2007). *Communication from the Commission to the Council and European Parliament: Improving the quality of teacher education.* COM (2007) 392 final, 2007. Brussels: CEC.

Cochran-Smith, M., & Fries, M. K. (2005). Researching teacher education in changing times: Paradigms and politics. In M. Cochran-Smith & K. Zeichner (Eds.), *Studying teacher education: The report of the AERA panel on research and teacher education* (pp. 69–110). Mahwah, NJ: Lawrence Erlbaum Associates.

Cochran-Smith, M., & Zeichner, K. M. (Eds.). (2005). *Studying teacher education: The report of the AERA panel on research and teacher education.* Mahwah, NJ: Lawrence Erlbaum Associates.

Darling-Hammond, L. (1999). *Teacher quality and student achievement: A review of state policy evidence.* Seattle: Center for the Study of Teaching and Policy, University of Washington.

Darling-Hammond, L., & Lieberman, A. (2013). *Teacher education around the world: Changing policies and practices.* Abingdon: Routledge.

Day, C. (2017). School leadership as an influence on teacher quality. In X. Zhu, A. L. Goodwin, & H. Zhang (Eds.), *Quality of teacher education and learning: Theory and practice* (pp. 101–117). Singapore: Springer.

Day, C., & Gu, Q. (2010). *The new lives of teachers.* Abingdon: Routledge.

Donaldson, G. (2011). *Teaching Scotland's future: Report of a review of teacher education in Scotland.* Edinburgh: Scottish Government.

Eisenschmidt, E. (2006). *Implementation of induction year for novice teachers in Estonia.* Dissertations on Social Sciences, 25. Tallinn: Tallinn University Press.

Eisenschmidt, E. (2010). Induction – Challenges and opportunities for improving teacher education in Europe. In O. Gassner, L. Kerger, & M. Schratz (Eds.), *The first ten years after Bologna* (pp. 121–136). Bucureşti: Editura Universităţii din Bucureşti.

ETUCE. (2008). *Teacher education in Europe: An ETUCE policy paper.* Brussels: ETUCE.

European Commission. (2005). *Common European principles for teacher competences and qualifications.* Brussels: European Commission.

European Commission. (2007). *Improving the quality of teacher education.* Brussels: European Commission.

European Commission. (2010). *Developing coherent and system-wide induction programmes for beginning teachers: A handbook for policymakers.* Brussels: European Commission.

European Commission. (2011a). *Literature review teachers' core competences: Requirements and development*. Brussels: European Commission.
European Commission. (2011b). *Literature review: Quality in teachers' continuing professional development*. Brussels: European Commission.
European Commission. (2012b). *Assessment of key competences in initial education and training: Policy guidance*. Strasbourg: European Commission.
European Commission. (2012c). *Supporting the teaching professions for better learning outcomes*. Strasbourg: European Commission.
European Commission. (2013a). *Supporting teacher competence development for better learning outcomes*. Brussels: European Commission.
European Commission. (2013b). *Supporting teacher educators for better learning outcomes*. Brussels: European Commission.
European Commission. (2015). *Shaping career-long perspectives on teaching: A guide on policies to improve initial teacher education*. Luxembourg: Publications Office of the European Union.
Eurydice. (2009). *Key data on education 2009*. Brussels: Eurydice.
Finn, A. (2017). The professional standing of teaching in Europe: Regulation or relegation? In B. Hudson (Ed.), *Overcoming the fragmentation in teacher education policy and practice* (pp. 153–178). Cambridge: Cambridge University Press.
Flores, M. A. (2016). Teacher Education curriculum. In J. Loughran & M. L. Hamilton (Eds.), *International handbook of teacher education* (Vol. 1, pp. 187–230). Singapore: Springer.
Grosmann, P., & McDonald, M. (2008). Back to the future: Directions for research in teaching and teacher education. *American Educational Research Journal, 45*(1), 184–205.
Harford, J., & Gray, P. (2017). Emerging from somewhere: Student teachers, professional identity and the future of teacher education research. In B. Hudson (Ed.), *Overcoming the fragmentation in teacher education policy and practice* (pp. 27–48). Cambridge: Cambridge University Press.
Hargreaves, A., & Shirley, D. (2017). *The fourth way: The inspiring future for educational change*. Thousand Oaks, CA: Corwin.
Hattie, J. (2003, October). *Teachers make a difference: What is the research evidence?* Paper presented at the ACER Research Conference 'Building Teacher Quality: What does the Research Tell us', Melbourne, Australia. Retrieved from http://research.acer.edu.au/research_conference_2003/4/ (accessed 10 June 2017).
Hattie, J. (2008). *Visible learning: A synthesis of meta-analyses relating to achievement*. Abingdon: Routledge.
Hudson, B. (Ed.). (2017). *Overcoming fragmentation in teacher education policy and practice*. Cambridge: Cambridge University Press.
Livingston, K. (2012). Teachers as learners at the centre of system, culture and practice change. In J. Madalińska-Michalak, H. Niemi, & S. Chong (Eds.), *Research, policy and practice in teacher education in Europe* (pp. 27–41). Łódź: University of Łódź Publishing House.
Loughran, J. (2017). Quality in teacher education: Challenging assumptions, building understanding through foundation principles. In X. Zhu, A. L. Goodwin, & H. Zhang (Eds.), *Quality of teacher education and learning: Theory and practice* (pp. 69–84). Singapore: Springer.
Madalińska-Michalak, J. (2017). Teacher education in Poland: Towards teachers' career-long professional learning. In B. Hudson (Ed.), *Overcoming the*

fragmentation in teacher education policy and practice (pp. 73–100). Cambridge: Cambridge University Press.

Madalińska-Michalak, J., Niemi, H., & Chong, S. (2012). *Research, policy, and practice in teacher education in Europe*. Łódź: University of Łódź Publishing House.

OECD. (2009). *Creating effective teaching and learning environments. First results from TALIS*. Paris: OECD. Retrieved from www.oecd.org/dataoecd/17/51/43023606.pdf (accessed 10 June 2017).

OECD. (2010). *Teaching and learning international survey (TALIS), technical report: Creating effective teaching and learning environments*. Paris: OECD.

OECD. (2011). *Building a high-quality teaching profession: Lessons from around the world*. Paris: OECD.

OECD. (2014). *TALIS 2013 results: An international perspective on teaching and learning*. Paris: OECD.

OECD. (2016). *Global competency for an inclusive world*. Paris: OECD. Retrieved from www.oecd.org/education/Global-competency-for-an-inclusive-world.pdf (accessed 6 June 2017).

OECD. (2005). *Teachers matter: Attracting, developing and retaining effective teachers*. Paris: OECD. Retrieved from www.oecd.org/edu/teacherpolicy (accessed 10 June 2017).

Russel, T., & Martin, A. K. (2016). Exploring the complex concept of quality in teacher education. In J. Loughran & M. L. Hamilton (Eds.), *International handbook of teacher education* (Vol. 2, pp. 143–180). Singapore: Springer.

Schleicher, A. (2012). *Preparing teachers and developing school leaders for the 21st century: Lessons from around the world*. Paris: OECD.

Schratz, M. (2010). What is a 'European Teacher'? In O. Gassner, L. Kerger, & M. Schratz (Eds.), *The first ten years after Bologna* (pp. 97–102). București: Editura Universității din București.

Schratz, M. (2014). The European teacher: Transnational perspectives in teacher education policy and practice. *CEPS Journal, 4*, 11–27.

Shirley, D., & MacDonald, E. (2016). *The mindful teacher* (2nd ed.). New York, NY: Teachers College Press.

Zgaga, P. (2014, May). *Fragmentation in teacher education vs. fragmentation in higher education*. Keynote lecture presented at TEPE 2014 conference 'Overcoming Fragmentation in Teacher Education Policy and Practice', Zagreb, Croatia.

Zhu, X., Goodwin, A. L., & Zhang, H. (Eds.). (2017). *Quality of teacher education and learning: Theory and practice*. Singapore: Springer.

Part 2
Tackling challenges and opportunities in teacher education

3 Developing teachers' competences to work in a European context

The HOWBET experience

Nilza Costa

Introduction

This chapter describes and discusses the HOWBET Summer School with respect to its rationale, implementation, and impact on participants. Finally, it highlights areas where actions are still needed for continuing to promote a European dimension in teacher education.

The HOWBET Summer School, an IP funded under the ERASMUS Lifelong Learning Programme (reference no. 2013-2011-PT1-ERA10-16688-P AVEIRO01), and designed in the scope of the Teacher Education Group of Campus Europae (http://campuseuropae.org), took place at the University of Aveiro, in Portugal, from 14 to 25 July 2014. This IP, coordinated by the University of Aveiro, involved eight European universities (the University of Aveiro, in Portugal; the University of Eastern Finland; the University of Hamburg, in Germany; the University of Latvia; the University of Lódz, in Poland; the University of Novi Sad, in Serbia; the University of Vienna, in Austria; and the University of Vytautas Magnus, in Lithuania), 36 pre-service teachers from those universities, and 11 teacher educators. This innovative formative experience deserves, from our point of view, its broad dissemination, as we explain in this chapter.

The rationale behind the HOWBET Summer School

Historically, teacher education had been focused on national education needs, and ruled by national policy and legislation (Darling-Hammond, 2017; Darling-Hammond & Sykes, 2003). However, teacher education, professionalism, and teachers' work have gained an increasing international dimension, namely due to globalisation and the consequent complexity of the educational challenges teachers have been facing (see, for instance, Paine & Zeichner, 2012). As far as Europe is concerned, this tendency has been building since the late 1990s, namely by the work of ENTEP, which was formed at the initiative of the Portuguese Minister of Education in 1999 (Gassner, Kerger, & Schratz, 2010). The generalised ideas, shared by European researchers and policymakers, of the importance of teacher education as a public good, of teachers' role in the support of a cohesive European space, and of the development of a European identity and citizenship, all justify the investment which has been and is currently being done in the field of teacher education (ITE, CPD, and teachers' professionalism). A brief summary of the main ideas which have emerged from this investment, and which constituted the rationale of the HOWBET Summer School, is put forward hereafter.

The concepts of 'European teacher', 'European dimensions', and 'Europeanness', and their relevance for teacher education, have been presented and discussed in several texts written by Austrian professor Michael Schratz, a researcher in education and representative of ENTEP in the European Commission (Schratz, 2005, 2010, 2014), and taken on board by several other studies, either focusing on a cross-border European perspective or on a national one (see, for instance, Donnelly & Watkins, 2011; Halinen & Holappa, 2013; Kearney, 2012). These same concepts are still significant in recent literature (see Alexiadou, 2017; Public Policy and Management Institute, 2017), which shows that they continue to be present in teacher education research and policy agenda.

Following the pioneering work of Schratz (2005), 'European teacher' means 'a teacher working within a European context of professionalism' (p. 1). The idea behind the development of such a concept is not to create a 'standardized teacher model', but to look for commonalities and values desired in a cohesive Europe, in the diversity of national identities. The concept of 'European dimension' has been used, according to the same author 'to balance national and transnational values in educational policy making' (Schratz, 2005, p. 4). Finally, 'Europeanness' 'constitutes a teacher within an understanding of European professionalism' (p. 1). In order to develop a European professionalism, (future) teachers should know and act according to six competences: *European identity, European knowledge, European multiculturalism, European language competence, European professionalism, and European citizenship* (Schratz, 2005, pp. 4–6). For that to occur it is necessary to introduce those domains in the curriculum of ITE and CPD, as well as to create learning environments for their development, which the HOWBET Summer School attempted to do.

In addition to what was mentioned earlier, the HOWBET Summer School also took on board several guidelines from the European Union (EU) policy documents in teacher education and the teaching profession (see http://ec.europa.eu/education/node_en), as for example 'Education and Training (ET) 2010' and 'Education and Training (ET) 2020'. It is worth noticing that the EU education policy documents have been (and still are) designed to support national actions and guide them to address European common challenges. They are often the result of academic studies and consultation of experts in education and teacher education. The four key ideas from those documents, which were incorporated in the HOWBET Summer School rationale, are summarised as follows.

1   Two strategic goals/priorities guided what the member states of the EU defined for its development. The first, launched in 2000, stated that the EU should 'become the most dynamic and competitive, knowledge-based economy in the world, capable of sustaining economic growth, employment and social cohesion' (cited by Agostini & Capano, 2013, p. 154). The second, launched in 2009 when Europe was emerging from an economic and financial crisis, stated that the EU should go for a 'smart growth' (developing

an economy based on knowledge and innovation), 'sustainable growth' (promoting a more resource efficient, greener, and more competitive economy), and 'inclusive growth' (fostering a high-employment economy delivering social and territorial cohesion) economy (Agostini & Capano, 2013, p. 156). Without prioritising the economic orientation of the two strategic goals/priorities of the EU, and considering the scope of HOWBET Summer School, we selected three key 'flags' to be present in Europe: social cohesion, sustainability development, and inclusive society.

2   The educational priorities defined in the two frameworks for European cooperation, namely 'Education and Training (ET) 2010' and 'Education and Training (ET) 2020' were also incorporated into the HOWBET rationale. The three strategic objectives of EU policies, defined in ET 2010, concerned 'a) improvements to the quality and effectiveness of education and training systems; b) the facilitation of access to education and training; and c) the opening up of the education and training system to the wider world' (Agostini & Capano, 2013, p. 153). ET 2020 included and expanded those objectives to four updated strategic ones, namely 'a) making lifelong learning and mobility a reality; b) improving the quality and efficiency of education and training; c) promoting equity, social cohesion and active citizenship; d) enhancing creativity and innovation, including entrepreneurship, at all levels of education and training' (Agostini & Capano, 2013, p. 153). Following the three key 'flags' stated earlier for the rationale of the HOWBET Summer School, as well as the educational priorities of ET 2010 and ET 2020, we added an additional three which education and training should promote: lifelong learning and mobility; equity, social cohesion, and active citizenship; and entrepreneurship.

3   The four priorities areas for European cooperation in education and training for the period 2012–2014, as defined by the Joined Report (Council of the European Union and the European Commission, 2012), are as follows (adapted from Agostini & Capano, 2013, pp. 162–163):

   a)   making lifelong learning and mobility a reality (lifelong learning strategies, European reference tools, and learning mobility);
   b)   improving the quality and efficiency of education and training in basic skills (literacy, mathematics, science, and technology); languages; professional development of teachers, trainers, and school leaders; modernising higher education and increasing tertiary attainment levels; attractiveness and relevance of vocational education and training; and efficient funding and evaluation;
   c)   promoting equity, social cohesion, and active citizenship (early school dropout, early childhood education and care, and equity and diversity); and
   d)   enhancing creativity and innovation, including entrepreneurship, at all levels of education and training (partnerships with business, research, and civil society; transversal key competences; entrepreneurship education; e-literacy; media literacy; and innovative learning environments).

4 The nine key competences and the three transversal skills identified as necessary for personal fulfilment, active citizenship, social cohesion, and employability through lifelong learning in a knowledge society, and the way to promote them, are, respectively: communication in the mother tongue, communication in foreign (multiple) languages, foreign language learning, maths competence and basic competences in science and technology, digital competence, learning to learn, social and civic competences, sense of initiative and entrepreneurship, and cultural awareness and expression; critical thinking, creativity, and collaboration; and problem solving and self-management (Arjomand et al., 2013, pp. 14–18).

In the next section, we will present how the HOWBET Summer School operationalised this rationale.

The HOWBET Summer School implementation

Thirty-six students from the eight participant Universities enrolled in the HOWBET Summer School. They were attending a degree in ITE (first or second cycle of Bologna, since the cycle level which grants a professional certificate varies among countries). Table 3.1 provides information about the students enrolled in the summer school, namely, university of origin, gender, age, and cycle of study. As the data show, each university had five participating students, except the University of Aveiro, where six students were allowed to enrol. The majority of the students were female, aged between 22 and 27 years old, and attending a second cycle of Bologna.

Table 3.1 Data concerning students enrolled in the HOWBET Summer School

University of origin	Number of students
University of Vienna (Austria)	5
University of Eastern Finland (Finland)	5
University of Latvia (Latvia)	5
University of Vytautas Magnus (Lithuania)	5
University of Lódz (Poland)	5
University of Aveiro (Portugal)	6
University of Hamburg (Germany)	5

Gender		Age		Cycle of study	
Female	Male	Range	Majority	Cycle of study	Number of participants
27	8	21–51 years old	22–27 years old	First cycle Second cycle Third cycle	7 28 1

Taking on board the rationale presented earlier, the HOWBET Summer School was designed, as it is presented in Table 3.2, with (a) three main goals; (b) eight competences and learning outcomes (content-related and transversal competences for lifelong learning), and (c) eight topics (in accordance with the IP 'flags'; see Agostini & Capano, 2013).

The methodology used in the HOWBET Summer School during the 10-day eight-hour sessions, generally included: (a) a morning session with a presentation by the teacher educator(s), but where students' participation was always encouraged; (b) an afternoon session following group-work strategy (varying with national or mixed-country groups, according to the proposed activity); and (c) an evening session with a social and cultural event prepared by the students of each country. Each day, apart from the first and the last, was centred on a specific topic under the responsibility of one or two teacher educator(s) from each university according to his/her/their expertise. The first session was dedicated to the presentation of the summer school and of each participant, where students shared their initial expectations and previous experiences, and a workshop about the Moodle online learning management system. The last session was devoted to the final evaluation of the summer school.

Table 3.2 Main goals, competences, and learning outcomes of the HOWBET Summer School

Goals	Competences and learning outcomes
Develop an understanding of 'Europeanness' in (future) teachers' profile work	Understand the main European trends in education and teacher education policies
Develop competences for teaching and acting as a 'European teacher'	Understand commonalities and differences in approaches to a 'European teacher' profile
Improve the quality of multilateral cooperation between participant European higher education institutions	Improve teaching and learning skills under conditions of diversity (cultural, social, linguistic, and economic)
	Show sensitivity towards differences in a multicultural environment
	Become aware of the main trends of the education systems of different European countries
	Enhance foreign language skills (English, but also other languages as a natural result of mobility)
	Gain the ability to act, work, and communicate in diverse multicultural situations
	Become open to changes and lifelong learning in the teaching profession

HOWBET was supported by Moodle learning management system: before the summer school, students registered in the virtual platform; during the summer school, Moodle was used for downloading documents suggested by the teacher educators, and for submitting and sharing students' work; after the summer school students could stay connected and exchange experiences.

Table 3.3 presents a list of the HOWBET Summer School topics. A more detailed description and analysis of these topics, their theoretical roots, and examples of activities carried out, are the focus of the majority of the chapters of this book.

Student assessments had a continuous and formative dimension, according to which the teacher educators gave feedback to the students about their participation and performance in the daily tasks, often in a written format after the session; and a summative dimension, consisting in the elaboration of an individual e-portfolio, which included a daily reflection on the work developed. The criteria used to assess students are listed in Table 3.4.

In accordance with the rationale of the HOWBET Summer School, the criteria used focused not only on content knowledge, but also on the students' attitudes and on their learning and development process. Table 3.5 presents the qualitative grades level, correspondent quantitative grades, and respective indicators for the e-portfolio. This instrument was presented and negotiated with the students at the beginning of the summer school, as a way to share responsibilities in the assessment process.

Table 3.3 Topics of the HOWBET Summer School and teacher educators responsible

Topics	Teachers responsible for the topic
Comparative analysis in education	Wilfried Hartmann (University of Hamburg, Germany)
Literacy competences in a multicultural context	Margarita Teresevičienė and Elena Trepulė (Vytautas Magnus University, Lithuania)
European citizenship education	Ana Raquel Simões (University of Aveiro, Portugal)
Learners' needs in multicultural contexts	Ilze Kangro and Ilze Ivanova (University of Latvia, Latvia)
Linguistic diversity in the classroom	Seija Jeskanen (University of Eastern Finland, Finland)
Diversity and social inclusion in education	Judith 't Gilde (University of Vienna, Austria)
Profile of European teachers' characteristics today and tomorrow	Joanna Madalińska-Michalak (University of Łódź, Poland)
Teaching with a European dimension: examples for the classroom	Nilza Costa and Mónica Lourenço (University of Aveiro, Portugal)

Table 3.4 Criteria for assessment

Criteria used and negotiated with the students to assess them
Deepness in the understanding of the topics
Fulfilment of the tasks required by the teacher educators
Participation in the discussions during the sessions
Critical thinking
Sharing national and trans-European experiences about the European dimension in teacher education
Contribution to a collaborative working environment
Integration in a multicultural environment

Table 3.5 Grading system to assess students' individual e-portfolios (adapted from Costa, 2014)

Grades level	Grades	Indicators
Outstanding	17–20	Identifies clearly the main topics dealt with each day of the IP, reflecting thoroughly about them and questioning critically
		Presents results from the group work developed during all the days of the IP, as well as materials created and presented during the course, and reflects upon them
Very good	14–16	Identifies the main topics dealt with each day of the IP, reflecting in some way about them
		Presents results from the group work developed during all the days of the IP, as well as materials created and presented
Good	10–13	Identifies some of the main topics dealt with each day of the IP, but only within a descriptive approach
		Presents only some of the results from the group work developed in the course, as well as some materials created and presented

All the students succeeded in the HOWBET Summer School, the majority with Very Good, followed by Good; and only three students earned Outstanding. Students' difficulties in presenting a critical reflection, in opposition with a descriptive one, was the main reason for the grades obtained.

In order to learn from the IP experience, three evaluation instruments were used: two questionnaires were filled in by the students in the first and in the last sessions of the summer school, and one was completed by the teacher educators at the end of the programme. The three questionnaires had a similar format, which included closed questions (some of them using a Likert scale) and open questions. The timing of the application of each questionnaire, to whom it was addressed, and its main aims are summarised in Table 3.6.

Table 3.6 Questionnaires used to evaluate the HOWBET Summer School (adapted from Costa, 2014)

Questionnaires	Target audience and timing	Main aims
Questionnaire A	– Applied to students on the first day of the IP	To characterise the participant students and to identify their opinions about (a) expectations of the IP, and (b) views on the IP (present and future).
Questionnaire B	– Applied to students on the last day of the IP	To evaluate if students' expectations were fulfilled, and to collect suggestions for future work related to the IP and their educational and formation path.
Questionnaire C (adapted from the questionnaire in the LLP–ERASMUS programme–IP; final participant report from the teachers)	– Applied to teacher educators at the end of each teacher mobility experience within the IP	To identify characteristics of the teacher educators' mobility period (MP) (e.g., hours of teaching), and to collect teachers' opinions about (a) the period before the MP (e.g., support from the home institution, motivations to teach in an ERASMUS IP), (b) during the MP (e.g., the kind of activities included), and (c) the evaluation of the MP (e.g., the level of satisfaction with which the MP is recognised by the home institution).

In addition to these formal moments, frequent informal assessment moments occurred, namely through daily discussions and reflections between the IP coordinator, the students, and the teacher instructors.

The HOWBET Summer School impact

This section presents the evaluation of the short-term impact of the HOWBET Summer School, given that the analysis is based on data collected at the beginning and at the end of the IP, and in informal moments. Although it would be relevant to follow up the participants' educational and professional path after the summer school (at a medium and long term), and therefore to be able to access its longer impact, this has not been done so far. There is only one indicator at a medium term that may provide some data on the extended impact of the summer school, which is the collaboration of six participating students in the writing of Chapter 9 of this book.

Next a summary of the results is presented, following a descriptive statistical analysis of the answers to the closed questions and a content analysis of the answers to the open questions. The evaluation of the HOWBET Summer School by the students was generally positive. Nearly 90% of the participants considered that the summer school corresponded positively to their expectations. The host city culture and the diversity of participants were the strongest reasons for this positive evaluation, followed by knowledge they acquired and the experiences they had of different perspectives about European education systems and teacher education approaches.

However, students considered some lectures to be (a) less interesting than others, (b) a bit elementary, and (c) with too much theory and not enough practical situations. Concerning the weakest aspect mentioned, students emphasised the heavy daily workload, but also some organisational aspects, such as the delay in receiving the travel costs, and some unexpected problems with their accommodation. Despite these opinions, when questioned if they would like to continue to collaborate with their peers and teachers, around 94% answered positively, stating that they would like to keep in touch with all the participants in the HOWBET Summer School (through, for example, Facebook, Skype conferences, or mailing lists), in order to be able to continue sharing experiences, doubts, concerns, and challenges facing education. They also showed a positive opinion concerning the organisation of future editions of this summer school. The main suggestions given to improve future editions are linked with the weakest aspects mentioned earlier. For example, students suggested that the daily workload should be reduced and the practical dimension of the topics should be increased.

The majority of the participating teacher educators evaluated the summer school as 'very good', highlighting aspects such as the richness of the mobility experience, in terms of the way it is recognised by their own university and in their annual evaluation performance. They also mentioned the positive impact of the summer school on their professional and personal development, as it broadened their understanding of different education and teacher education systems and practices; improved their teaching competences and skills; increased their awareness of linguistic, social, and cultural diversity; and enhanced their motivation and job satisfaction. Also with this experience, teachers stated that they would encourage students and colleagues to go on ERASMUS mobility, as it may develop new cooperation projects, new areas of research and increase the quality of their teaching.

In terms of the main difficulties met by the partnership when organising and managing the HOWBET Summer School, teacher educators highlighted the following by order of significance: to deal with the shortage of budget, to cope with the heavy workload of the IP, and to deal with some cultural differences.

In summary, and despite the weaknesses highlighted by the participants (students and teacher educators), we can say that the HOWBET Summer School attained its three main goals.

Final considerations

We hope that the evidence provided in this chapter, together with a more detailed approach given in some other chapters of this book, may serve as a springboard for other initiatives concerning the issue of teacher education in Europe. Before finishing, we would like to point out one last consideration concerning the pioneering experience of HOWBET Summer School and its relevance.

Despite the fact that the IP was developed in 2014, some key ideas remain up-to-date and should be studied further. Concepts such as 'Europeanness' still continue to be present in recent studies (for example, see the study of Kirpitchenko & Voloder, 2016). In addition, data from the United Nations (UN) (2016) emphasise the existence of 40 million international migrants in Europe, which highlights teachers' challenges in dealing with this context in schools, namely concerning diversity and inclusion. Furthermore—and despite all the advances undertaken in teacher education in European countries—the recently published *Education and training monitor report* (European Commission, 2017) provides evidence for the positive impact of the European dimension of teacher education in the attainment of the priorities defined in ET 2020, both in the EU educational area and in each member state, which, as referred to earlier, had a central role in the rationale of the HOWBET Summer School and in its operationalisation. This report also highlights areas where actions are still needed, and which were already taken on board by the HOWBET Summer School, namely the development of better and more inclusive schools; the need to support teachers for excellent teaching and learning; and the improvement of the effectiveness, equitability, and efficiency of governance of the school education systems. The EU continues to support the professional development of teachers (e.g., through ERASMUS+, new publications as the 2017 report *Preparing teachers for diversity: the role of initial teacher education*). However, teacher education research and programmes promoted by European higher education institutions need to go further in such enterprise. We hope that the HOWBET Summer School may be a source of inspiration for this.

References

Agostini, C., & Capano, G. (2013). Education policy: Comparing EU developments and national policies. In D. Natali & B. Vanhercke (Eds.), *Social developments in the European Union 2012* (pp. 147–180). Belgium (Brussels): ETUI.

Alexiadou, N. (2017). Equality and education policy in the European Union: An example from the case of Roma. In S. Parker, K. Gulson, & T. Gale (Eds.), *Policy and inequality in education* (pp. 111–131). Singapore: Springer.

Arjomand, G., Erstad, O., Gilje, O., Gordon, J., Kallunki, V., Kearney, C., . . . von Reis Saari, J. (2013). *KeyCoNet 2013 literature review: Key competence development in*

school education in Europe. Retrieved from http://keyconet.eun.org/c/document_library/get_file?uuid=060f39a1-bd86-4941-a6ca-8b2a3ba8548e&groupId=11028 (accessed 29 October 2017).
Costa, N. (2014). *Final report of the HOWBET IP. Aveiro: Universidade de Aveiro* (unpublished report delivered to the ERASMUS+ National Agency Education and Training).
Council of the European Union and European Commission (2012). Joint Report of the Council and the Commission on the implementation of the Strategic Framework for European cooperation in education and training (ET 2020). Education and training in a smart, sustainable and inclusive Europe (2012/C 70/05).
Darling-Hammond, L. (2017). Teacher education around the world: What can we learn from international practice? *European Journal of Teacher Education, 40*(3), 291–309.
Darling-Hammond, L., & Sykes, G. (2003). Wanted: A national teacher supply policy for education: The right way to meet the 'Highly Qualified Teacher' challenge. *Education Policy Analysis Archives, 11*(33), 1–55.
Donnelly, V., & Watkins, A. (2011). Teacher education for inclusion across Europe. *La nouvelle revue de l'adaptation et de la scolarisation, 3*(5), 17–24.
European Commission. (2017). *Education and training monitor 2017*. Luxembourg: Publications Office of the European Union.
Gassner, O., Kerger, L., & Schratz, M. (Eds.). (2010). *The first ten years after Bologna*. Romania: Editura Universității din București.
Halinen, I., & Holappa, M. (2013). Curricular balance based on dialogue, cooperation and trust – The case of Finland. In W. Kuiper & J. Berkvens (Eds.), *Balancing curriculum regulation and freedom across Europe* (pp. 39–62). The Netherlands: SLO Netherlands Institute for Curriculum Development.
Kearney, C. (2012). *KeyCoNet's review of the literature: Key competence development in school education in Europe*. Brussels: European Schoolnet.
Kirpitchenko, L., & Voloder, L. (2016). Student mobility from Central/Eastern Europe: Towards a shared Europeanness. In M. Chou (Ed.), *Proceedings of the Australian sociological association conference* (pp. 176–182). Australian: TASA.
Paine, L., & Zeichner, K. (2012). The local and the global in reforming teaching and teacher education. *Comparative Education Review, 56*(4), 569–583.
Public Policy and Management Institute. (2017). *Preparing teachers for diversity: The role of initial teacher education*. Luxembourg: Publications Office of the European Union.
Schratz, M. (2005). What is a 'European Teacher'? A discussion paper. *ENTEP Papers*. Retrieved from www.sdcentras.lt/pla/res/Schratz.pdf (accessed 10 October 2017).
Schratz, M. (2010). What is a 'European Teacher'? In O. Gassner, L. Kerger, & M. Schratz (Eds.), *The first ten years after Bologna* (pp. 97–102). București: Editura Universității din București.
Schratz, M. (2014). The European Teacher: Transnational perspectives in teacher education policy and practice. *CEPS Journal, 4*(4), 11–27.
United Nations Department of Economic and Social Affairs, Population Division (2016). International Migration Report 2015 (ST/ESA/SER.A/384). Retrieved from www.un.org/en/development/desa/population/migration/publications/migrationreport/docs/MigrationReport2015.pdf (accessed 1 November 2017).

4 Future needs of learners in a European context

Ilze Ivanova and Ilze Kangro

Introduction

The 21st century has brought diverse and rapid socio-economic changes for everybody in the world. Due to fast and wide technological progress, the traditional working environment is gradually disappearing. Work today is becoming more intellectual than physical, requiring employers and employees to possess new skills, such as digital and social skills, foreign languages, and entrepreneurship. Nowadays people are likely to have a variety of careers during their lifetime, and both professional occupations and workplaces are changed quite frequently. Creativity, strong critical thinking, and interpersonal communication skills, for instance, will be essential for success in a rapidly changing, interconnected, and complex world.

According to data from *World population prospects: The 2015 revision* (UN, 2015b), between 2015 and 2030, the number of people in the world aged 60 and above will grow by 56%, from 901 million to 1.4 billion; by 2050, the world's senior population is projected to more than double its 2015 size, reaching nearly 2.1 billion. This situation will clearly affect education and the life of generations to come, making it imperative to devise a well-developed lifelong education programme to encourage students to learn and develop new skills necessary for the current century.

Currently there are many different factors and circumstances that exist simultaneously influencing education, learning, and everyone's life, such as globalisation, localisation, and internationalisation. The expression 'local and global' prompts people to learn how to think globally but at the same time to act locally. Therefore, thinking and acting are also the skills to be acquired and to be activated during one's lifetime. Information and technology opportunities are also increasing day by day, requiring new knowledge and skills. As the amount of information increases exponentially, education systems can no longer focus primarily on memorising a core body of knowledge. Knowledge has to be acquired and used as a tool to develop new skills and attitudes in order to be successful in life. Today, the Internet creates opportunities for the growth of new industries. Creativity and innovation determine success in work and in one's academic life. Consequently, learning is a necessity for everybody in a globalised, rapidly changing, and diverse world: it is an essential life skill to keep up with developments. Thus, a new type of a teacher is required to promote the education of the future citizens of the 21st century.

This chapter includes a theoretical analysis of learners' needs in the 21st century and, correspondingly, the characteristics of future teachers to support the implementation of those needs. As the authors of this chapter represent Latvia, a short overview about teacher education in Latvia is given as well. Finally, the chapter offers insights into the views of prospective teachers participating in a workshop of the HOWBET Summer School about students' needs for the future, the characteristics of the contemporary student and teacher, future professions, and the role of the school in the preparation for the future.

Theoretical background

Learners' needs and competences in the 21st century

Studies addressing changes in education, learning, and teaching; skill development; general and professional competences; and learners' needs have been conducted by different authors in different periods and at different levels: theoretical and practical; European, global, and local; and from the point of different non-governmental and self-governing organisations (see, among others, Fadel, Trilling, & Bialik, 2015; Fullan & Langworthy, 2014; Hozjan, 2009; Kennedy, Hyland, & Ryan, 2007; Schleicher, 2015; Trilling, 2007; Wagner, 2008, 2015). In the previous century, psychologist Abraham Maslow summarised the developmental goals for an individual in his well-known 'pyramid of needs' (Maslow, 1943). The pyramid demonstrates the idea that lower-level needs are more fundamental to a person's well-being than higher-level needs. If those needs are not fulfilled, the higher-level needs will not be easily reached. Physiological and biological needs are at the basic level, the lack of which results in disfunction of the biological organisms. These needs include safety and security, love and belonging, and esteem. The highest two levels in the pyramid are allocated to self-actualisation and self-transcendence. Self-actualisation could be understood as the realisation of one's full potential. The highest self-transcendence need is defined as the need of helping others to achieve self-actualisation (Maslow, 1943).

Maslow's theory has been highly popular in business management; and it has also been applied to motivate learners in the classroom setting. In this respect, teachers should structure their lessons and the classroom learning environment to meet as many of the needs of students as possible, especially the safety, belonging, and esteem needs. When all levels of the pyramid are met, students are able to show their full ability and eagerness for learning.

Despite the popularity of Maslow's theory, rather than focusing on a pyramid of needs, recent studies have addressed the competences required by learners to feel effective at meeting everyday challenges and opportunities, demonstrating skill over time, and feeling a sense of growth. The *European qualifications framework for lifelong learning* (European Parliament and Council, 2008) presents a definition of the concept of 'competence' as the ability to use knowledge, skills, and personal and/or methodological abilities in work or study environments and in professional and personal development. 'Skill' is defined as the ability to apply knowledge and use know-how to complete tasks and solve problems. 'Skills' are described as both cognitive and practical. 'Knowledge' is described as the outcome of information through learning and is distinguished as the body of facts, principles, theories, and practices that are related to a field of work or study. The authors of this chapter consider knowledge, skills and abilities, attitudes, values, and behaviours to be the essential components of the concept of competence. All of these components are learning outcomes to be reached in the learning process. Learning outcomes demonstrate learner's knowledge, understanding, and ability to complete and accomplish a process of learning.

The development of competences as learning outcomes in the learning process has become of the utmost importance in education, drawing the attention of several organisations and researchers. In 1992 Agenda 21 of the UN (UN, 1992) proposed a comprehensive plan of action to be taken globally, nationally, and locally, aiming to prepare the world for the challenges of the 21st century. It highlighted the following:

> All the individuals should have competence to support the development that meets the needs of the present without compromising the ability of future generations to meet their own needs. [. . .] The individual learner should have the knowledge, values and skills to be an active, democratic and responsible citizen and to participate in decisions at the personal level as well as at different levels within society locally and globally, in order to contribute to creating a sustainable society.
>
> (UN, 1992, pp. 3–4, 61)

Alongside Agenda 21, the UN's 2030 Agenda (UN, 2015a) puts forward big tasks for the next 15 years. All of its 17 goals are connected, leading to peace, mutual understanding, cooperation, and better lives for everybody. Goal 4 defines the specific tasks for education: to 'ensure inclusive and equitable quality education and promote lifelong learning opportunities for all' (UN, 2015a, p. 12). It puts forward that by 2030 all learners should:

> acquire the knowledge and skills needed to promote sustainable development, including, among others, through education for sustainable development and sustainable lifestyles, human rights, gender equality, promotion of a culture of peace and non-violence, global citizenship and appreciation of cultural diversity and of culture's contribution to sustainable development.
>
> (UN, 2015a, pp. 14–15)

In the European context, the Europe 2020 strategy acknowledges that a transformation of education and learning is needed to produce the new skills and competences required, if Europe is to remain competitive, overcome the current economic crisis, and seize new opportunities. However, to determine how education policy can adequately prepare learners for life in the future society, it is necessary to determine what competences will be relevant and how they will be acquired in the future (European Commission, 2010, p. 1).

Similar ideas are expressed by the UN Educational Scientific and Cultural Organization (UNESCO), which states that quality education systems have to enable learners to continuously adapt their competences while continuously acquiring and even developing new ones (UNESCO, 2012). These competences are considered to be diverse in scope, ranging from core skills, content knowledge, cognitive skills, and soft skills, to occupational skills, and to enable learners to meet a complex demand or carry out a complex activity or task successfully or effectively in a certain context. Their typologies and approaches are as diverse as the entities – countries, organisations and individuals – that define them. UNESCO gives a very wide view on core competences in different countries, which suggests that different models of education are explored to develop these competences.

In the 2010 eTwinning Conference, which took place in Seville, Spain, the participating teachers were consulted about the future challenges and changes for education and training. The ensuing report, titled *The future of learning: European teachers' visions* (Ala-Muthka et al., 2010), revealed that teachers foresaw that in 15 years' time learning objectives would focus on competences rather than knowledge. Teachers confirmed the importance of emphasising the European Union key competences in future educational objectives, and highlighted the fact that analytical and critical skills, problem solving, collaboration, negotiation, innovation, and self-management would become important basic skills in the future. Developing one's personality and managing one's identity were identified as new important key competences, together with awareness of environmental challenges and understanding and managing one's place in a changing world and society. Languages, mathematics, and ICT were considered crucial for developing one's competences over the course of a lifetime.

In the eTwinning Conference it was argued that everyone needs to obtain the basic skills necessary for citizens in Europe, such as:

- communication in the mother tongue;
- communication in a foreign language;
- mathematical skills;
- digital skills;
- social skills, citizenship skills;
- learning skills;
- self-initiative and entrepreneurship skills; and
- understanding of culture and reflection.
    (European Parliament and Council, 2006)

Furthermore, the participants in the conference stressed that learning has to be more tailored to the needs of individuals. To keep learners motivated and to improve their educational attainment and performance, they should be encouraged to develop their own talents and interests.

Considering learning and competences for the future, Trilling (2007) articulates the new learning formula for the 21st century, highlighting the essential learning skills, the mastering of which will help ensure everyone's success in the 'knowledge age'. The author points out that the basic '3Rs' of reading, 'riting, and 'rithmetic, multiplied by the lifelong skills most needed for the upcoming times – called here the '7Cs' (critical thinking and doing, creativity, collaboration, cross-cultural understanding, communication, computing, and career and learning self-reliance) – have become the new formula for success in the 21st century (Trilling, 2007). Regarding competencies, Wagner (2008, 2015) speaks about 'survival skills' such as critical thinking and problem solving; collaboration across networks and leading by influence; agility and adaptability; initiative and entrepreneurship; and effective written and oral skills.

More recently, the 21st century skills required by every student have been widely discussed in the World Economic Forum report *New vision for education: Fostering social and emotional learning through technology* (World Economic Forum, 2016). The report stresses 16 skills that are necessary for the 21st century, including foundational literacies, competencies, and character qualities. *Foundational literacies* are the skills necessary to perform everyday tasks, such as literacy, numeracy, scientific literacy, financial literacy, ICT literacy, and cultural and civic literacy. *Competencies* relate to the means through which students approach complex challenges, and include critical thinking/problem solving, creativity, communication, and collaboration. *Character qualities* are the ways in which students approach their changing environment, and consist in curiosity, initiative, persistence, adaptability, leadership, and social and cultural awareness. It is argued that all these competencies are acquired from learning and throughout life.

The World Economic Forum (2016) states that today's job candidates must be able to collaborate, communicate and solve problems – skills developed mainly through social and emotional learning. Combined with traditional skills, social and emotional proficiency will equip students to succeed in the evolving digital economy. The forum concludes that good leadership skills, as well as curiosity, are equally important for students to learn for desired jobs.

Schools, creativity and innovative pedagogical strategies

Considering the needs and competences that have been identified by several researchers and organisations, the question arises – do schools satisfy the individual and common needs of learners and prepare them to acquire necessary competences for life? Together with this question, the following should also be addressed:

- Is the future certain or uncertain?
- Do we teach for the future?
- Do we know what professions will be needed in the future?

- What competences will be necessary in the future?
- What values should be promoted?
- Are we teachers creative enough to support students' learning needs?
- Does the school provide opportunities for the development of competences, such as creativity, which is needed for everyday life and career building?

Furthermore, considering that the journey of life starts in the family, there is also another very important question to be answered: Are we all – family, school, and society – cooperating and collaborating in providing opportunities for our children to be well prepared for life after 20 years? Do we pay balanced attention to the development of competences and character of the personality?

Ken Robinson considers that insufficient attention is paid to the development of creativity that is an essential feature of this century. In his talk 'Do schools kill creativity?' (2006) he touches upon this problem and considers that it is very important to solve it in the nearest future. He states that 'creativity now is as important in education as literacy, and we should treat it with the same status' (Robinson, 2006, n.p.). He also believes that 'we are educating people out of their creative capacities, that we do not grow into creativity, we grow out of it, or rather, we get educated out of it' (ibid.).

Andreas Schleicher, Director for Education and Skills of the OECD, puts forward more radical tasks for schools:

> Schools need to drive a shift from a world where traditional knowledge is depreciating rapidly in value, towards a world in which the enriching power of deep competencies is increasing, based on a relevant blend of traditional and modern knowledge, along with skills, character qualities, and self-directed learning.
>
> (Schleicher, 2015, p. 2)

Along these lines, Fadel, Trilling, and Bialick (2015) consider that

> We will need to leverage best practices from education systems around the world (and from industry where applicable). We will need to carefully re-examine the relevance of what we teach, curate the traditional disciplines, add relevant modern disciplines, and place emphasis on more holistic learning – not just knowledge but also skills, character, and meta-learning. Finally, we will need the courage to innovate, letting go of the comfort of an existing system and working under conditions of uncertainty toward a better one.
>
> (Fadel, Trilling, & Bialick, 2015, p. 28)

To fulfil the mission of learning (i.e., to promote the development of competences for the 21st century) requires deep understanding of the contemporary student. In recent decades, a new type of student has emerged – the 'digitally native student'. A 'digital native' is someone who grows up in the digital age, rather than acquiring familiarity with digital systems as an adult, and is shaped and formed by world events and various changes in society and the economy, such as globalisation, internationalisation, and localisation. This digital native is demanding, sometimes egocentric, with very diverse values. Trilling (2007, p. 12) very aptly characterises digital natives by saying that they have a very rich online life, namely through:

> *searching* multiple search engines and info sites, and Googling people and interests;
> *collecting* graphics, animations, MP3s, videos, and sensor data, e.g., skin conductance (fitness trackers);
> *creating* stories, websites, avatars, and games;
> *sharing* web pages, blogs, drawings, music, videos, webcams, and humour;
> *communicating* via email, instant messaging, chat, and cell phone calls;
> *coordinating* projects, travel plans, and workgroups;
> *meeting* via forums, chat rooms, online multiplayer games, and dating sites;
> *socialising* via a wide variety of socialising methods learned online;
> *evaluating* via reputation systems, rating systems, and online advisors;
> *buying and selling* on auction sites, forums, and online markets;
> *gaming* solo, one-on-one, and in small and large groups; and
> *learning* by conducting online research on topics of personal interest.

To attract the attention of digital natives to learning and to address the global job market needs it is necessary to create an educational environment conducive to learning. New tools and processes – characterised by sociability, collaboration, simplicity, and connections – are of great importance for teachers to involve the contemporary student in a learning process that takes place in a collaborative environment characterised by the recognition of common goals, the understanding of the process of collaboration, the definition of clear roles for participants in the learning process, careful assigning of tasks and reflection; and quality assurance at all levels.

Educators, therefore, have to employ some innovative pedagogical tools and strategies that spring from the knowledge-based economy: active (cooperative) learning, technology enhancement, or 'just-in-time learning' (Traylor, Heer, & Fiez, 2003) are but some examples. Active cooperative learning presupposes that teachers employ instructional activities that engage students in doing and thinking instead of passive listening. Technology enhancement involves using hardware and software tools, such as ICT, which represent a significant opportunity for knowledge creation. Just-in-time learning is a pedagogical strategy that uses feedback between classroom activities and work that students do at home, in preparation for the classroom meeting. The goals are to increase learning during classroom time, to enhance student motivation, to encourage students to prepare for class, and to allow the teacher to organise the classroom activities to best meet students' needs. Thus, a new type of a teacher is required to promote the education of the future citizens of the 21st century.

The 21st century teacher: the case of Latvia

In order for learners to acquire knowledge, and to develop skills and character for lifelong learning, a new type of teacher is needed who acts as a guide and an assistant to students' learning in this turbulent and changing world. An essential question that we have to answer, then, is: What is required from 21st century teachers to be able to satisfy learners' needs? ENTEP has set the task to develop the following teacher competences (see Schratz, 2005):

- organising competences (school level and class level);
- relationship competences;
- communicative competences;
- planning competences;
- psycho-pedagogical competences;
- methodological-didactic competences;
- competences of management of external resources;
- reflective competences; and
- European competences.

In the ENTEP report *The first ten years after Bologna*, Schratz (2010) defines the European teacher as a teacher working within a European context of professionalism, who has the same competences as any other 'good teacher' and possesses specific competences in the European dimension concerning European identity, knowledge, multiculturalism, European language competence, European professionalism, and citizenship (see Chapters 1 and 2 in this book for a discussion on the concept and profile of European teachers). All of these competences are developed in the framework of teacher education, as well as through participating in exchange programmes and projects, and developing practice in diverse schools.

The structure of teacher education in Europe and in countries world-wide can be characterised with the help of two main models: the integrated model and the consecutive model (Buchberger, Campos, Kallós, & Stephenson, 2002; Busch, 2002; Galton & Moon, 1994). In the integrated model a student simultaneously studies both one or more academic subjects, and the ways of teaching that subject, leading to a combined Bachelor's degree and teaching credential to qualify as a teacher of that subject. This means that within its framework the academic, pedagogical, psychological, professional practice, and other components are linked together. In the consecutive model the teacher first obtains a qualification in one or more subjects (often a Bachelor's degree), and then studies for a further period to gain an additional qualification in teaching (this may take the form of a Master's degree programme). Hence, in the integrated model Bachelor's studies (for instance, in Physics, History, or English Philology) are very little connected with the teacher's profession; whereas in the consecutive model the student first masters the foundations of science (at Bachelor level) and after that how to teach this subject to pupils (i.e., pedagogy, methods of teaching the subject, or teaching practices at a school).

Every country has its own traditions regarding teacher education. In Latvia the Bologna declaration does not contradict the acquisition of teacher's qualification in four-year professional Bachelor study programmes, which allows implementing the integrated teacher education model. After receiving a teacher diploma, teachers may increase the level of academic education by obtaining a Master's degree in Education Sciences or in a professional Master's degree program. The integrated approach allows future teachers to be more in contact with real life – and that is very important for the teaching profession. Nowadays, universities, teacher organisations, and the Ministry of Education and Science of Latvia are working on the development of a new system of teacher education, sustained on a competence-based approach (National Centre for Education, 2016).

Today the task of the teacher is no longer to be a knowledge transmitter and to check to what extent the pupil has mastered this knowledge. Today the role of the teacher is to encourage pupils to acquire knowledge actively and in a conscious way, to provide possibilities for the pupils to learn, to teach 'learning to learn' skills at school, and to help pupils acquire many competences necessary for life. A teacher's readiness to implement such aims is more adequately ensured by a qualitative integrated teacher education programme and not by the consecutive teacher education model. The integrated model, certainly, does not mean that young teachers lack knowledge in their subject(s). The question is about the key aims of one and the other model (Kangro & Kangro, 2012, p. 131).

Dunn (2005) also stresses that the teachers of the 21st century need to become assistants to learners in constructing their own knowledge. This provides more effective learning, as it helps students organise pieces of information into a system of knowledge (Siau, Sheng, & Nah, 2007). McKinsey's 2007 report suggests that one of the main factors for providing qualitative education in schools is the teacher: if there are problems in the teaching profession, the education quality in schools decreases. This also influences higher education and the development of the country (Barber & Mourshed, 2007). Summarising these results and searching for answers to the question of how the state school system is able to achieve the highest quality level in the world, Kangro and James (2008) suggest that the best students should become teachers because in the countries that get the best results in international comparative studies, the best secondary school graduates continue studies in teacher education programmes (5% in South Korea, 10% in Finland, and 30% in Singapore and Hong Kong).

The movement 'The possible mission' could be mentioned as a positive example in Latvia that attracts and educates the most gifted, motivated, flexible graduates of the Bachelor study programmes in different spheres of science to the teaching profession (for more information see www.iespejamamisija.lv). The number of students involved in the programme is small (between 15 and 20 young teachers every year). The participants are selected as a result of a large competition. Their education is deeply rooted in practice in schools. 'The possible mission' has involved the most recognised business and finance structures to support the programme ideologically and financially. Its organisation is based on the experience of similar foreign organisations, like Teach for America (USA), Teach First (Great Britain), *Renkuosi mokyti* (Lithuania), and *Noored Kooli* (Estonia).

Looking back to the HOWBET Summer School seminar (see Chapter 3 in this book for a detailed description of this IP), the authors consider that, through performing different activities and reflecting on their outcomes, future teachers demonstrated the understanding of this rapidly changing world, the needs of learners in the 21st century, and the role of the teacher in managing the teaching and learning process. This is described in the following section.

The HOWBET Summer School: a description and reflection on the workshop 'Future needs of learners in a European context'

Thirty-six prospective teachers and 11 teacher educators from eight European countries participated in the workshop 'Future needs of learners in a European context', carried out during the HOWBET Summer School. The aim of this workshop was to develop both knowledge and skills that learners and teachers will need in the future, and to gain a better understanding of the problems of the 21st century across Europe, stressing the role of the teacher in the learning process and sharing the experiences from different countries. The students worked in six international groups in order to practice showing respect for different views and acting in a multicultural environment, as well as to reach the goals set for the workshop. The students were actively involved in tasks and discussions on how they saw the changes in the world, how they characterised the contemporary student and teacher, as well as how they could influence the learning process and their personal development. They also discussed learners' needs, and how teachers can support learning and develop each and every student's potential. Table 4.1 presents an overview of the activities given to students in the workshop.

In Task 1, students were invited to discuss learners' needs and their priorities in life. Therefore, students had to write their own needs on separate sheets of paper, using colours to highlight their priorities (e.g., first priority, red; second priority, green; third priority, yellow). Then, they read their priorities and discussed them within the group. Later, a whole-group discussion ensued about personal needs, the needs of contemporary students, and the needs of society in general. Students had to agree upon five needs that are critical for all people. In all six groups, the 36 participants pointed out 'education' as a need for everybody, stressing it as fundamental for the development of every citizen and every country in the world. Education was characterised as a powerful tool for social progress leading to more empowered, skilful, flexible, and happy individuals; more sustainable and peaceful societies' and more economic growth.

In Task 2, students discussed the keywords they would use to characterise the world of the 21st century. For this matter, they analysed a word cloud provided by the teacher educators and authors of this article, and proposed their own version of the word cloud. The 21st century word cloud made by the students during the seminar included the needs of this century, as well as what is expected from education and from individuals (Figure 4.1). This word cloud suggests that students see 'innovation', 'creativity', and 'adaptation' as most important in the 21st century world.

Table 4.1 Overview of the workshop entitled 'Future needs of learners in a European context'

Tasks	Description
Task 1. What are your needs in life?	1. Write five of your needs on separate sheets of paper. Use colours: First priority – red Second priority – green Third priority – yellow 2. Glue the priority sheets on the blackboard, grouping them according to colours. 3. Read the needs of your fellow group members, and discuss them within the group. 4. Present your reflections to the whole group.
Task 2. What keywords would you apply to the 21st century?	1. Analyse the word cloud presented by the teachers. 2. Make your own version of the 21st century word cloud.
Task 3. What is the meaning of 'competence'?	1. Define the concept of 'competence'. 2. Compare different models for developing competences using the pictures that are given under the following Internet links: www.p21.org/our-work/p21-framework https://sites.google.com/a/fargoschools.org/discovery-library-technology/21st-century-skills 3. Find more competence models.
Task 4. What are the professions of the future?	1. Name the future professions in 20–30 years' time. 2. Write the advertisement for these professions.
Task 5. What is the aim of education today?	1. Answer to the following question: What is the aim of education today? 2. Discuss this within the whole group to write a collective response.
Task 6. What does the contemporary learner look like?	1. Within your group make a portrait of the contemporary learner and its characteristics (consider different age groups).
Task 7. How is teaching and learning in the contemporary school?	1. Characterise teaching and learning in the contemporary school.
Task 8. What is creativity and innovation?	1. Define the concepts of creativity and innovation. 2. Name the innovations (initiatives, projects, etc.) that have taken place last year at your university.
Task 9. How can my school satisfy learners' needs?	1. Name three ideas that could help your school satisfy learners' needs, thus making it more distinctive and competitive in Europe and beyond. a) Every participant writes three ideas in five minutes on small sheets of paper. b) Every participant glues his/her ideas on separate sheets of paper (i.e., first idea on one sheet of paper, the second idea on another sheet of paper, etc.)

(*Continued*)

Table 4.1 (Continued)

	2. In international-mixed groups, every group chooses a sheet of paper with ideas, reads the ideas and then chooses one idea from the paper that they would like to implement. 3. Visualise the idea! 4. Describe your visualised idea in three minutes.
Task 10. What is the mission of the 21st century teacher?	1. Describe the mission and role of the 21st century teacher.

Figure 4.1 The 21st century word cloud: expectations from education

Task 3 was to define the concept of 'competence'. The definitions included knowledge, quality, skills, attitudes, and learning outcomes, which suggests that there is no unified understanding of the same concept in different countries. In the discussions, students used the concept of 'development of personal traits', which can be considered a synonym to 'development of a character' or 'personality'. To offer insights into different perspectives of developing competences, students compared models available online. Students were very quick in finding and characterising the models, revealing good skills in the use of modern technologies.

In Task 4, the students were asked to name some future professions in 20–30 years' time. All the named professions were connected with modern technologies and digitalisation (ICT system manager, virtual consultant, digital manager, or digital dentist). Some students even named virtual teacher and virtual medical doctor as professions. After that, they had to write an advertisement for specialists with the given professions. This caused problems for the participants, as they did not know the skills necessary for these future professions, and they had never thought about the so-called 'soft skills' for different professions. During the discussion, all students stressed the desire to learn throughout their lives. This suggests that students understand the meaning of learning and the value of education in life. They also argued that changes are necessary in education to satisfy the needs of the 21st century especially in the context of education.

Task 5 included a reflection around the aim(s) of education today. Students' answers were very different: to obtain knowledge corresponding to 21st century demands, to learn to live in the society of the 21st century, or to equip pupils with knowledge and skills. Taking into account all the students' responses, the aim of education was collectively composed as follows: to prepare students to use their knowledge and competence in the innovative, creative, and rapidly changing economy and society. It was agreed that learning objectives have to be based more on competences, as well as on developing one's personality and identity. In defining the needs and the objectives of today's student, it is important to know and understand the student, his/her future prospects, and different processes in society. Furthermore, in order to organise and reorganise the learning process it is important to know and understand the learner.

In Task 6 students were asked to make a portrait of the contemporary learner. In making these portraits in international working groups the participants stated that learners are very open-minded, sometimes egocentric, and very demanding from society and from other people; they discuss very personal matters in different social networks, and spend a lot of time on the Internet. Sometimes they prefer communicating on the Internet to communicating face-to-face; thus, they tend to lose real connections and opportunities to develop communication skills. Their life is fast-paced, diverse, dynamic, and rich. It was pleasant to see students' portraits of different age groups. This allows us to conclude that prospective teachers are aware of age differences and their needs.

Task 7 was related to the characterisation of teaching and learning in the contemporary school. Groups came to the conclusion that the teacher needs to promote an interest in learning, because students are no longer expected to be passive recipients of knowledge. This entails:

- engaged doing, creating, and sharing;
- learning by doing,
- the use of rich, multiple-media representations;
- exploring multiple sources of information;
- playing and creating ways for others to play in order to learn new things; and
- creative problem-solving and answer-finding methods.

In Task 8 students had to define the concepts of creativity and innovation and name innovations (i.e., initiatives, projects, etc.) that had taken place at their university in the previous year. Students were good at defining the concepts; however, they named very few examples from their universities. This means that universities and other higher education institutions need to think about how to include and promote innovation in the teaching-learning process. This might allow prospective teachers to transfer these innovations to their own school contexts.

Task 9 aimed to promote students' ability to learn together, make quick decisions, and present ideas in a concise and concrete way. Therefore, students were asked to present three ideas that could help their schools satisfy learners' needs and make them more distinctive and competitive in Europe and beyond. This task involved several steps: first, every participant had to write three possible ideas on small sheets of paper; then, all participants had to glue their ideas on separate sheets of papers; finally, students worked in international-mixed groups and chose one idea from the paper that they would like to implement. To develop their idea, student had to visualise it. Therefore, an explanation was provided on methods of visualisation as a secret to successful implementation. Afterwards, students described their visualised ideas.

In Task 10, students were asked to characterise the mission of the 21st century teacher. This teacher was characterised by students as someone who:

- organises learning opportunities;
- manages learners' progression;
- deals with learners' heterogeneity;
- develops learners' commitment to working and learning;
- works in teams;
- participates in school curriculum and organisation development;
- promotes parent and community commitment to school;
- uses new technologies in their daily practice;
- tackles professional duties and ethical dilemmas; and
- manages their own professional development.

Students' involvement in the activities reveals that they developed the ability to work in groups, particularly in multicultural environments; they were responsive, active, and showed a good command of ICT skills.

Conclusions

Learning for the future has to begin in the family, in kindergarten, and in schools. Members of future generations should learn to grow and develop as part of society and should be aware of what takes place around them, so that they can become responsible and independent global citizens. Thus, learning has to become more active and constructive, with an emphasis on learning by doing; it has to take place in social interaction with other learners, teachers, and third parties; and it has to be connected to real life, the workplace, and nature, within the local and global community. This means that modern technologies and creativity have to be an integral part of learning at the present moment, not 20 years from now.

The use of different modern technologies will increasingly require the development of different skills, such as creativity, cooperation, communication, collaboration, critical thinking, and sharing of ideas. Teachers have to acquire new roles to understand young learners and make learning active and attractive. This means that schools and higher education institutions have to revise their curricula to prepare future learners who have 'a creative head', 'skilful hands', and 'a warm and kind heart'.

Besides teacher education, it is very important to think about the new contemporary subjects in the school curriculum, which have not been changed for many years. School has to become a centre of culture and education not only for students, but also for their parents. Furthermore, it needs to put forward unified requirements for all students and support students in understanding learning objectives and learning needs.

References

Ala-Mutka, K., Redecker, Ch., Punie, Y., Ferrari, A., Cachia, R., & Centeno, C. (2010). *The future of learning: European teachers' visions. Report on a foresight consultation at the 2010 eTwinning Conference.* Retrieved from http://ftp.jrc.es/EURdoc/JRC59775_TN.pdf (accessed 30 June 2017).

Barber, M., & Mourshed, M. (2007). *How the world's best-performing school systems come out on top.* McKinsey & Company. Retrieved from http://mckinseyonsociety.com/downloads/reports/Education/Worlds_School_Systems_Final.pdf (accessed 30 June 2017).

Buchberger, F., Campos, B. P., Kallós, D., & Stephenson J. (Eds.). (2002). *Green paper on teacher education in Europe 'High quality teacher education for high quality education and training'.* Retrieved from www.cep.edu.rs/sites/default/files/greenpaper.pdf (accessed 30 June 2017).

Busch, F. W. (2002, August). *New structures for teacher training? Integrative versus consecutive models.* Paper presented at the ATEE 27th Conference 'Teacher Education and Educational Reform', Warsaw, Poland.

Dunn, S. G. (2005). *Philosophical foundations of education: Connecting philosophy to theory and practice.* Upper Saddle River, NJ: Pearson Education.

European Commission. (2010). *Europe 2020 strategy.* Retrieved from https://ec.europa.eu/info/strategy/european-semester/framework/europe-2020-strategy_en (accessed 30 June 2017).

European Parliament and Council. (2006). *Key competencies for lifelong learning – A European reference framework.* Retrieved from http://eur-lex.europa.eu/legal-content/EN/TXT/HTML/?uri=CELEX:32006H0962&from=EN (accessed 30 June 2017).

European Parliament and Council. (2008). *Recommendation of the European Parliament and the Council on the establishment of the European qualifications framework for lifelong learning.* Retrieved from http://eur-lex.europa.eu/legal-content/EN/TXT/PDF/?uri=CELEX:32008H0506(01)&from=EN (accessed 30 June 2017).

Fadel, Ch., Trilling, B., & Bialik, M. (2015). *Four-dimensional education: The competencies learners need to succeed.* Boston, MA: Center for Curriculum Redesign.
Fullan, M., & Langworthy, M. (2014). *A rich seam: How new pedagogies find deep learning.* Retrieved from www.michaelfullan.ca/wp-content/uploads/2014/01/3897. Rich_Seam_web.pdf (accessed 30 June 2017).
Galton, M., & Moon, B. (1994). *Handbook of teacher training in Europe: Issues and trends.* London: David Fulton Publishers.
Hozjan, D. (2009). Key competences for the development of lifelong learning in the European Union. *European Journal of Vocational Training, 46*(1), 196–207.
Iespējamā misija [The Possible Mission web page]. Retrieved from www.iespe jamamisija.lv (accessed 30 June 2017).
Kangro, A., & James, D. (2008). Rapid reform and unfinished business: The development of education in independent Latvia 1991–2007. *European Journal of Education. Research, Development and Policy, 43*(4), 547–562.
Kangro, A., & Kangro, I. (2012). Teachers in Latvia: Topical problems and solutions in times of changes. In P-M. Rabensteiner & E. Ropo (Eds.), *Education and nature in European education* (pp. 128–153). Baltmannsweiler: Schneider Verlag.
Kennedy, D., Hyland, A., & Ryan, N. (2007). *Writing and using learning outcomes: A practical guide.* Cork: University College Cork.
Maslow, A. H. (1943). A theory of human motivation. *Psychological Review, 50*(4), 370–396.
National Centre for Education. (2016). *Kompetenču pieeja mācību saturā (2016–2012)* [Competence-based approach in education]. Project supported by the European Social Fund. Retrieved from http://visc.gov.lv/visc/projekti/esf_831.shtml (accessed 30 June 2017).
Robinson, K. (2006, February). *Do schools kill creativity?* Presented at TED Talks, Monterrey, CA [Video lecture]. Retrieved from www.ted.com/talks/ken_robinson_says_schools_kill_creativity?language=en (accessed 30 June 2017).
Schleicher, A. (2015). Prologue: Why rethinking the what of education matters. In Ch. Fadel, B. Trilling, & M. Bialik (Eds.), *Four-dimensional education: The competencies learners need to succeed.* Boston, MA: Center for Curriculum Redesign.
Schratz, M. (2005). What is a 'European Teacher'? A discussion paper. *ENTEP Papers.* Retrieved from www.sdcentras.lt/pla/res/Schratz.pdf (accessed 30 June 2017).
Schratz, M. (2010). What is a 'European Teacher'? In O. Gassner, L. Kerger, & M. Schratz (Eds.), *The first ten years after Bologna* (pp. 97–102). București: Editura Universității din București.
Siau, K., Sheng, H., & Nah, F. F-H. (2007). Use of a classroom response system to enhance classroom interactivity. *IEEE Transactions on Education, 50*(2), 398–403.
Traylor, R. L., Heer, D., & Fiez, T. S. (2003). Using an integrated platform for learning to reinvent engineering education. *IEEE Transactions on Education, 46*(4), 409–419.
Trilling, B. (2007). Towards learning societies and the global challenges for learning with ICT. *Australian Educational Computing, 22*(1), 10–16.
UN. (1992). *United Nations Conference on environment and development – Agenda 21.* Retrieved from https://sustainabledevelopment.un.org/content/documents/Agenda21.pdf (accessed 30 June 2017).
UN. (2015a). *Transforming our world: The 2030 agenda for sustainable development.* Retrieved from www.un.org/ga/search/view_doc.asp?symbol=A/RES/70/1&Lang=E (accessed 30 June 2017).

UN. (2015b). *World population ageing: Highlights.* Retrieved from www.un.org/en/development/desa/population/publications/pdf/ageing/WPA2015_Highlights.pdf (accessed 30 June 2017).

UNESCO. (2012). *Competencies.* Retrieved from www.unesco.org/new/en/education/themes/strengthening-education-systems/quality-framework/desired-outcomes/competencies/ (accessed 30 June 2017).

Wagner, T. (2008). *The global achievement gap: Why even our best schools don't teach the new survival skills our children need?* New York, NY: Basic Books.

Wagner, T. (2015). *Tony Wagner's seven survival skills.* Retrieved from www.tonywagner.com/7-survival-skills (accessed 30 June 2017).

World Economic Forum. (2016). *New vision for education: Fostering social and emotional learning through technology.* Geneva, Switzerland: World Economic Forum, Boston Consulting Group. Retrieved from www3.weforum.org/docs/WEF_New_Vision_for_Education.pdf (accessed 30 June 2017).

5 Linguistic diversity
How to deal with it in a classroom

Seija Jeskanen

Introduction

What is my cultural and linguistic background? What is my language proficiency? Am I monolingual, bilingual, multilingual or, possibly, plurilingual? Am I aware of my students' linguistic and cultural background? Do I have the intercultural skills that a teacher needs in the new Europe characterised by linguistic and cultural diversity? What about my students? Does the education system provide them with opportunities to develop their language knowledge and intercultural competence? These are the questions we, European teachers and teacher educators, must ask ourselves.

Many European countries are changing rapidly from comparatively homogeneous monolingual and monocultural societies to linguistically and culturally diverse societies. The aim of this chapter is to discuss and clarify such concepts as linguistic and cultural diversity, multicultural education, and plurilingualism. The focus is on teacher education. This chapter consists of five sections, the first being this introduction. The second section, 'Linguistic diversity: definitions', discusses how linguistic and cultural diversity can be defined and measured. The third, 'Languages in European schools', outlines the aims of language education in Europe and the current status of language education. The fourth, 'Immigrant children in European schools', focuses on immigrant children and the types of problems they face in school. The fifth, 'Linguistic diversity and teachers' work' considers the skills and competencies required by European teachers working in linguistically and culturally diverse schools. Finally, the last section, 'Tools for dealing with linguistic and cultural diversity', deals with some tools developed for language education by the Council of Europe and the European Centre for Modern Languages.

Linguistic diversity: definitions

There are at least three related perspectives of linguistic diversity: language diversity, phylogenetic diversity, and structural diversity (Harmon & Loh, 2010; Van Parijs, 2007). Language diversity consists of language richness: i.e., how many different languages are spoken in a particular country, town, or neighbourhood.

Phylogenetic diversity refers to the distance between spoken languages or to the number of different language families in a certain area. Structural diversity refers to structural variations, such as phonology, morphology, or syntax, within languages. Two well-known indexes measure linguistic diversity: the Linguistic Diversity Index (LDI) (Simons & Fennig, 2017) and the Index of Language Diversity (ILD) (see Harmon & Loh, 2010). UNESCO published the LDI in 2009. This index, also called Greenberg's diversity index, assesses the probability that two randomly selected people from any country will speak the same language. According to the LDI, the language diversity in Europe is highest in Belgium and lowest in Malta. The ILD, developed by Terralingua, an independent organisation, measures the changes in language demographics. According to the ILD, a decline in language diversity is a major trend worldwide, whereas the share of the top 10 languages in the world is growing. About 500 languages face extinction, and thousands of other languages are at risk (Harmon & Loh, 2010). As UNESCO (2009) has stated, culture and language are closely related, and languages play a vital role in the development and survival of a culture and in ensuring cultural diversity. If a language dies, then the culture also disappears.

Europe is a linguistically poor continent compared to Africa, which has more than 2,000 languages, or Asia, with 2,300 languages. Although Europe has a population of about 750 million, or about 11% of the world's population, there are only 38 official state languages and about 140 indigenous languages in Europe. All the European languages count for less than 4% of the world's languages. The five most commonly spoken languages by number of mother-tongue speakers (i.e., Russian, German, English, French, and Italian) all belong to the Indo-European language family. Other language families in Europe are the Uralic language family, which includes Finnish, Estonian, Hungarian, and Sámi; the Caucasian language family (e.g., Georgian); and the Altaic language family (e.g., Tatar, Western Turkic). The Basque language, which is spoken in Spain and France, does not belong to any language family; it is a genealogically isolated language (Haarmann, 2011; see also Simons & Fennig, 2017).

After a long process, which started in the 1950s, multilingualism has become an official policy within the European Union (EU). However, in the official EU context, multilingualism means the parallel use of the official languages of its member states. In January 2017, 66 languages had official status in the EU, and 26 of these languages were state languages. Most European countries recognise only one language as the state language; two languages had this status in four countries (i.e., Ireland, Cyprus, Malta, and Finland). Luxembourg, Belgium, and Bosnia and Herzegovina had three state languages. Linguistic diversity in Europe is a many-sided concept that includes official national languages, regional minority languages (e.g., Sámi in Finland, Sweden, and Norway), immigrant languages (e.g., Punjabi in the UK or Turkish in Germany), non-territorial languages (e.g., Yiddish and Romani), and sign languages (European Commission/EACEA/Eurydice, 2017; Extra, 2007).

It was impossible to say how many different languages people living in Europe spoke in 2017. According to the Valuing All Languages in Europe project

(VALEUR) (McPake & Tisley, 2007) undertaken by the European Centre for Modern Languages in 21 European countries, about 440 spoken languages and 18 sign languages were in use. The project found that the range of languages was very wide: from Inuktitut, which originated in Greenland, to Maori, which originated in New Zealand. The traditional picture of Europe as a linguistically homogeneous continent is quickly changing. Linguistic and cultural diversification is becoming a reality throughout Europe. On the one hand, European integration processes have made it possible for Europeans to move freely inside Europe. On the other hand, immigration from outside Europe has drastically increased. Many former seemingly mono- or bilingual societies have become *de facto* multilingual and multicultural. The European map of languages has become a colourful patchwork of official state languages, indigenous or regional languages, and immigrant languages.

Language and culture are closely connected. Multiculturalism is a broad concept, which includes cultural diversity, as well as educational, linguistic, and socio-economic factors. The education, housing, and language policies that a state adopts have a great impact on the lives of different minority groups. The Multiculturalism Policy Index (Tolley, 2016) is a research project which aims to provide information about multiculturalism policies in 21 countries. The project provides an index at three points in time (1980, 2000, and 2010) for three types of minorities: immigrant groups, historic national minorities, and indigenous peoples. The index includes eight indicators of multiculturalism: legislative affirmation of multiculturalism, multiculturalism in school curricula, exemptions from dress codes, the inclusion of ethnic sensitivity in public media, dual citizenship, funding of cultural activities organised by different ethnic groups, funding of bilingual education or mother-tongue instruction, and affirmative action for disadvantaged immigrant groups (Tolley, 2016). Table 5.1 presents two education-correlated indicators and the total score of the eight indicators mentioned for immigrant minority policies of some European countries.

Table 5.1 The Multicultural Policy Index for some European countries (adapted from Tolley, 2016, p. 6)

Country	School curriculum 1980	2000	2010	Bilingual education 1980	2000	2010	Total score (max. 8) 1980	2000	2010
Austria	0	0	0.5	1	1	1	0	1	1.5
Belgium	0	0	0.5	0	0.5	0.5	1	3	5.5
Denmark	0	0	0	0	0	0	0	0	0
Finland	0	0	1	0	1	1	0	1.5	6
France	0	0	0	0	0	0	1	2	2
Germany	0	0	0.5	0	0.5	0.5	0	2	2.5
Netherlands	0	0	1	0	0	0	2.5	5.5	2
Portugal	0	0.5	0.5	0	0	0	1	2	3.5
Spain	0	0	0.5	0	1	1	0	1	3.5
UK	0	0.5	0.5	0	0	0	2.5	2.5	5.5

Note: 0 = no such policy, 0.5 = partial policy, 1 = clear policy

The results of the Multicultural Policy Index project revealed no dramatic changes between 1980 and 2000 or between 2000 and 2010 in multiculturalism policies in the 21 investigated countries. Some countries have moved forward in some aspects of multiculturalism policies, whereas others have taken backward steps.

Languages in European schools

The Council of Europe (2014) has published the aims of language education in European schools. The first aim states that the member states of the Council of Europe should promote plurilingualism, which means that everyone has the right to develop communicative skills in more than one language in accordance with his/her needs. A plurilingual person has competence in more than one language and can switch between these languages according to the circumstances at hand. There is a distinction between plurilingualism and multilingualism. A plurilingual person has more than one linguistic and cultural identity. For instance, children may become plurilingual and have multiple identities if they have grown up in a family where the parents are from different cultures and speak different languages with the children. A multilingual person is someone who is competent in more than one language but usually has only one cultural identity (Council of Europe, 2001).

The second aim decrees that the member states should contribute to linguistic diversity, which means that everyone should have the right to learn languages and to use one's own language or languages. Thirdly, the member states should encourage mutual understanding, which presupposes intercultural communication and acceptance of cultural differences. Democratic citizenship is the fourth aim. As the Council of Europe (2014) has stated, an individuals' plurilingual competence facilitates his/her participation in democratic and social processes in multilingual societies. The last aim is social cohesion, which means that all the individuals living in Europe should have equal opportunities for personal development, education, and employment (Council of Europe, 2001).

In 2002, the European Commission proposed an ambitious goal: all schoolchildren in Europe should have the opportunity to learn at least three languages from an early age (the mother tongue or native language and two foreign languages). According to the report *Key data on teaching languages at school in Europe* (European Commission/EACEA/Eurydice, 2017) in most EU countries, children start to learn a foreign language at 6–9 years of age. At the same time, the duration of compulsory foreign language learning has increased, and furthermore, in most European countries, students learn two foreign languages at least at some point during their schooling. English is the most commonly taught foreign language in European schools, with more than 79% of pupils in primary education and more than 97% of pupils in lower secondary and general upper secondary education learning English. German, French, and Spanish are the most popular second foreign languages. Additionally, in many European countries, non-language subjects can be taught in foreign or regional languages in some schools. In theory, Content and Language Integrated Learning (CLIL) exists in most European countries. However, in reality, CLIL is not yet widespread. Furthermore, pupils in many European schools speak many more mother tongues (first languages, home languages, native languages, languages of origin, and heritage languages) than official or regional languages in Europe or languages of instruction in schools.

The importance of good proficiency in the mother tongue (home language, first language) for children's cognitive development and learning is a commonly accepted fact. One of the most important aims of the UNESCO is to promote mother tongue-based bilingual or multilingual early education (Ball, 2011). The mother tongue can be used as the language of instruction, or it can be taught as a subject. The best results ensure the use of the mother tongue in both ways. Fostering mother tongue skills among immigrant children is also a matter of human rights. In addition, the development of language skills of immigrants may give such children better access to the labour market and, at the same time, increase societies' linguistic and cultural capital and economical welfare (Little, 2010).

Immigrant children in European schools

There are two main models of the integration of newly arrived immigrant children into schools in Europe: the integrated model and the separated model. In the integrated model, the immigrant children study in mainstream education classes with the children of the same age (or younger, depending on the circumstances). The immigrant children follow the same methods and curricular content as those of the native pupils. Support measures (usually linguistic) are implemented on an individual-needs basis during school hours. There are two forms of the so-called separated model. In the first type, immigrant children are schooled separately from native-born children for a limited period to enable them to receive special attention tailored to their needs, especially intensive language learning. However, these children may attend some lessons in mainstream classes with the other pupils. This model is called 'preparatory classes', and is nowadays the dominant model in European schools. The second form of the separate model includes long-term measures: special classes can be formed within schools for one or several school years. The immigrant children are often grouped together according to their competence in the language of instruction. The course content and teaching methods are adopted to the needs of the immigrant pupils (European Commission/EACEA/Eurydice, 2009, 2017).

A key concept, when we think about the education in a linguistically diverse Europe, is multicultural education. In one quite well-known definition, multicultural education is defined as follows: 'Multicultural education is a field of study and an emerging discipline whose major aim is to create equal educational opportunities for students from diverse racial, ethnic, social-class, and cultural groups' (McGee Banks & Banks, 1995, p. xi). The concept of culturally responsive teaching is theoretically connected with the concept of multicultural education and it provides one of the practical solutions to the teaching of culturally and linguistically diverse classrooms (see Gay, 2010).

Equity is one of the main components of multicultural education. Research, statistics and, for example, the results of PISA (see Dustmann, Frattini, & Lanzara, 2012; OECD, 2015) have shown that European school systems have partly failed to fulfil the educational needs of immigrant children and achieve the aim of equity. Immigrant students are disadvantaged in education in many ways compared with native-born students: the type of school in which students from immigrant families are enrolled is often academically less demanding, the duration of schooling is shorter, indicators of achievement are worse, dropout rates are higher, and immigrant students attain fewer school diplomas. The tests of achievement show that already at the end of primary school education, the scores of immigrant pupils are substantially lower than native-born students' scores. As a result, immigrant children more often select academically less demanding secondary tracks. They are over-represented in vocational education, which does not prepare the students for further academic education. Immigrant pupils are also over-represented in special education schools. Immigrant students stay for a shorter time in secondary education than native-born students, and many immigrant students leave secondary school without any diploma (Heckman, 2008a, 2008b).

There are many reasons for the underachievement of immigrant children. The school system itself may cause underachievement. The educational attainment of immigrant pupils is lower in countries with economic inequality, low investments in childcare, and undeveloped preschool education. The educational attainment of immigrant students is better in comprehensive systems with late tracking and worse in systems of strong tracking. One reason for underachievement is school segregation. European countries do not officially have segregated schools for immigrant pupils on a legal basis. School segregation is primarily the result of the concentration and segregation of immigrants in housing. A large concentration of immigrant pupils in schools has a negative impact on all the pupils' academic performance. Peers have a considerable influence on the academic achievements of immigrant pupils. Research has shown that minority children who study with classmates who have higher educational aspirations increase their own achievement (Heckman, 2008a, 2008b).

The national school systems matter, but so does every school, when we think of the education of immigrant pupils. In a 'good' school, children – immigrant children included – learn more. In terms of the education of immigrant pupils, not only the school curriculum but also the leadership of the school is important. The head of the school is not only the administrative but also the pedagogical leader of the school. The duty of the school principal is, among other things, to ensure that the school staff work together and share common aims. The teachers in a 'good' school have high expectations for their students, including immigrant children, and are ready to give them support when needed. In a 'good' school, the quality of teaching is high, and the teachers use modern and effective teaching methods and materials, according to the needs of both native-born and immigrant pupils. In a 'good' school, the physical learning environment is well-organised, safe, and culturally diverse, and it has good equipment. The social learning environment is positive, encouraging, and equitably demanding for all pupils. The last feature of a 'good' school is high involvement of parents in school life. The teachers and the school administration listen to parents and cooperate with them. Good and respectful communication with parents helps the school to meet the needs of the immigrant children and helps them to integrate into school life (Heckmann, 2008a, 2008b).

Linguistic diversity and teachers' work

School systems in European countries are very different. However, all schools and teachers have the same responsibility: to take care of the needs of all the children, regardless of their cultural and linguistic backgrounds. Today, teaching immigrant children from inside and outside Europe is an essential part of any European teacher's work. This work is very important not only from the perspective of the child but also from the perspective of society. Teachers who work in multilingual and multicultural classes find it interesting and enormously rewarding, but also demanding and frustrating to teach immigrant children. To be able to meet the challenges of multicultural education, teachers need good training. To operate in a linguistically and culturally diverse context, teachers require intercultural competence. According to Byram, Nichols, and Stevens (2001), teachers' intercultural competence consists of attitudes, knowledge, skills, and critical cultural awareness. They also noted that teachers should be able to suspend disbeliefs about other cultures and beliefs about one's own culture. Teachers should be also able to see how things are from the perspective of a person who has a different set of values, beliefs, and behaviours. In addition, Byram, Nichols, and Stevens (2001) state that teachers should have knowledge about how different social or ethnic groups function. Teachers should have also skills of comparison, interpreting, and relating, so that they are able to interpret events and appearances from another culture and to relate them to their own culture. Teachers also require skills of discovery and interaction. They should be able to acquire new knowledge of cultures and cultural practices and use positive attitudes, skills, and knowledge in communication and interaction with individuals from other cultures. In addition, teachers need critical cultural awareness. All these 'shoulds' place new demands on teacher education programmes throughout Europe. The concept of intercultural education is often used in conjunction with the concept of multicultural education, although there is a difference in the meanings of these concepts. While the aim of multicultural education is to produce acceptance or tolerance of other cultures, intercultural education emphasises understanding of, respect for, and dialogue between cultures and cultural groups. Interculturality includes the idea of a mutual learning process. Immigrants learn about the host countries' culture and language and, at the same time, the native citizens learn about the immigrants' culture and languages (Council of Europe, 2009).

UNESCO has developed and published a vast amount of materials on intercultural and multicultural education. As early as in 1992, an International Conference on Education organised by UNESCO suggested the following aims of intercultural education: 'the reduction of all forms of exclusion, the furthering of integration and school achievement, the promotion of respect for cultural diversity, the promotion of understanding of the cultures of others, and the promotion of international understanding' (UNESCO, 2006, p. 27). These aims should be implemented in curricula, teaching methods and materials, language teaching, school life, teacher training, and the interaction between schools and society.

According to UNESCO (2006, p. 32), there are three principles on which intercultural education should be centred. The first principle relates to respect for the cultural identity of the learner through providing culturally appropriate and responsive high-quality education for all. Secondly, intercultural education should provide every learner with the cultural knowledge, attitudes, and skills which are necessary for achieving active and full participation in society. Thirdly, intercultural education should promote respect, understanding, and solidarity among individuals, and different ethnic, social, cultural, and religious groups and nations.

Intercultural education is not possible without teachers who know these principles. Teacher training should familiarise student teachers with their own cultural heritage, which is the basis for understanding other cultures. Furthermore, student teachers need to become aware of the educational and cultural needs of minority groups. For this aim, students in teacher training programs need to gain knowledge of the history of civilisation, so that they are able to adapt educational contents, methods, and materials to the needs of diverse ethnic and linguistic groups. Furthermore, student teachers need critical awareness of the role of education in the struggle against racism and discrimination. Lastly, teacher students need to gain linguistic skills in more than one foreign language. In short, student teachers need to gain good intercultural communication competence for their future career as teachers (UNESCO, 2006).

The awareness of cultural and linguistic diversity is the foundation of intercultural communication, and it requires awareness of our own cultural values, beliefs, and perceptions. Cultural awareness and sensitivity become central when we interact in culturally and linguistically diverse environments. People interpret and evaluate things in different ways in accordance with their cultural background (e.g., an appropriate behaviour in one culture can be viewed as inappropriate in another culture). Misunderstandings arise when we are not aware of the impact of our own culturally related assumptions when we are trying to understand another person's reality. Several definitions of cultural awareness reflect how people perceive cultural differences. One of these definitions (Quappe & Cantatore, 2007) consists of four stages of awareness. In the first stage (called the 'parochial stage'), people are aware of their own way of doing things, which they consider the only right way. These people ignore the impact of cultural differences on their way of thinking. In the second stage (the 'ethnocentric stage'), people are aware of other ways of doing things, but they still consider their own way as the best one.

These people consider cultural differences as a source of problems. In the third stage (the 'synergistic stage'), people are aware of their own way of doing things and others' ways of doing things. These people are able to choose the best way, depending on the situation. At this stage, people consider cultural differences not only the cause of problems, but also a benefit. This stage is close to the concept of multiculturalism. In the fourth stage (the 'participatory stage'), people from different cultural backgrounds come together for the creation of shared meanings. This stage is close to the concept of interculturality, which refers to the ability to experience and analyse cultural otherness. Interculturality refers also to openness to, interest in, curiosity about and empathy towards people from other cultures. According to Byram (2009, p. 6), '[i]nterculturality enables people to act as mediators among people of different cultures'.

Tools for dealing with linguistic and cultural diversity

The Council of Europe and the European Commission have made considerable efforts to promote all the languages in Europe, and even outside Europe. These efforts have led to the development of several tools for promoting language education, plurilingual and pluricultural competence, and intercultural education.

Common European framework of reference for languages

The *Common European framework of reference for languages: learning, teaching, and assessment* (CEFR) (Council of Europe, 2001) was compiled in collaboration with several educational specialists and researchers from different European countries. The process started in the 1970s, and the final document was published in 2001. The CEFR is now available in 40 European and non-European languages (Council of Europe, 2017a). The CEFR describes foreign language proficiency at six levels. Using the CEFR levels helps to compare curricula, tests, and examinations across languages and national boundaries. It also provides a basis for recognising language qualifications, and thus facilitates educational and occupational mobility. In 2002, the EU recommended the use of the CEFR in setting up systems for the validation of language competences. Today, the CEFR is used to evaluate language proficiency in most of European countries. In more than half of the countries where the CEFR is used, the education authorities have advocated regulations or recommendations to establish levels of proficiency in foreign languages using the proficiency levels of the CEFR, although only in seven European countries the CEFR is used to report student attainment level at the end of upper secondary education (Council of Europe, 2001; European Commission/EACEA/ Eurydice, 2012, 2017).

The European Language Portfolio

The European Language Portfolio (ELP), developed by the Council of Europe, was also published in 2001 (Council of Europe, 2017b). The ELP serves two functions: pedagogical and reporting. The pedagogical aim of the ELP is to make the language learning process more transparent and to enhance learner autonomy. The second function is to provide evidence of learners' proficiency in languages. The ELP provides a record of a learner's linguistic and cultural skills. Additionally, the ELP is intended to promote plurilingualism and communication skills in additional languages to the person's native tongue. The ELP is linked to the CEFR. Learners use the language proficiency levels of the CEFR to assess their language skills. The Council of Europe has published materials to aid the development of ELPs in different countries. Between 2001 and 2010, when the accreditation of ELPs ended, 118 ELP models were validated and accredited. After 2011, nine more ELP models were registered. The ELP models are designed for use by different age groups of learners: from 4-year-olds to adults. The EPLs are also available in paper and electronic formats (Council of Europe, 2017b).

Framework of Reference for Pluralistic Approaches

In 2008–2011, the European Centre for Modern Languages established a project entitled 'Framework of Reference for Pluralistic Approaches' (FREPA). The aim of the FREPA was to develop a tool for teachers of all subjects, teacher trainers, decision makers, curriculum or programme designers, and textbook writers, which could help raise learners' awareness, as well as the other stakeholders' awareness about the importance of developing plurilingual and pluricultural competence and intercultural education. The framework consists of a list of descriptors (knowledge, skills, and attitudes) considered necessary in plurilingual and intercultural education. The framework also provides teaching materials. The FREPA is published in its entirety in English, French, and German, and the materials of the framework are in the process of translation in many countries (Candelier et al., 2012).

Promoting language awareness and plurilingualism in teacher education: the HOWBET Summer School activities

The HOWBET Summer School brought together student teachers and teacher educators from eight European universities to discuss some current topics in teacher education, and to learn from each other, broadening experiences in international collaboration (see Chapter 3 for a more detailed description of this summer school). The aim of the workshop titled 'Language diversity: how to deal with it in a classroom' was to increase student teachers' knowledge about language diversity in Europe, to motivate them to think about linguistic and cultural diversity, to elaborate on the topic from the educational point of view of each country, and to become aware of the student teachers' own linguistic and cultural diversity, as well as of the diversity in the summer school group.

To achieve this, the students were asked to participate in the 'draw your own language tree' activity.

The idea of using the language tree activity is adopted from the ELP materials (European Centre for Modern Languages, 2015). The activity can be used in any classroom to increase language awareness. Instead of a tree, teachers can ask the learners to draw a flower, a house, or a map that includes all languages that learners know at some level of proficiency. As part of the activity, the teacher can draw his/her own language tree. Teachers can also ask the learners to indicate their mother tongue or home language(s) in the drawing, what languages the learners have learned and used at school, and those they have learned and used outside school to illustrate the idea of plurilingualism and the ubiquity of learning: all language skills count, not only those learned at school.

The student teachers in the HOWBET Summer School were also asked to indicate in what context and in what kinds of situations and places they had learned and used different languages. Furthermore, they were asked to evaluate their language proficiency in different languages using the proficiency levels of the CEFR.

After the students had drawn their individual language trees and discussed them in smaller groups, they compiled a collaborative language tree of the whole group on the classroom blackboard and discussed it. The group of student teachers was relatively small, since there were only 36 students. Nevertheless, the language tree activity provided a good picture of the current European linguistic and cultural diversity: 10 mother tongues and a vast amount of second, third, and even fourth languages. This experience shows that plurilingualism is not an abstract and academic concept but part of everyday life in Europe and present in every kind of situations.

Concluding remarks

Teaching in culturally and linguistic diverse environments requires new approaches in teacher education. All European teachers and teacher educators need new skills in teaching students from different cultural and linguistic backgrounds. Teachers need knowledge about different cultures and languages, not to forget their own culture and language. Cultural and language awareness based on knowledge is needed, but it is not enough; positive attitudes, acceptance, and understanding diversity as an opportunity to develop and grow, instead of dealing diversity as a problem, are also essential.

The UNESCO, the Council of Europe, and other European institutions and organisations have developed recommendations and materials to support teachers' work in culturally and linguistically diverse learning environments. Furthermore, teacher education programmes in many European countries have taken measures to meet the challenges of the new situation. Some teacher training programmes include compulsory courses abroad, and different student exchange programmes have been developed to encourage student teachers to go abroad, and to participate in intercultural exchange programmes and courses to develop their intercultural competence. In addition, many short courses are organised, of which the HOWBET Summer School was an excellent example of European cooperation in teacher education. Still, in the future, considerable efforts are demanded to achieve the aims of equal and inclusive education for all children, included immigrant and minority children, in Europe.

References

Ball, J. (2011). *Enhancing learning of children from diverse language backgrounds: Mother-tongue based bilingual or multilingual education in the early years*. Paris: UNESCO.

Byram, M. (2009). *Multicultural societies, pluricultural people and the project of intercultural education*. Strasbourg: Council of Europe, Language Policy Division. Retrieved from www.coe.int/lang (accessed 7 January 2015).

Byram, M., Nichols, A., & Stevens, D. (2001). Introduction. In M. Byram, A. Nichols, & D. Stevens (Eds.), *Developing intercultural competence in practice* (pp. 1–8). Clevedon: Multilingual Matters.

Candelier, M. (coord.), Camilleri-Grima, A., Castellotti, V., de Pietro, J-F., Lörincz, I., Meißner, F-J., Schröder-Sura, A., Noguerol, A., & Molinié, M. (2012). *FREPA – A framework of reference for pluralistic approaches to languages and cultures: Competences and resources* (revised ed.). Graz: European Centre for Modern Languages. Retrieved from http://carap.ecml.at/Start/tabid/3577/language/en-GB/Default.aspx (accessed 23 November 2017).

Council of Europe. (2001). *Common European framework of reference for languages: Learning, teaching, assessment*. Cambridge: Cambridge University Press.

Council of Europe. (2009). *Autobiography of intercultural encounters. Context, concepts and theories*. Strasbourg: Council of Europe, Language Policy Division. Retrieved from www.coe.int/t/dg4/autobiography/Source/AIE_en/AIE_context_concepts_and_theories_en.pdf (accessed 7 November 2017).

Council of Europe. (2014). *Education and languages, language policy*. Retrieved from www.coe.int/t/dg4/linguistic/division_EN.asp? (accessed 7 November 2017).

Council of Europe. (2017a). *Common European framework of reference for languages: Learning, teaching, assessment* (revised ed.). Retrieved from www.coe.int/en/web/common-european-framework-reference-languages/ (accessed 17 May 2017).

Council of Europe. (2017b). *European Language Portfolio*. Retrieved from www.coe.int/en/web/portfolio (accessed 7 May 2017).

Dustmann, C., Frattini, T., & Lanzara, G. (2012). Educational achievement of second generation immigrants: An international comparison. *Economic Policy, 27*(69), 143–185.

European Commission/EACEA/Eurydice. (2009). *Integrating immigrant children into schools in Europe*. Brussels: Education, Audiovisual and Culture Executive Agency. Retrieved from http://eacea.ec.europa.eu/education/eurydice/documents/thematic_reports/101EN.pdf (accessed 15 November 2017).

European Commission/EACEA/Eurydice. (2012). *Key data on education in Europe 2012*. Brussels: Education, Audiovisual and Culture Executive Agency. Retrieved from http://eacea.ec.europa.eu/education/eurydice/documents/key_data_series/134EN.pdf (accessed 22 November 2017).

European Commission/EACEA/Eurydice. (2017). *Key data on teaching languages at school in Europe – 2017 Edition*. Luxembourg: Publications Office of the European Union. Retrieved from https://webgate.ec.europa.eu/fpfis/mwikis/eurydice/images/0/06/KDL_2017_internet.pdf (accessed 22 November 2017).

Extra, G. (2007). Dealing with new multilingualism in Europe: Immigrant minority languages at home and at school. *Australian Review of Applied Linguistics*, 30(2), 1–38.

Gay, G. (2010). *Culturally responsive teaching: Theory, research, and practice* (2nd ed.). New York, NY: Teachers College Press.

Haarmann, H. (2011). Europe's mosaic of languages. In *European history online (EGO)*. Mainz: Institute of European History. Retrieved from www.ieg-ego.eu/haarmannh-2011-en (accessed 23 November 2017).

Harmon, D., & Loh, J. (2010). The index of linguistic diversity: A new quantitative measure of trends in the status of the world's languages. *Language Documentation and Conservation*, 4, 97–151. Retrieved from www.christensenfund.org/wp-content/uploads/2013/11/harmonloh.pdf (accessed 23 November 2017).

Heckman, F. (2008a). *Education and the integration of migrants: Challenges for European education systems arising from immigration and strategies for the successful integration of migrant children in European schools and societies* (NESSE Analytical Report 1 for EU Commission DG Education and Culture). Bamberg: European Forum for Migration Studies. Retrieved from www.efms.uni-bamberg.de/pdf/NESEducationIntegrationMigrants.pdf (accessed 23 November 2017).

Heckmann, F. (Ed.). (2008b). *Education and migration strategies for integrating migrant children in European schools and societies: A synthesis of research findings for policy-makers* (An independent report submitted to the European Commission by the NESSE network of experts). Retrieved from www.nesse.fr/nesse/activities/reports/activities/reports/education-and-migration-pdf (accessed 23 November 2017).

Little, D. (Ed.). (2010). *The linguistic and educational integration of children and adolescents from migrant backgrounds*. Strasbourg: Council of Europe, Language Policy Division.

McGee Banks, C., & Banks, J. (1995). Equity pedagogy: An essential component of multicultural education. *Theory into Practice*, 34(3), 152–158.

McPake, J., & Tinsley, T. (Eds.). (2007). *Valuing all languages in Europe*. Graz: European Center for Modern Languages.

OECD. (2015). *Immigrant students at school: Easing the journey towards integration*. Paris: OECD. Retrieved from www.wib-potsdam.de/wp-content/uploads/2016/06/Immigrant_Students_at_Schools.pdf (accessed 23 November 2017).

Quappe, S., & Cantatore, G. (2007). *What is cultural awareness, anyway? How do I build it?* Retrieved from http://yuin.mgoals.com.au/wp-content/uploads/sites/3/2013/02/What_is_Cultural_Awareness_.pdf (accessed 23 November 2017).

Simons, G., & Fennig, C. (Eds.). (2017). *Ethnologue: Languages of the world* (20th ed.). Dallas, Texas: SIL International. Retrieved from www.ethnologue.com (accessed 2 May 2017).

Tolley, E. (2016). *Multiculturalism policy index: Immigrant minority policies* (revised ed. by M. Vonk). Kingston: Queen's University, School of Policy Studies. Retrieved from http://queensu.ca/mcp/sites/webpublish.queensu.ca.mcpwww/files/files/immigrantminorities/evidence/ImmigrantMinoritiesEvidence2016web(1).pdf (accessed 23 November 2017).

UNESCO. (2006). *Guidelines on intercultural education.* Paris: UNESCO. Retrieved from http://unesdoc.unesco.org/images/0014/001478/147878e.pdf (accessed 23 November 2017).

UNESCO. (2009). *Investing in cultural diversity and intercultural dialogue.* Paris: UNESCO. Retrieved from http://unesdoc.unesco.org/images/0018/001847/184755e.pdf (accessed 23 November 2017).

Van Parijs, P. (2007). Linguistic diversity as curse and as by-product. In X. Arzoz (Ed.), *Respecting linguistic diversity in the European Union* (pp. 17–46). Amsterdam: John Benjamins.

6 European teachers and inclusive education

Judith 't Gilde

Introduction

In 2006, countries from all over the world signed the Convention of the United Nations on the Rights of Persons with Disabilities. Since then even more countries have signed, committing themselves to making their education system inclusive. This has important consequences in general and in particular for teachers. An inclusive education system would mean that, when possible, all children go to the same school. It requires teachers who are able to deal with a diverse student population more than ever. It also raises many questions: Should special needs schools entirely disappear? Is it realistic for teachers to be able to teach everyone? How will inclusive education be implemented? It certainly requires a reform of many current education systems, teacher training, and the involvement of teachers, who are at the centre of inclusive education. Austria is a very relevant example, since it signed the Convention early on and over the last few years has been making serious steps towards a more inclusive education system.

This chapter will focus on European teachers and inclusive education. Inclusion is not only about children with disabilities, as many people tend to think. It is about diversity and dealing with each child and his/her uniqueness, strengths, and weaknesses. As this chapter will show, inclusion is a human right and therefore the question should not really be whether it will happen, but rather when it will happen. Each European teacher should know about inclusion and its current development, but more importantly, young teachers should get practical opportunities to discuss and learn how to deal with diversity in the classroom. The HOWBET Summer School gave a group of international students this opportunity for a day and was a step in that direction (see Chapter 3 in this book for a description of this summer school).

In the first section, this chapter will discuss the background of inclusive education. It will clarify the difference between integration and inclusion, show that inclusion is a human right and illustrate inclusion and its different faces by examining different examples. It will focus on teachers and inclusive education by reviewing the current preparedness of teachers for inclusion and looking at the notions of fixed ability and transformability. In the second section, the activities developed for the HOWBET Summer School will be described. Finally, the main challenges and opportunities for the present and the future of teacher education in relation to inclusive education will be presented.

Theoretical background

Terminology: inclusion versus integration

Inclusion is a fairly new and challenging concept. In the early 90s, the notion of 'inclusion' emerged to replace the terms 'mainstreaming' and 'integration' in the USA, Australia, and England (Biewer, 2010). The book entitled *Effective schools for all* from Mel Ainscow (1991), as well as the educational programme 'Special needs in the classroom: Teacher education resource pack' developed by UNESCO in 1993, both presented a foundation for the creation of inclusive schools, even though the notion of 'inclusion' was not yet mentioned. The major impetus for using the term 'inclusion' was the development of the Salamanca Declaration, supported by a group of British consultants working for UNESCO (Biewer, 2010). At the World Conference on Special Needs Education: Access and Quality, held in Salamanca, Spain, in 1994, the Salamanca Declaration that promoted the approach to inclusive education was adopted and endorsed by 92 countries (UNESCO, 1994). It laid the foundation for transformation within the education systems to realise inclusion. A group of involved British academics then started to use the term 'inclusion' and spread it. For instance, in 1995, the book *Towards inclusive schools* was published (Clark, Dyson, & Millward, 1995). Since then, the English term 'inclusion' has been used more and more all over the world.

It is worth looking at the development of the term 'inclusion' in German-speaking countries, since the change happened differently from that in English-speaking countries. One of the concerns pointed out by the Committee on the Rights of Persons with Disabilities is the German translation of the Convention on the Rights of Persons with Disabilities, in which 'inclusion' is translated as 'integration'. Already in the translation of the Salamanca Declaration, made by the Austrian UNESCO committee in 1996, 'inclusion' was translated as 'integration' and 'inclusive schools' as *'integrative Schule'* (integrated schools) (Biewer, 2010). Some years later, the term 'inclusion' started being translated by the German word *'inklusion'* (Biewer, 2010). As a consequence, in German-speaking countries, and more specifically in Austria, the two notions of 'integration' and 'inclusion' are often used as synonyms or confused with each other, without a clear separation. This then leaves the question as to whether inclusion and integration mean the same thing or whether inclusion is something new.

In the Salamanca Declaration the notion of inclusion focused on special needs children (UNESCO, 1994). Over the years, the notion of inclusion has been broadened to include working children, religious minorities, child soldiers, HIV/AIDS orphans, ethnic and linguistic minorities, poverty-stricken children, migrants, nomadic children, abused children, and refugees or displaced children (UNESCO, 2005). As such, children with special needs are one group among many others who should be taken into account when considering inclusion. However, very often, when talking about inclusive education, people take into account children with special needs only. The UNESCO guidelines define inclusion as:

> a process of addressing and responding to the diversity of needs of all learners through increasing participation in learning, cultures and communities, and reducing exclusion within and from education. It involves changes and modifications in content, approaches, structures and strategies, with a common vision which covers all children of the appropriate age range and a conviction that it is the responsibility of the regular system to educate all children.
> (UNESCO, 2005, p. 13)

This definition is very similar to the one given by the *Index for inclusion*, mentioning that inclusion is an 'unending process [. . .] of increasing participation' (Booth & Ainscow, 2002, p. 3), where three dimensions – inclusive policies, inclusive practices, and inclusive cultures – are at the centre. The two definitions have in common that they do not see the child as a problem, but rather it is the education system or the school that has to change. The guidelines of UNESCO (2005, p. 27) explain the process of what happens when education is seen through the lens of exclusion and inclusion. When looking through the lens of exclusion, the fact that a child is different from other children is considered an issue. That child needs special materials, special help, and special teachers in order to learn. As a result, the child is excluded from the school. Now, looking from the lens of inclusion, the education system is seen as the issue. It is not equipped to handle diversity. There is a lack of appropriate materials and curriculum and parents' involvement. These factors are environmental and are the root of the problem, not the child.

The two points mentioned earlier – the broadening of the definition and the fact that inclusion is a process of change for schools, institutions, and education systems – points towards the difference between integration and inclusion. Hinz (2002, p. 360) explains that with integration, the child firstly has to be labelled as an 'integration child' ('I-Kind') and then the school will get supplementary resources such as a teacher that comes in twice a week. The classroom teacher has to adapt the curriculum, so that this child can also participate. Hinz describes it as '*Auch-Pädagogik*', or translated in English 'also-Pedagogy'. In reality, the child is seen as different from the others, even though he/she attends a mainstream school.

Inclusion aims at general pedagogics where the different dimensions of heterogeneity are taken into account and where a whole school approach is applied in order to change attitudes, conceptions, and ways of thinking and teaching in a whole institute. In other words, the idea of inclusive education is that all children work on the same curriculum, but with some adaptations depending on each child's needs. For instance, the children could all be working on a circus project, where each child contributes to the project in his/her own way. Some children could be making the decorations, others writing a song, and others designing the costumes.

In integration, a large part of the class will follow one curriculum, whereas special education needs (SEN) children will work on something totally different, which does not follow the idea of inclusion. Hinz (2002, p. 359) gives an overview of the differences between integration put into practice versus inclusion put into practice. I would like to briefly discuss some of these examples:

1. Children with specific disabilities attend regular schools versus learning and living for all children in regular schools.

    Attending a regular school does not necessarily mean that the children are all learning and living together. During my research in integration classes in Vienna, Austria, many times I saw how a group of children went and sat outside of the classroom with a teacher and did something entirely different from the rest of the class. That is integration and not inclusion.

2. In the two-groups-theory, SEN and no SEN is contrasted to the theory of heterogeneous groups, meaning many minorities and majorities.

    UNESCO's (2005) broad definition of inclusive education says that every child is unique and different. Every child has particular strengths and weaknesses. One suit does not fit all, or in other words, there is no such thing as two groups, but rather there are many individuals with different learning needs. This theory promotes thinking in terms of inclusive education as something meant for all and not limited to SEN.

3. Resources for children with a label versus resources for schools.

    This refers to the issue of the school versus the child seen as the issue. When resources go to the schools, the schools can change and adapt themselves in order to receive all kinds of children.

4. SEN teachers are seen as support for children with SEN versus SEN teachers as support for school teachers, classes, and schools.

    Heading towards a more inclusive system means changing the role of SEN teachers and 'regular' teachers. Teachers will need support in the classroom and advice. In Austria for instance, starting from 2015, there is no longer a specific training that leads to a degree for SEN teachers. Instead, teacher training offers the possibility for specialisation on inclusive pedagogy with a focus on SEN. This is in addition to the skills and knowledge that all teachers will get in inclusive education.

This section discussed how the concept of inclusion has made its appearance over the last decades. Inclusion and inclusive education are not only about children with disabilities, but about the inclusion of all children. As explained in this section, integration is different from inclusion even though the terms are often confused. The following section will show that inclusive education is a right of every child. Some countries have legally bound themselves to create inclusive education systems, which is not an easy task, as the example of Austria will show.

Inclusive education as a human right and a philosophy

In 1948, the Universal Declaration of Human Rights stated in Article 26 that 'everyone has the right to education' (United Nations, 1948). Since then, different conventions and statements have implicitly advocated for inclusive education. Following is an overview of the most important ones.

- 1989: the UN Convention on the Rights of the Child, ensuring the right of children to receive education without discrimination (UN, 1989)
- 1990: the World Declaration on Education for All (UNESCO, 1990)
- 1994: the Salamanca Statement and Framework for Action on Special Needs Education (UNESCO 1994)
- 2000: The World Education Forum (UNESCO, 2000) and the UN Millennium Declaration (UN, 2000). The largest gathering of world leaders in history committed their nations to a global partnership to reduce poverty and set time-bound targets, such as ensuring that all children have access to and complete free compulsory primary education, with a particular focus on girls and marginalised children.
- 2006: the Convention on the Rights of Persons with Disabilities (UN, 2006)

An important step towards inclusive education was taken in 2006, when the Convention on the Rights of Persons with Disabilities was adopted. Article 24 specifically advocates for inclusive education: 'States Parties shall ensure an inclusive education system at all levels and lifelong learning' (UN, 2006). It is important to point out that the Convention includes an 'Optional Protocol' and that each document can be signed and ratified. The Optional Protocol was created because it became clear during the discussion that countries had different views on the extent of the rules for inspection and communication (Biewer, 2010). Countries who sign and ratify the Optional Protocol commit to dealing with controlling mechanisms. There is a critical difference between signing and ratifying. By signing, a state expresses the intention to comply with the convention, but this is not binding. It is usually the first step. Once a country ratifies the Convention, the Convention is officially binding. In the case of the Convention of the Rights of Persons with Disabilities and its Optional Protocol, many countries signed, but did not ratify, meaning that they are not legally bound to the Convention or its Optional Protocol.

The example of Austria will again be used to illustrate this. Austria has signed and ratified both the Convention and the Optional Protocol. This means that Austria is legally obliged to implement legislations that promote, protect, and ensure the full and equal enjoyment of all human rights by persons with disabilities education. It also signifies that Austria has to deal with controlling mechanisms that follow the process (Biewer, 2011). An example is the creation of an independent monitoring committee that supports the creation of an Austrian inclusive school system (Monitoringausschuss, 2010).

In its guidelines for inclusion, UNESCO (2005) mentions an interesting point that I would like to briefly discuss: inclusion should not be seen as just an organisational or technical change. It is a philosophy, where inclusion is seen as a 'dynamic approach of responding positively to pupil diversity and of seeing individual differences not as problems, but as opportunities for enriching learning' (UNESCO, 2005, p. 12). However, often this is not how children with special needs are seen in society. For the process of inclusion to happen, a change of attitudes in society is required. The UNESCO guidelines describe how moving from exclusion towards inclusion is a process, and how societal attitudes towards disabilities have an impact on the services provided for excluded groups. For instance, in Austria and Germany, special needs schools were not common until the second half of the twentieth century (Biewer, 2010). When society ignores children who are excluded, this results in their exclusion from the educational system. Once there is some acceptance of the children with special needs, or children from excluded groups, organisations or charities start taking care of the education of these children. This leads to segregation: on one side are children who attend regular school and, on the other side, children who go to schools run by these organisations or charities. With the understanding by society that children with special needs also have the right to quality education, special needs schools and integration classes appear. Finally, with the help of knowledge, inclusion sees the light. Although UNESCO does not specify this, in my opinion knowledge is often created through positive experiences for teachers, parents, and children with special needs. For instance, by experiencing an integration class, children with special needs can positively contribute. It is when teachers, parents, and schools start to work together on a school for all that inclusion sees the light.

This section of the chapter discussed inclusive education as a human right and a philosophy. For inclusion to happen, a change in societal attitudes is required. This is a process that may differ per country. The following section will use some examples from different countries to show how inclusion might encounter different issues depending on the country.

The different faces of inclusion: Austria, Pakistan, and Nigeria

The principles of inclusion are described in various international declarations, but in the end each country has to adapt and interpret these to suit its own context. Each country faces different challenges when trying to implement inclusion. I discussed the example of Austria in detail during the HOWBET Summer School, since this is where I do my research in relation to the topic of inclusion.

My research is about the processes of professional development of teachers working in integration classes, in secondary academic schools in Vienna, Austria.

After primary school, there are a range of secondary schools to which a student can apply; for example, the *Allgemeinbildende Höhere Schule* (AHS), meaning the academic secondary schools, where only academically gifted children can gain admittance. The AHS is composed of eight years of schooling: four at lower levels and four years at a higher level. At the completion of the AHS, students obtain a high-school degree, the *Matura*, which allows them to go to university. In the lower four years, some of the secondary academic schools have integration classes. In 2014–2015, in Vienna, four out of 69 AHS public schools had integration classes. In total there were seven integration classes at the AHS level. These integration classes were composed of regular students, four to five SEN students, and an integration teacher in addition to the subject teacher. I researched the developmental tasks of the teachers in the integration classes.

The concept of developmental tasks comes from the American sociologist and educationalist Havighurst (1972), who devised the concept of developmental stages and tasks from infanthood to old age. Almost three decades later, the German educator Hericks (2006) identified four developmental tasks which pre- and in-service teachers in their first years of teaching are confronted with: (a) the development of competence; (b) the development of the ability to mediate or transfer acquired knowledge and competence to others; (c) the development of the ability to acknowledge the student's otherness; and (d) the development of the ability to interact within the school system. My research aimed at finding out how these developmental tasks are given shape in relation to inclusive education for subject teachers working in integration classes of academic secondary schools in Vienna. I have analysed three cases in depth, each case representing a teacher who deals differently with his/her developmental tasks: not at all, still working on them, or finished.

It is interesting to look at how integration started in the mid-80s in Austria, because parents played an important role in advocating for the integration of children with disabilities in mainstream schools. From a historical perspective, Austria did not differ much from many other European countries: for a long time, children with disabilities had no option but to attend a special needs school. However, in the mid-80s parents of children with and without disabilities started initiatives to support integration, for instance, by involving the media and organising a symposium about integration on a yearly basis with experts from all over the world. It was not an easy task, since parents of children without disabilities, teachers, and headmasters needed to be convinced of the advantages of integration (Feyerer & Prammer, 2002). In 1984, the first integration class was created in an elementary school in Oberwart (Feyerer, 2013). Then, the efforts of the parents' initiatives first resulted in a working group at the Ministry, which was to work on the topic of integration, and finally, in 1993, in a law that gave parents the right to choose where the child is educated (Altrichter & Feyerer, 2011; Luciak & Biewer, 2011). Integration was then made possible at primary and lower levels of secondary school (Buchner, Feyerer, & Flieger, 2009). It was only in 2012 that integration was made legal for the ninth grade, but with restrictions (Feyerer, 2013).

Children in Austria have the right to integration if they have a *sonderpädagogischer Förderbedarf* – a requirement of SEN. Usually a special education teacher diagnoses a student with SEN in the first or second year of elementary school. The diagnosis is mostly based on performance deficits in mathematics and German. Once the parents agree with the diagnosis, the school can receive extra resources (Gebhardt, Krammer, Schwab, Rossmann, & Gasteiger Klicpera, 2013). If in an integration class in an elementary school there are three to five children with SEN, then an integration class teacher is employed full-time. If there are fewer than three pupils with SEN in the regular class, it gets more complicated, since the amount of time a support teacher will be paid to be there depends on the type of disability of the child with SEN. The support teacher will be there a maximum of 10 hours per week, per child (Gebhardt et al., 2013). In secondary school, the special needs teacher will be there for 22 hours if there are three to five children in the integration class. However, the children with SEN sometimes have a few more hours of courses to follow, and with the consent of the teacher and parents, the SEN child will be in the regular classroom without the integration teacher for those hours.

In Austria, the laws concerning the integration of SEN children are suggestions rather than obligations. They describe what could be done to foster integration, instead of being compulsory. Some states (*Bundesländer*) promote integration, whereas others give it a low priority (Altrichter & Feyerer, 2011; Buchner et al., 2009). Buchner and Gebhardt (2011) calculated the integration quota for the year 2009–2010, per *Bundesland*, with a range from 77.3% in Steiermark, to 54.6% in Vienna, to 27.1% in Niederösterreich. This shows the differences in integration per *Bundesländer*, and that in Vienna, the capital, about one child out of two with a SEN is integrated. These contrasts can be explained by the variations in regional traditions and the attitude and willingness of school boards, teachers, and SEN leaders to make changes (Buchner et al., 2009). In general, 58% of students with SEN are integrated, which situates Austria in the middle range in comparison to other European countries: France (9%), Germany (21%), the Netherlands (38%), Ireland (80%), and Norway (90%) (European Agency for Development in Special Needs Education, 2012).

It is striking that although Austria ratified the convention in 2008, no reform of the Austrian education system was discussed in relation to inclusion until 2010. Then, the monitoring committee wrote a statement expressing serious concern that the ratification had not triggered any discussion so far and that no plans for reforms had been submitted. The committee stated the need for a reform and plans to make education inclusive, including the closure of special schools (Monitoringausschuss, 2010). The production of a 'roadmap for inclusive schools' written by the Austrian organisation *Lebenshilfe Österreich*, led to the first public discussions in 2011. This roadmap describes how by 2016 there should be no more special needs schools (Lebenshilfe Österreich, 2010). However, in 2012, the National Action Plan for Disability ('Nationale Aktionsplan Behinderung') promoted the creation of regions that should become models for inclusion until 2020 (Bmask, 2012). Guidelines for these models issued by the Ministry for

Education and Women state that by 2020 regular schools should be able to offer quality support to all children so that special schools are used as little as possible (BMBF, 2015). Whether all special needs schools should be abolished or not and whether this is realistic is much debated in Austria and in other countries where inclusive education is a current topic. For instance, Ahrbeck (2014) argues that special needs schools are a form of inclusion: it allows children with special needs who otherwise would be excluded to join society and go to a school. Speck (2010) and Ahrbeck (2014) state that the abolishment of special needs schools is not prescribed in the United Nations' Convention on the Rights of Persons with Disabilities.

During the HOWBET Summer School workshop on inclusion not only was the example of Austria presented, but also Pakistan, Nigeria, and Bosnia and Herzegovina were mentioned, since I have worked in those countries in the field of education. These countries were brought up, to point out that each country struggles with different problems when it comes to exclusion and inclusion. Furthermore, examples were used to illustrate the broadness of the term 'inclusive education' and that it is not only limited to special needs children.

In Pakistan and Nigeria, many girls are excluded from the educational system. Some of the reasons given are that they need to stay at home to look after younger children, school is too far away from home, there are no female teachers, or there are no separate toilets for girls. Another excluded group are working children. Families need their income to survive and education is not a priority. Including these children means that schools, organisations, and communities need to make some changes. Simple solutions are sometimes building toilets for girls or employing female teachers. In some schools that I visited in Nigeria in 2010, working children came to school, and during breaks they were allowed to sell the food items (for example) which they would normally sell all day long.

The case of Bosnia and Herzegovina is very complex and cannot be explained in a few lines. In this country, alongside other systems there is a school system that is called 'two schools under one roof', which means that children from different ethnic groups are attending classes in the same building. For example, in the morning Bosniak children are taught according to the Bosniak curriculum by Bosniak teachers, whereas in the afternoon Serbian children are taught according to the Serbian curriculum by Serbian teachers. In Bosnia and Herzegovina, making education inclusive would require a lot of thought about the inclusion of different ethnic and religious groups.

It goes without saying that issues in these countries are much more complex than they are discussed here, but it is important to realise that inclusion has many faces and that the excluded groups differ per country. In addition, these examples show that inclusion is not only about children with disabilities, but also about ethnic and religious groups, girls, child labourers, and migrants.

This section tried to explain and illustrate the terms 'inclusion' and 'inclusive' education by using the examples of different countries. An important question that so far has not been addressed is how teachers, the key actors in formal education, should implement and deal with inclusion.

Teachers and inclusive education

Often – like many other teachers, I am sure – I have asked myself how teachers are supposed to implement inclusive education. Although teachers are key actors in inclusive education, international researchers mention the lack of appropriate training and skills for teachers to manage inclusive classes (Donnelly & Watkins, 2011; Forlin, Loreman, Sharma, & Earle, 2009; Kershner, 2007; Pijl, 2010). Teachers do not feel well prepared for managing diversity and inclusive education in their classroom. Thus, there is a need for appropriate training of teachers to be able to cope with diversity and meet the needs of all learners in their classroom. Pijl (2010) argues that reforming the initial training only is not enough. Teachers need to be supported in the classroom by colleagues, support staff, and governing bodies. It is important to support teachers in order for them to have successful experiences of inclusive education, which will generate teacher's positive attitudes and self-confidence (Pijl, 2010).

Some years ago, Salend and Duhaney (1999) did a literature review about the impact of inclusion on students with and without disabilities and their educators. They reported that teachers' perception of inclusion seems to be related to their success in implementing inclusion, the availability of financial resources, supportive service, student characteristics, and time to collaborate and communicate with others. Teachers are concerned that the students without disability might suffer in an inclusive classroom. Interestingly, the literature review reveals that placement in an inclusive classroom can have a positive impact for students with and without disabilities. Examples are increased acceptance and understanding, and respect for individual differences. However, a successful experience for every child in an inclusive setting depends on many factors, such as a good collaboration between the teachers, assistance for the SEN children, and the willingness and skills of the teacher.

Hart, Drummond, and McIntyre (2007) and the *Index for inclusion* from Booth and Ainscow (2002) express a common worry, which is about the influence and power of language on children, teachers, and the curriculum. The authors argue for the development of an appropriate language for inclusion. In many schools, when children are having difficulties in education, these are interpreted as deficits or impairments situated in the child, and the child might end up getting the label 'SEN'. This way of viewing things in terms of 'able' and 'not able' is called the 'medical model' (Booth & Ainscow, 2002). Hart et al. (2007) use the term 'fixed-ability thinking', which assumes that learning capacity is a fixed and internal property. It conveys to teachers the message that they cannot do much to change anything, because the problem is coming from within the child. Not only teachers are affected by this way of thinking, but also the child and the curriculum. For instance, teachers view children as bright, average, or less able, and adapt their teaching strategies to this – a practice that prevents from being creative and thinking about many ways to promote learning. Ability labelling undermines the hopes, expectations, and self-perceptions of children. It limits the range of learning opportunities for children, as the curriculum is restricted for some of them (Hart et al., 2007).

In contrast, thinking in terms of 'barriers of learning and participation' and 'transformability' allows teachers and children to see a potential for change. Booth and Ainscow (2002) advocate for the use of the concept 'barriers of learning and participation', because these barriers can arise at a certain time, but they can also be transformed and changed. An example from my own research is how a child in a wheelchair was not allowed to participate in gym classes until the gym teacher decided to adapt his course and convince everyone that the child should participate. Transformability is the opposite of fixed ability. Transformability challenges the view of individual deficits as learning difficulties. It implies that every child has the potential to grow, change, and improve, and that teachers can influence the learning capacity of the student. Teachers try to discover how the learning capacity of each and every student can be enhanced, and which conditions should be created to support this (Hart et al., 2007).

An article by Hart et al. (2007) is in my opinion very interesting for teachers. Firstly, it makes teachers reflect on their own pedagogical principles. A teacher is part of a dynamic, ever-changing society. Ideas about education, teaching methods, and teachers' roles change over time. For inclusion to happen, teachers need to be willing to look at themselves, to reflect, to develop themselves, and to be creative. Secondly, the article tries to find a way forward for inclusion by discussing transformability and the important role the teacher has in this process. Thirdly, it discusses the following three pedagogical principles in relation to transformability and thus to inclusion.

1   *The principle of everybody*: a teacher is there for everyone, equally and fairly; no child should be left out.
2   *The principle of co-agency*: learning is described as a common enterprise between teachers and students. Both students and teachers can contribute and share responsibility for the learning process.
3   *The principle of trust:* students will engage in learning activities if the conditions are right. If not, the teacher will search for other ways to reach out to the students.

This article puts teachers in the centre of inclusive education, as it should be. I believe that it is important for future teachers also to focus on the practical side of teaching and inclusion and not just to learn about theories. Thus, during the HOWBET Summer School I tried to actively engage the students through different activities as the following section will describe.

The HOWBET workshop on European teachers and inclusive education

The HOWBET Summer School workshop on European teachers and inclusive education aimed at getting the student teachers to discuss, exchange, and reflect on inclusive education in their country and classroom and, more generally, to compare and learn from other countries and future European teachers. After the different examples of countries had been discussed with the students, they were asked to do some research about their own countries. Some questions to help the students were:

- What did your country do with the Convention on the Rights of Persons with Disabilities?
- Which steps are or are not taken towards inclusion in your country?
- What happens to children with disabilities in your county?
- Which groups are excluded from the education system in your country and what is being done to include them?

In relation to the topic of 'How to Become a European Teacher', we discussed the role that the participants thought they might have in inclusive education, and what they thought of inclusive education. Several participants expressed their fears and scepticism. They worried about the tendency of European governments to reduce expenditures on education. They also wondered if they would have the resources, experience, and time to put inclusive education into practice, and if inclusive education is a realistic plan.

The next part of the workshop about inclusive education aimed at getting students to discuss and reflect on inclusive education in the classroom in a more practical way. They were asked to form mixed national groups and to follow the instructions for discussion on the assignment. The first part of the assignment consisted of a discussion about inclusive pedagogy versus individual pedagogy, based on the article from Florian and Black-Hawkins (2011). They researched how teachers try to make meaning of the concept of inclusion in their practice, and they discussed the concept of 'inclusive pedagogy' in opposition to 'individual pedagogy'. Inclusive pedagogy focuses on everybody in the classroom, whereas individual pedagogy focuses only on the student who has been identified as in need for additional support (Florian & Black-Hawkins, 2011, p. 820). In their article, the authors use some examples of individualised approach to inclusion versus an inclusive pedagogy approach to inclusion. The students were asked to discuss the following questions:

- Which pedagogy have you experienced, applied or seen so far in your classrooms? Is it more individual or more inclusive?
- Which one do you prefer and why?

In the second part of the assignment, some teaching strategies were presented, in particular those described in the book *What really works in special and inclusive education* from Mitchell (2008) such as the following.

> *Co-teaching*: a general teacher and a special education teacher work together on an equal level. This does not mean that the special education teacher is responsible for children with SEN only, but it means that each other's expertise is respected. For instance, the teachers could prepare together a

mathematics lesson, then one of them explains a concept, while the other shows the same concept in another way. Both of them walk around and help children when they are doing their exercises.
- *Cooperative group teaching*: learners work together in small learning groups, helping each other to carry out individual and group tasks. This is different from mutual assistance groups, where the more able learners assist less able learners. In cooperative group teaching, all members of the group have something unique to contribute. All members have to participate to achieve a group goal. For example, in a project each child could have a task that would help to complete the project.
- *Peer tutoring*: This is based on the idea that children can learn a great deal from each other. One learner (the 'tutor') provides a learning experience for another learner (the 'tutee'). The tutor could get a 'training' (how to give feedback, how to encourage the student to find the answer himself/herself), the sessions need to be supervised, and both tutor and tutee could get a certificate at the end of the process. It can be applied in many areas, such as reading, maths, or science.

The students were given the following question to support a discussion: 'Which teaching strategies could help to increase the achievement of *all* children?' The students could either discuss the topic freely or use the following prompts:

- What do you think of these strategies? Are they doable?
- Which ones have you already used, and did they really promote the inclusion of *all* children?
- Discuss the advantages and disadvantages of each strategy.
- Which other teaching strategies that promote inclusive pedagogy can you think of?

Finally, the last part of the workshop consisted of a plenary discussion about the relation between the 'European teacher' and inclusive education, with the help of the following questions:

- How would you relate inclusion to this topic?
- Which qualities, skills would a teacher need?
- Which challenges does inclusion present to the European teacher?
- And which challenges does the European teacher present to inclusion?

In their discussions, the students focused on the skills and qualities that the European teacher would need in relation to inclusion. They concluded that learning how to deal with diversity and differentiation is quite a challenging task, especially when you are at the beginning of your teaching career. They also realised that teacher education in different countries puts more or less focus on learning skills to deal with inclusion in the classrooms. Finally, the students pointed out that opportunities in which you can discuss educational issues, such as this seminar, should be more common. They found it particularly interesting to get a chance to talk to and to learn from people from different countries in Europe and to reflect on their own practices and the practices in their country.

Concluding remarks

Not only in our society, but also in education, 'diversity' has become a keyword. Inclusion is about embracing diversity and the right of all children to have access to the same education. However, I feel that the concept of inclusive education is a top-down one, where even though teachers are the ones who need to put it into practice, they are often not clearly included. As a matter of fact, I worked with more than 40 teacher trainers in 2012–2013 in Vienna, but none of them could explain the meaning of inclusive education. This has now changed with the transformation of teacher education in Austria.

Teacher training content is often imposed on teachers following what society or expert committees have decided should be done. However, it is important to figure out which needs teachers have for training and development, also in relation to inclusive education, by taking teachers into account. I believe that more research should be done in cooperation with teachers, to uncover what their reality in the classroom looks like and what their needs are. During my research in Austria, I have been able to see that teachers have a personal, biographical background that influences their choices in becoming a teacher and in particular their choice in working in the integration class. Many of them are creative and strive to do their best for each and every child. There is a treasury of knowledge and skills among them that should be given more attention. The HOWBET Summer School was a great opportunity to work with future teachers on the topic of inclusion and to highlight the different issues that inclusive education is facing depending on the country. The education scene is changing now maybe more than ever, but teachers need to be consciously made and be a part of it. To become a European teacher, they should know about inclusion and be able to learn how to include as many children in their classroom as possible, and how to offer them the best learning possibilities so that each child can thrive. However, teachers should also be entitled to state their limits and be taken seriously.

An important skill for teachers to succeed in a classroom that is more and more diverse (see Chapter 5 in this book for a discussion on linguistic diversity in Europe) is to be able to cooperate and work together with many professionals in their field, to be open-minded and learn from others, in their country and outside. A European teacher should know that inclusion is not just about children with disabilities, but it is also about how to include each and every child. To become a European teacher, he/she needs to value diversity, be able to reflect on his/her teaching and to be given the right support, so that not only the children but also the teacher can succeed.

References

Ahrbeck, B. (2014). *Inklusion. Eine Kritik [Inclusion. A critique]*. Stuttgart: Kohlhammer.

Ainscow, M. (1991). *Effective schools for all*. London: Fulton.

Altrichter, H., & Feyerer, E. (2011). Auf dem Weg zu einem inklusiven Schulsystem? Die Umsetzung der UN-Konvention in Österreich aus der Sicht der Governance-Perspektive [On the way to an inclusive school system? The implementation of the UN Convention in Austria from the point of view of the governance perspective]. *Zeitschrift für Inklusion, 4*. Retrieved from www.inklusion-online.net/index.php/inklusion/article/view/131/127 (accessed 16 June 2017).

Biewer, G. (2010). *Grundlagen der Heilpädagogik und Inklusiven Pädagogik* [Fundamentals of specials needs education and inclusive pedagogy] (2nd ed.). Bad Heilbrunn, Germany: Klinkhardt.

Biewer, G. (2011). Die UN-Behindertenrechtskonvention und das Recht auf Bildung [The UN convention on the rights of persons with disabilities]. In O. Dangl & T. Schrei (Eds.), *Hochschule, Bildungsrecht für alle?* (pp. 51–62). Wien/Krems: Kirchliche Pädagogische.

Bmask (2012). *Nationaler Aktionsplan Behinderung 2012-2020. Strategie der Österreichischen Regierung zur Umsetzung der UN-Behindertenrechtskonvention. Inklusion als Menschenrecht und Auftrag* [National Plan of Action for Disability 2012–2020. Strategy of the Austrian Federal Government for the implementation of the UN Convention on the Rights of Persons with Disabilities. Inclusion as a human right and a mandate]. Wien: Bundesministerium für Arbeit, Soziales und Konsumentenschutz.

BMBF (2015). *Verbindliche Richtlinie zur Entwicklung von Inklusiven Modellregionen* [Compulsory guidelines for the development of inclusive model regions]. Retrieved from https://bildung.bmbwf.gv.at/schulen/bw/abs/rl_inklusive_modell_2015.pdf?61edru (accessed 12 March 2018).

Booth, T., & Ainscow, M. (2002). *Index for inclusion: Developing learning and participation in schools*. Centre for Studies on Inclusive Education. Retrieved from www.eenet.org.uk/resources/docs/Index%20English.pdf (accessed 16 June 2017).

Buchner, T., Feyerer, E., & Flieger, P. (2009). *Report on the social inclusion and social protection of disabled people in European countries*. Retrieved from www.disability-europe.net/downloads/293-at-social-inclusion-report (accessed 25 November 2015).

Buchner, T., & Gebhardt, M. (2011). Zur schulischen Integration in Österreich: Historische Entwicklung, Forschung und Status Quo [School integration in Austria: Historical development, research and status quo]. *Zeitschrift für Heilpädagogik, 62*(8), 298–304.

Clark, C., Dyson, A., & Millward, A. (1995). *Towards inclusive schools?* London: David Fulton Publishers.

Donnelly, V., & Watkins, A. (2011). Teacher education for inclusion in Europe. *Prospects, 41*, 341–353.

European Agency for Development in Special Needs Education. (2012). *Special needs education: Country data 2012*. Retrieved from www.european-agency.org/publications/ereports/sne-country-data-2012/SNE-Country-Data2012.pdf (accessed 16 June 2017).

Feyerer, E. (2013). *Inklusive Region in Österreich: Bildungspolitische Rahmenbedingungen zur Umsetzung der UN-Konvention* [Inclusive regions in Austria. Educational, political frameworks for the implementation of the UN convention]. Retrieved from http://bidok.uibk.ac.at/library/feyerer-regionen.html (accessed 16 June 2017).

Feyerer, E., & Prammer, W. (2002). *Gemeinsamer Unterricht in der Sekundarstufe 1* [Common teaching at the lower level of secondary school]. Retrieved from http://bidok.uibk.ac.at/library/feyerer-unterricht.html (accessed 16 June 2017).

Florian, L., & Black-Hawkins, K. (2011). Exploring inclusive pedagogy. *British Educational Research Journal, 37*(5), 813–828.

Forlin, C., Loreman, T., Sharma, U., & Earle, C. (2009). Demographic differences in changing pre-service teachers' attitudes, sentiments and concerns about inclusive education. *International Journal of Inclusive Education, 13*(2), 195–209.

Gebhardt, M., Krammer, M., Schwab, S., Rossmann, P., & Gasteiger Klicpera, B. (2013). What is behind the diagnosis of learning disability in Austrian schools? An empirical evaluation of the results of the diagnosis process. *International Journal of Special Education, 28*(2), 147–153.

Hart, S., Drummond, M. J., & McIntyre, D. (2007). Learning without limits: Constructing a pedagogy free from determinist beliefs about ability. In L. Florian (Ed.), *The SAGE handbook of special education* (pp. 486–498). London: Sage.

Havighurst, R. J. (1972). *Developmental tasks and education* (3rd ed.). New York, NY: Longman.

Hericks, U. (2006). *Professionalisierung als Entwicklungsaufgabe: Rekonstruktionen zur Berufseingangphase von Lehrerinnen und Lehrern* [Professionalisation as developmental task. Reconstructions of the starting phase of teachers]. Wiesbaden: VS Verlag für Sozialwissenschaften.

Hinz, A. (2002). Von der Integration zur Inklusion: Terminologisches Spiel oder konzeptionelle Weiterentwicklung? [From integration to inclusion. Terminological games or a conceptual development?] *Zeitschrift für Heilpädagogik, 53*, 354–361.

Kershner, R. (2007). What do teachers need to know about meeting special educational needs? In L. Florian (Ed.), *The SAGE handbook of special education* (pp. 486–498). London: Sage.

Lebenshilfe Österreich. (2010). *Gemeinsam lernen – Eine Schule für alle! Schritt für Schritt zur neuen Schule für alle: Stufenplan zur inklusiven Schule* [Learning together – One school for all! Step by step to a new school for all: A plan towards inclusive schools]. Vienna: Lebenshilfe Österreich.

Luciak, M., & Biewer, G. (2011). Equity and inclusive education in Austria: A comparative analysis. In A. J. Artiles, E. B. Kozleski, & F. R. Waitoller (Eds.), *Examining equity on five continents* (pp. 17–44). Cambridge, MA: Harvard Education Press.

Mitchell, D. (2008). *What really works in special and inclusive education: Using evidence-based teaching strategies*. Abingdon: Routledge.

Monitoringauschuss. (2010). *Stellungnahme des unabhängigen Monitoringausschusses zur Umsetzung der UN Konvention über die Rechte von Menschen mit Behinderungen* [Opinion of the Independent Monitoring Committee on the Implementation of the UN Convention on the Rights of Persons with Disabilities]. Retrieved from http://monitoringausschuss.at/stellungnahmen/inklusive-bildung-10-06-2010/ (accessed 21 September 2017).

Pijl, S. J. (2010). Preparing teachers for inclusive education: Some reflections from the Netherlands. *Journal of Research in Special Educational Needs, 10*(1), 197–201.

Salend, S. J., & Duhaney, L. M. G. (1999). The impact of inclusion on students with and without disabilities and their educators. *Remedial and Special Education, 20*(2), 114–126.

Speck, O. (2010). *Schulische Inklusion aus heilpädagogischer Sicht. Rhetorik und Realität* [School inclusion from a special education point of view. Rhetoric and reality]. München: Ernst Reinhardt Verlag München Basel.

UN. (1948). *The universal declaration of human rights.* Retrieved from www.un.org/en/universal-declaration-human-rights/ (accessed 21 September 2017).

UN. (1989). *The convention on the rights of the child.* Retrieved from www.ohchr.org/EN/ProfessionalInterest/Pages/CRC.aspx (accessed 21 September 2017).

UN. (2000). *United Nations millennium declaration.* Retrieved from www.un.org/millennium/declaration/ares552e.pdf (accessed 21 September 2017).

UN. (2006). *The convention on the rights of persons with disabilities.* Retrieved from www.un.org/disabilities/documents/convention/convention_accessible_pdf.pdf (accessed 25 November 2017).

UNESCO. (1990). *The world declaration on education for all.* Retrieved from http://unesdoc.unesco.org/images/0012/001275/127583e.pdf (accessed 21 September 2017).

UNESCO. (1993). *Teacher education resource package.* Paris: UNESCO. Retrieved from http://unesdoc.unesco.org/images/0009/000966/096636eo.pdf (accessed 21 September 2017).

UNESCO. (1994). *The Salamanca framework and statement for action on special needs education.* Paris: UNESCO. Retrieved from www.unesco.org/education/pdf/SALAMA_E.PDF (accessed 21 September 2017).

UNESCO. (2000). *The Dakar framework for action: Education for all: Meeting our collective commitments.* Retrieved from http://unesdoc.unesco.org/images/0012/001211/121147e.pdf (accessed 21 September 2017).

UNESCO. (2005). *Guidelines for inclusion: Ensuring access to education for all.* Retrieved from http://unesdoc.unesco.org/images/0014/001402/140224e.pdf (accessed 16 June 2017).

7 Teaching and learning for citizenship education

Ana Raquel Simões

Introduction

All human beings are at the same time individuals and citizens of a given society, thus linking human rights and citizenship rights. This interface creates new demands regarding education in general and citizenship education in particular, since there is a clear tension between the particular and the universal, the national and the international, the individual and society. Thus, citizenship education has the important role of making individuals more aware of the human and political issues at stake in society, in an intersection between knowledge, practice and values that constantly interact.

To reflect on this intersection, as well as on theoretical and methodological aspects of citizenship education, are two of the major aims of this chapter. Hence, this chapter focuses on the following issues: the notion, aims, and relevance of citizenship education and human rights education (HRE); the history of citizenship education; diverse approaches to citizenship education in different countries; teacher education programmes concerning citizenship education; European citizenship around Europe and data from Eurobarometer surveys; topics on citizenship education; and questions for reflection. A brief description of some of the tasks undertaken by the student teachers who participated in the HOWBET Summer School will also be provided, as well as a summary of the students' voices in the reflections they wrote at the end of the workshop, and a conclusion.

Citizenship education and human rights education

In this chapter, citizenship education is understood as 'the subject area that is promoted [. . .] with the aim of fostering the harmonious co-existence and mutually beneficial development of individuals and of the communities they are part of' (European Commission/EACEA/Eurydice, 2017, p. 9). Hence, citizenship education is important for the development of democratic societies, where individuals play an active and informed role in their communities (at local, regional, national, and international levels).

It is believed that citizenship education is constituted by four dimensions: political, social, cultural, and economic (Figure 7.1). The political dimension

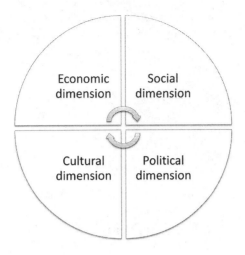

Figure 7.1 Dimensions of citizenship education

refers to the political rights and responsibilities related to the political system. In order to develop this dimension, work may be done in terms of improving knowledge of the political system and promoting democratic attitudes and participatory skills. The social dimension concerns interpersonal behaviour in society, and requires measures of loyalty and solidarity; hence, it is essential to develop social skills and the knowledge of social relationships. The cultural dimension refers to the consciousness of cultural heritage. This dimension should be developed through knowledge of history and basic skills (language competence, reading, and writing). The economic dimension concerns the relationship between the individual and the labour and consumer market, which requires skills appropriate for job-related activities and vocational training.

Intrinsically related to citizenship education is education for democratic citizenship (EDC), defined as

> education, training, dissemination, information, practices and activities which aim, by equipping learners with knowledge, skills and understanding and moulding their attitudes and behaviour, to empower them to exercise and defend their democratic rights and responsibilities in society, to value diversity and to play an active part in democratic life, with a view to the promotion and protection of democracy and the rule of law.
> (Council of Europe, 2010, n.p.)

HRE is also related to the former two concepts (citizenship education and EDC). The definition of HRE is

> education, training, dissemination, information, practices and activities which aim, by equipping learners with knowledge, skills and understanding

and moulding their attitudes and behaviour, to empower them to contribute to the building and defence of a universal culture of human rights in society, with a view to the promotion and protection of human rights and fundamental freedoms.

(Council of Europe, 2010, n.p.)

One can see a clear relationship between these concepts. As far as EDC and HRE are concerned, both are closely interrelated and mutually supportive, and intended to help individuals to play an effective role in their community (either at the local, national or European/international level). Both show people how to become informed about their rights, responsibilities, and duties, and help them to realise that they can make a difference. They differ in focus and scope rather than in goals and practices. While EDC focuses primarily on democratic rights and responsibilities, and active participation, in relation to the civic, political, social, economic, legal, and cultural spheres of society, HRE is concerned with the broader spectrum of human rights and fundamental freedoms in every aspect of people's lives.

As far as when and where EDC and HRE take place, one has to conclude that this does not just happen in schools during citizenship lessons: EDC and HRE cover all forms of education, from children up to young adults at college and university, and into adult education, vocational training, and the workplace, and thus are considered lifelong learning processes. Thus, one may find EDC and HRE in the work of campaigning groups and on Internet pages aimed at varied target audiences. EDC and HRE are not just about learning to vote or learning our rights in society; they involve issues such as learning how to sort out problems within a group, learning how to resolve playground disputes in a fair and sensible way, and how to keep one's environment clean and safe in a community. One may also conclude that EDC may happen everywhere: not only in schools, but also in the community in general (e.g., working with the local community, discovering and experiencing democratic participation in society, and addressing topical issues such as environmental protection and cooperation between generations and nations).

Based on the European Union (EU) reference framework on social and civic competences (European Parliament and Council, 2016), citizenship education is related to the development of competences that comprise knowledge, skills, and attitudes. The Council of Europe (2016) competences for democratic culture add a fourth dimension, 'values'. These dimensions are not of common agreement, since authors like Doğanay (2012) consider attitudes, values, and dispositions as a whole, whereas ten Dam, Geijsel, Reumerman, and Ledoux (2010, 2011) replace values (or dispositions) with reflections in the empirical testing of some of these competence areas.

This chapter follows the EU's reference framework of key competences for lifelong learning, as well as the European Commission/EACEA/Eurydice (2017) report *Citizenship education at school in Europe*, which uses knowledge, skills, and attitudes. According to this latter document, one may conclude that citizenship education needs to help students develop knowledge, skills, and attitudes in four broad competence areas: (a) interacting effectively and constructively with others; (b) thinking critically; (c) acting in a socially responsible manner; and (d) acting democratically.

History of citizenship education

Over the last decades, there has been a growing awareness of the role of education in the promotion of the core values of the Council of Europe: democracy, human rights, and the prevention of human rights violations. More generally, education is increasingly seen as a defence mechanism against the rise of violence, racism, extremism, xenophobia, discrimination, and intolerance. In the Second Summit of Heads of State and Government of the Council of Europe, held in October 1997 in Strasbourg, the heads of state and government of the member states decided to 'launch an initiative for education for democratic citizenship with a view to promoting citizens' awareness of their rights and responsibilities in a democratic society' (Council of Europe, 1997, p. 4). The Second Summit decisions were implemented, at the political level, through the preparation of a *Declaration and programme of action on education for democratic citizenship*, adopted by the Committee of Ministers who met in Budapest on 7 May 1999. This confirms the growing awareness of the role of education as: (a) a promotor of core values of the Council of Europe; (b) a defence mechanism against the rise of violence, racism, extremism, xenophobia, discrimination, and intolerance; (c) a contributor to social cohesion and social justice.

One may consider three major phases in the history of citizenship education. The first phase (1997–2005) was an exploratory phase, which consisted of a conceptual analysis of the concept (terminology and key competences). The results of this phase were disseminated by means of communication and networking, namely through the creation of a network of national EDC coordinators and the adoption of *Recommendation (2002) 12 on Education for democratic citizenship* by the Committee of Ministers. One important step taken during this phase was the launch of the European Year of Citizenship through Education in 2005.

The second phase (2006–2010) was called 'Learning and living democracy for all'. During this phase, the world programme on HRE of the UN for Europe was monitored, and a close relationship between EDC and HRE was established. In 2010 the Council of Europe's *Charter on education for democratic citizenship and human rights education* was adopted as a reference document on citizenship and HRE. This document contains a comprehensive description of the place and range of EDC by highlighting the following aspects: EDC embraces any formal, non-formal, or informal educational activity, including that of the family; EDC is a factor for social cohesion, mutual understanding, intercultural, and inter-religious dialogue, and solidarity; EDC contributes to promoting equality between men and women; EDC encourages the establishment of harmonious and peaceful relationships within and among peoples, as well as the promotion and development of democratic society and culture; EDC should be at the heart of the reform and implementation of education policies; EDC is an innovative factor in the organisation and management of overall education systems, as well as curricula and teaching methods.

The third phase (2010–2014) was called 'Education for democratic citizenship and human rights'. This period was dedicated to the implementation of the Charter (and its adaptation to children's rights), as well as to a new edition of *Compass: The manual for human rights education with young people* (Council of Europe, 2012).

Across these periods, some other measures were taken. The Human Rights Education Youth Programme was launched in 2000, and in 2004 the UN approved the World Programme for Human Rights Education, setting ambitious targets for strengthening and developing human rights. *Resolution (2008) 23 on the youth policy of the Council of Europe* was launched, which further strengthened the central role of HRE in youth policy, setting human rights and democracy as a priority, including 'ensuring young people's full enjoyment of human rights and human dignity, and encouraging their commitment in this regard' (Council of Europe, 2008, n.p.). The *White paper on intercultural dialogue: Living together as equals* was also released in 2008, which shows a growing interest of the Council of Europe in intercultural dialogue. In 2010 a Directorate General responsible for justice, legal rights, and citizenship was established, and 2013 was declared the 'European Year of Citizens'.

In 2014 the programme 'Europe for citizens: Remembrance and European citizenship/democratic engagement and participation' was launched; and will continue through 2020. This programme comprises four actions, titled Active Citizens for Europe, Active Civil Society in Europe, Together for Europe, and Active European Remembrance (European Commission, 2016). Several international organisations have also been promoting the development of citizenship education. The Council of Europe, for example, has published the reference framework *Competences for democratic culture: Living together as equals in culturally diverse societies* (Council of Europe, 2016), and has recently disseminated results from the second monitoring of the implementation of the *Charter on education for democratic citizenship and human rights education* (Council of Europe, 2017). UNESCO has also been promoting citizenship education through its Global Citizenship Education Model (see http://en.unesco.org/gced).

Approaches to citizenship education

Citizenship education has been included in the school curriculum of European countries in different ways that tend to reflect the importance that education decision makers attach to this area. The detailed objectives and content of citizenship education vary across Europe, but the main aim of the subject area is generally to ensure that young people become active citizens capable of contributing to the development and well-being of the society in which they live. Thus, one may say that citizenship education is part of national curricula and may be delivered in schools through three main approaches: (a) as a stand-alone subject, (b) as part of another subject or learning area, and (c) as a cross-curricular dimension.

However, a combination of these approaches is often used. According to the European Commission/EACEA/Eurydice (2017), most education systems use either the integrated or the cross-curricular approach, and may use both at all levels of general education. This means that most teachers, from different subject areas, are expected to be involved in citizenship education issues.

Citizenship education as a stand-alone subject

According to the European Commission/EACEA/Eurydice (2017) report *Citizenship education at school in Europe*, the approach that is the least used by the education systems in Europe is the one of a compulsory separate subject, which happens mostly at secondary level. In fact, the 20 education systems that have a compulsory separate subject use varied forms of implementation, sometimes starting at primary level but, more usually, at the lower secondary and/or upper secondary level. The countries where it is offered for a longer period of time are Estonia, France, Slovakia, and Finland (from 7 to 12 years of study). The compulsory period is especially long in France, where citizenship education is taught for the whole 12 years of schooling throughout primary, lower, and upper secondary education. Cyprus, Croatia, and Turkey, at the other end of the group, provide citizenship education in one year/grade only. A few countries have recently increased the compulsory possibility of citizenship education as a separate subject, as in the case of Belgium (French Community). Other countries have also extended the number of grades of citizenship education, such as Greece and Finland.

Citizenship education as part of another subject or learning area

In the vast majority of countries, citizenship education is integrated into several subjects or educational/learning areas, whether or not it is also taught as a separate compulsory subject. The subjects which incorporate aspects of citizenship education are mostly Social Sciences, History, Geography, Languages, and Ethics/Religious Education. A learning area brings together the content or objectives from several closely related disciplines or subjects into a discrete teaching bloc. In Hungary and the Netherlands, citizenship education is integrated into curriculum areas that can be organised into teaching blocs at the discretion of the school. In Latvia, there are four separate subjects (Ethics, Health Education, Introduction to Economics, and Civics), integrated into the social sciences curriculum area, which are taught during the whole period of compulsory education.

Citizenship education in a cross curricular approach

Citizenship education may have the status of a cross-curricular approach. Where it exists, this approach is always combined with other subject-based approaches. As a cross-curricular dimension, all teachers must contribute to implementing the related objectives as defined in national curricula.

In Germany, the policies are decided within each *Land*. In Belgium (Flemish Community), secondary school teams are collectively responsible for taking decisions on how to implement global curricular objectives concerned with citizenship education (e.g., taking responsibility, being critical, etc.) and more specific objectives. In Denmark, at upper secondary level, educational programmes and the school culture are supposed to prepare students for participation, responsibilities, and rights in a democratic society. In Croatia, schools have to implement the 2012 curriculum for citizenship education as a cross-curricular and interdisciplinary topic (even though they may also teach citizenship education as a separate subject). In Hungary, education for active citizenship and democracy is of core importance in the National Core Curriculum throughout the entire education system. In Iceland, in upper secondary levels, democracy and human rights are seen as fundamental pillars and included in all school subjects and activities. Finally, in Portugal, in 2012 the guidelines suggested that citizenship education could be implemented as a transversal curricular area, also provided the opportunity for it to be worked into projects and other activities involving the community, or as a compulsory separate subject in primary and lower secondary schools. In September 2017, the new national strategy for citizenship education was introduced, and is now being piloted. This includes a new subject – Citizenship and Development – in the form of a compulsory separate subject in the second and third levels of basic education (pupils aged 10–13), and as a cross-curricular area in the remaining academic pathway.

Teacher education and citizenship

In order to prepare teachers to work in the field of citizenship education, work has to be undertaken in terms of teacher education programmes:

> Without training in EDC/HRE of teachers and others both in the educational system and outside it, for example youth leaders, such education will be ineffective and worse than useless. The subject is very different from traditional subjects. Those who will teach it must first be taught it themselves. The best methods of teaching it are also different, and have to be learned.
> (Council of Europe, 2010, p. 32)

There is a huge diversity in terms of what happens as far as teacher education programmes on citizenship education are concerned. Generally, teachers of citizenship education at primary level are generalists, and the teaching skills required are common for all generalist teachers. In contrast, at secondary level, teachers of citizenship are specialists, usually qualified to teach one or two curriculum subjects.

According to the European Commission/EACEA/Eurydice report (2017), increased efforts have been taken by many countries in recent years to develop teachers' professional competences concerning citizenship education. The number of countries where it is possible to specialise in citizenship education has increased. Before, it was possible only in the UK and now it is a possibility also in Belgium, Ireland, Luxembourg, the Netherlands, and Denmark. Seven other countries (the Czech Republic, Estonia, Latvia, Lithuania, Austria, Poland, and

Slovakia) offer the possibility to train teachers to become semi-specialists in citizenship education.

Nine countries have defined a set of common competences directly linked to citizenship for all secondary teachers, whatever their subject specialisation may be. In most countries, central-level regulations on ITE and/or their qualifications define areas of specialisation for secondary teachers according to the courses they take. Generally, the area of citizenship education is integrated within ITE courses for specialists in History, Geography, Philosophy, Ethics/Religion, Social Science, or Economics.

European citizenship across Europe and data from Eurobarometer surveys

The *Standard Eurobarometer 85* survey (European Commission, 2016) was carried out in May 2016 in 34 countries or territories: the 28 member states of the EU, five candidate countries (the former Yugoslav Republic of Macedonia, Turkey, Montenegro, Serbia, and Albania), and among the Turkish Cypriot Community in the part of the country that is not controlled by the government of the Republic of Cyprus. This Eurobarometer aimed to collect data on:

1 *Perceptions of the EU's achievements*: What do Europeans regard as the EU's most positive results?
2 *The concept of European citizenship*: Do Europeans see themselves as European citizens? Do they know their rights as European citizens? Do they want more information on this subject?
3 *Values*: Do Europeans feel that they have a good understanding of what is currently happening in the world? Do they think there are shared values in their country? What are the economic and social values of Europeans?

In terms of what is perceived as the main positive results of the EU, the free movement of people, goods, and services is pointed out by most people (56%), just 1% above the reference to peace among the member states of the EU (55%). In the third position is the Euro (25%), and in fourth place come student exchange programmes, such as ERASMUS (23%). Some references tally a percentage lower than 20%: the political and diplomatic influence of the EU in the rest of the world (19%), the economic power of the EU (18%), and the level of social welfare (health care, education, and pensions) in the EU (17%).

Concerning European citizenship, 66% of respondents feel a sense of European citizenship. Twenty-eight per cent even state that they 'definitely' feel like citizens of the EU. One must notice that the sense of European citizenship is slightly stronger among respondents in the eurozone countries (68%) than in non-eurozone countries. In terms of differences between countries, Greece is now the only country where a minority of respondents feel that they are citizens of the EU (46% versus 54%), and in Italy the opinions are divided (both 49%). This sense of European citizenship seems to be higher than average among respondents born after 1980 (73% 'yes' versus 26% 'no'), decreasing with age. The most significant differences reflect the respondents' level of education: the sense of European citizenship is very widespread among Europeans who studied up to the age of 20 or beyond (76%), but it is the minority view among Europeans who left school before the age of 15 (49% versus 49%). Close to six in ten respondents have a sense of European citizenship (59% say they feel 'nationals and European', 'European and nationals', or 'European only'). Men (63%) are more likely than women (55%) to see themselves as European citizens, and this sense of European citizenship is more widespread among the younger respondents, as previously highlighted.

As far as the economic and social values of Europeans are concerned, 40% of the Europeans think immigrants contribute a lot to their country, which shows that more than half of the respondents disagree. When asked whether or not they agree with some given statements reflecting their economic and social values, the statement '(Our Country) should help refugees' is supported by 63% of Europeans, while 30% are against it; 65% of Europeans agree that 'the State intervenes too much in our lives'; 52% of Europeans disagree that 'immigrants contribute a lot to (Our Country)'. However, 40% of respondents believe they do.

Comparing the Eurobarometer survey results of 2012 and 2016, as far as openness of Europeans to others is concerned, the extent to which Europeans are open to other EU countries remained stable: almost half of Europeans had socialised with people from another EU country during the 12 months preceding the survey. However, the proportion of Europeans who has visited another EU country in the past 12 months has fallen. The proportions of Europeans who have watched a TV programme (35%) or read a book, magazine, or newspaper (25%) in a language other than their mother tongue have not changed since autumn 2012. The number of Europeans who have used the Internet to buy a product or service in another EU country has increased slightly (22%, +2). In the Flash Eurobarometer 365 – 'European Union Citizenship' (EACEA, 2012), and concerning EU citizens' awareness of their status as citizens of the EU, the vast majority of respondents (81%) said they were familiar with the term 'citizen of the European Union', a percentage that has increased when compared with data from previous years. Almost all respondents knew that it is true that they can be both a citizen of the EU and of their own country (89%).

Considering all the data presented in these studies, one sees that work still has to be done in terms of developing educational actions for European citizenship and HRE. There are some principles that can be used in the definition of these educational actions, which will be considered in the next section.

Principles in European democratic citizenship and human rights education

Three principles in European democratic citizenship and HRE may be considered: (a) teaching 'about' European democratic citizenship and human rights, (b) teaching 'for' European democratic citizenship and human rights, and (c) teaching 'through' European democratic citizenship and human rights.

Regarding teaching 'about' European democratic citizenship and human rights (cognitive dimension), students need a clear understanding of what democracy and citizenship mean, what human rights they enjoy and how to defend them. They need to know how their country's and EU's political system work, as well as to study key documents. It is also important that they are aware that each individual enjoys the right of free thought and expression, free access to information through uncensored media, and the key principle of equality and non-discrimination: women and men, rich and poor, young and old, nationals and immigrants equally possess these rights.

Concerning teaching 'for' European democratic citizenship and human rights (participative dimension), young citizens need to learn how to participate in their ('glocal') communities and how to exercise their human rights and freedoms – for example, their right of free access to information and of free thought, opinion and expression. They should also have active experience in interacting with others – such as promoting their interests, negotiating for compromise, or agreeing on how to define 'the general welfare' (Human Rights Declaration, Article 29). In this respect, there are some values and practices that have to be learned:

> To become full and active members of society, citizens need to be given the opportunity to work together in the interests of the common good; respect all voices, even dissenting ones; participate in the formal political process; and cultivate the habits and values of democracy and human rights in their everyday lives and activities. As a result, citizens come to feel useful and recognized members of their communities, able to participate in and make a difference to society.
> (Hartley & Huddleston, 2009, p. 8)

As far as teaching 'through' European democratic citizenship and human rights is concerned, one must acknowledge the importance of allowing students to exercise their human rights (for instance, freedom of thought and expression), which requires opportunities for them to take part in governing their school, exercising their human rights, and fulfilling their responsibilities. In all of these dimensions, democratic citizenship and human rights serve as a pedagogical guideline.

While teaching 'about' European democratic citizenship and human rights may be assigned to special subjects (such as Social Studies, History, and Civic Education), the cultural dimension of EDC/HRE – teaching 'through' democracy and human rights – is a challenge for the whole school: human rights and democracy become the school community's pedagogical guideline and the lens through which all of the elements of school governance are judged. Thus, one may conclude that a combination of instruction (listening to a lecture, reading), training (demonstration, practice, and coaching) and experience should be undertaken, since knowledge may be acquired through instruction, but competences and attitudes need some training experience in order to be developed.

How to develop European citizenship and human rights education?

As mentioned before, teaching through and for European democratic citizenship and human rights requires, first of all, that teachers develop their own competencies on this issue (Keating-Chetwynd, 2009). In terms of school activities, citizenship education is usually undertaken by means of active learning (e.g., task-based learning), considering activities such as role plays, debates, decision-making games, interviews with experts, producing reports, or other forms of presentation. It is important for the teacher to see how the students cope with the problems they encounter, so that they understand that they should not give in quickly. They should observe the students at work, with two different perspectives of assessment in mind: the process of learning and the achievements at work. Thus, teachers have an important role in helping students decide when and on what topic they want to work, helping them to define what should be briefing within the group (Council of Europe, 2010). In order to discuss these issues, the students from the HOWBET Summer School were invited to undertake activities either individually or in groups.

HOWBET Summer School: activities and reflection

During the workshop on citizenship education which was part of the HOWBET Summer School, students were asked to undertake five tasks (see Table 7.1).

Table 7.1 Overview of the workshop entitled 'Citizenship education in Europe'

Tasks	Description
1. *What is citizenship education for me?*	Group work (students organised in groups according to their nationalities) 1. Create a word cloud on citizenship education (www.tagxedo.com/app.html). 2. Is citizenship education or a similar subject included in your country's curriculum? 2.1. If so, at which levels (pre-primary/primary/lower/upper secondary)? 3. Please provide a statement of how the subject is defined in your country or a brief outline of the aims and coverage of the subject.

2. *How is citizenship education included in teacher education programmes?*	Group work (mixed groups as far as nationality is concerned)
	1. Is (European) citizenship education or a similar subject included in your teacher education curriculum?
	  1.1. If so, which is the coverage of the subject?
	  1.2. If not, which topics could be included?

3. *How do I define my identity?*	Individual work (followed by small-group and then whole-group discussion) 1. Please answer the following questions: Who are we? Who am I? Which is my community? Which communities do I belong to? Am I a local citizen? Am I a national citizen? Am I a European citizen? What does 'European' mean? Am I a 'glocal' citizen? (Glocal = global + local.)

(*Continued*)

Table 7.1 (Continued)

4. How would I answer to the Eurobarometer?	Group work (mixed groups)
	1. Answer Eurobarometer questions:
	  1.1. What do you expect from the EU?
	  1.2. What are the EU's main achievements from which Europeans feel that they have benefited?
	  1.3. Do you see yourselves as European citizens today? And in the near future?
	  1.4. Do you know your rights as European citizens? Do you want more information about these rights and, if so, in which areas in particular?
	  1.5. What are the most important values in the eyes of Europeans? And which values do they consider best represent the EU?

5. Which activities can promote citizenship and HRE?	Group work
	1. Think about educational activities to promote citizenship and HRE. Consider the following topics:
	  1.1. Context
	  1.2. Target audience
	  1.3. People/institutions involved
	  1.4. Description of the activity(ies)
	  1.5. Resources to be used
	  1.6. Assessment

Task 1 was undertaken right at the beginning of the workshop, in order to discuss the concept of citizenship education and how it is included in the different national education systems. Besides the personal view of the concept, the discussion of the different realities in the diverse countries was a means of comparative reflection on this issue.

When the students were invited to write three words they related to citizenship education, their answers were entered into a programme to create a word cloud, which included the input from the different groups (Figure 7.2). The words that came up with high relevance included rights, (social) cohesion, democratic, education, citizen, and partnership. The order of appearance is shown in the size of the letters; i.e., the larger the font, the higher the number of occurrences the word has.

After discussing the concept, it was important to see how the different countries deal with citizenship education, namely those of the participants in the HOWBET Summer School. Thus, Task 2 was suggested as group work, where the students were invited to reflect not only on citizenship education, but also more specifically on European citizenship education and how it is included in their teacher education programmes.

In order to interrelate the concepts of identity and citizenship, as well as to promote students' reflection on what the expression 'European' may convey, the students were asked to undertake Task 3 individually, followed by small-group and then whole-group discussion. The reflection focused on individual identity(ies) and sense of citizenship, and on discussing concepts such as national, European, and 'glocal' citizenship.

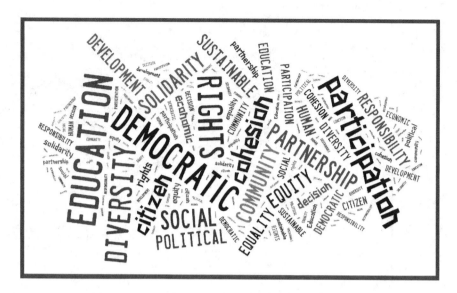

Figure 7.2 Word cloud created by HOWBET students on citizenship education

So as to get acquainted with the Eurobarometer surveys concerning the topic of citizenship education, the students were asked to undertake Task 4, organised in mixed groups (in terms of nationalities), where they had to answer and reflect about some questions from the Eurobarometer. Besides getting in touch with the instrument used, they also had to answer to the questions themselves and discuss their answers with their colleagues.

It was our intention in the HOWBET Summer School to create the opportunity for students (all enrolled in teacher education degrees) to think about possible educational activities to develop citizenship education. This was the aim of Task 5, which was presented and discussed within each group. Finally, some examples of resources and activities that may be undertaken to promote citizenship and HRE were analysed, namely: Council of Europe (2010, 2012); Gollob and Krapf (2007, 2008, 2009); and Gollob, Krapf, and Widinnge (2010a, 2010b).

The students' voices

During the workshop students were able to question themselves about how they perceive citizenship and HRE. There were opportunities to reflect upon these issues, according to the tasks they were given (some of them presented in this chapter). Some questions puzzled the students, such as: How democratic is our community/society? When we think of 'Europeans' and 'European citizenship', are we considering Europe (as a continent) or the EU? When asked to write a reflection at the end of the workshop, the student (ST) responses demonstrated the following.

1   They understand the importance and complexity of citizenship education: "European citizenship, for me, means the feeling of belonging to a group and being a part of something that I can relate to. European citizenship means participation and, to a certain extent, common values – or at least the will to find common ground" (ST1).
2   They show awareness and ability to reflect about the difference between being European and EU-citizens.
3   They are able to identify the (co)existence of different European curricula, as far as European citizenship is concerned: "When looking at the different curricula, the topic of European citizenship is mostly implemented either in the form of an overall teaching principle in the general curriculum, or/and within a specific subject such as Geography or Political Science, whereas a special subject of European Citizenship is still the exception" (ST8).
4   They are aware of the importance to work these themes with children in formal, non-formal, and informal educational settings, involving diverse partners: "I myself have enormous expectations concerning the future of our planet. The environmental disaster we have created has to be dealt with. I do not believe we can prevent this catastrophe but we can do something to help diminish it, especially as teachers. This is a really important expectation because as a union we have more power to make a difference than we would as single nations" (ST14).
5   They recognise the four main dimensions of European citizenship education (political, social, cultural, and economic).
6   They are keen to present the approaches of differentiating teaching about, for, and through European citizenship: "One of the best ways to reach the aim of European Citizenship might be to actually teach through citizenship education. To me, this means not only to teach on an abstract level but also to conduct concrete projects (preferably with a visible outcome) in the class, such as the ones which were drafted in the last group activity of the day; see Chapter 9 in this book" (ST9).
7   The responses discussed how much each participant identifies himself/herself with the EU.
8   The students reflected on their role as European teachers to work on human rights and democracy in order to avoid ethnocentrism and nationalism and incorporate a glocal point of view.

Conclusion

As we have seen previously in this chapter, it is very important to develop knowledge, experience, and reflection on citizenship education in general, and more specifically, as far as teacher education in particular is concerned. This seems to be an issue that is currently in the spotlight of many European countries. In fact, some countries have increased the teaching hours for a compulsory subject, others have introduced a compulsory separate subject of citizenship education, and even others have revised its status at national level, like Portugal. In some countries guidance and support resources on this subject have also been provided (for instance, in France, Italy, Cyprus, and Luxembourg). The majority, if not all countries also have recommendations concerning student and parent participation in school governance.

As seen in recent reports and studies, there are significant differences in countries' policies in terms of the implementation of citizenship education in schools. We have seen that most countries, according to Eurydice latest report on this issue (European Commission/EACEA/Eurydice, 2017), choose to have citizenship education integrated in other subjects, involving a numerous amount of teachers at European level.

However, as we have seen, work still has to be undertaken concerning the regulation or recommendations on the competences teachers must develop within the area of citizenship education, as well as on the definition of possible guidelines concerning students' continuous assessment. The discussion on the use of national evaluation in this area is also a very recent theme, since it may be arguable if the data collection instruments are able to guarantee the evaluation of all the core dimensions of citizenship education.

Work has also to be done concerning initial and in-service teacher preparation for citizenship education. Actually, a clear policy gap seems to exist in some nations as far as the definition of teacher's competences in this area is concerned. The role and importance of training in this area is decided by higher education institutions in some of the countries, which leaves room for very diverse scenarios. Hence, we see that the possibility to create fora of discussion on citizenship education is very important. HOWBET constituted one of these fora, offering future teachers the possibility to develop knowledge on the theme, as well as to interact with others, and discuss their own and their countries' situation regarding citizenship education. Thus, mobility programmes or other international projects (namely on teacher education) may be an important opportunity for the development of citizenship education in the European arena.

References

Council of Europe. (1997). *2nd summit of heads of state and government of the Council of Europe, final declaration and action plan*. Strasbourg: Council of Europe. Retrieved from https://rm.coe.int/168063dced (accessed 22 November 2017).

Council of Europe. (2008). *Resolution (2008) 23 on the youth policy of the Council of Europe*. Retrieved from http://pjp-eu.coe.int/documents/1017981/9907025/CM_Res_08_youth_policy_en.pdf/7df7229a-3c5b-90bf-3eea-22900881b71f (accessed 10 October 2017).

Council of Europe. (2010). *Charter on education for democratic citizenship and human rights education*. Retrieved from www.coe.int/t/dg4/education/edc/Source/Charter/Charterpocket_EN.pdf (accessed 10 October 2017).

Council of Europe. (2012). *Compass: Manual for human rights education with young people*. Strasbourg: Council of Europe.

Council of Europe. (2016). *Competences for democratic culture – Living together as equals in culturally diverse democratic societies*. Strasbourg: Council of Europe.

Council of Europe. (2017). *Learning to live together: Council of Europe Report on the state of citizenship and human rights education in Europe*. Retrieved from https://rm.coe.int/the-state-ofcitizenship-in-europe-e-publication/168072b3cd (accessed 24 April 2017).

Doğanay, A. (2012). A curriculum framework for active democratic citizenship education. In M. Print & D. Lange (Eds.), *Schools, curriculum and civic education for building democratic citizens* (pp. 19–39). Rotterdam: Sense Publishers.

EACEA (Education, Audiovisual and Culture Executive Agency). (2012). *Citizenship education in Europe*. Brussels: EACEA. Retrieved from http://eacea.ec.europa.eu/education/eurydice/documents/thematic_reports/139EN.pdf (accessed 10 October 2016).

European Commission. (2016). *Standard Eurobarometer 85 Report European citizenship*. Luxembourg: Publications Office of the European Union. Retrieved from http://ec.europa.eu/COMMFrontOffice/publicopinion/index.cfm (accessed 18 May 2017).

European Commission/EACEA/Eurydice. (2017). *Citizenship education at school in Europe – 2017: Eurydice report*. Luxembourg: Publications Office of the European Union.

European Parliament and Council. (2016). *Recommendation 2006/962/EC of the European parliament and of the council of 18 December on key competences for lifelong learning*. Retrieved from http://enil.ceris.cnr.it/Basili/EnIL/gateway/europe/EUkeycompetences.htm (accessed 4 June 2017).

Gollob, R., & Krapf, P. (Eds.). (2007). *Exploring children's rights*. Strasbourg: Council of Europe.

Gollob, R., & Krapf, P. (Eds.). (2008). *Living in democracy*. Strasbourg: Council of Europe.

Gollob, R., & Krapf, P. (Eds.). (2009). *Teaching democracy – A collection of models for democratic citizenship and human rights education*. Strasbourg: Council of Europe.

Gollob, R., Krapf, P., & Weidinge, W. (Eds.). (2010a). *Taking part in democracy*. Strasbourg: Council of Europe.

Gollob, R., Krapf, P., & Weidinge, W. (Eds.). (2010b). *Educating for democracy – Background materials on democratic citizenship and human rights education for teacher*. Strasbourg: Council of Europe.

Hartley, M., & Huddleston, T. (2009). *School-community-university partnerships for a sustainable democracy: Education for democratic citizenship in Europe and the United States*. Strasbourg: Council of Europe.

Keating-Chetwynd, S. (Ed.). (2009). *How all teachers can support citizenship and human rights education: A framework for development of competencies*. Strasbourg: Council of Europe. Retrieved from http://dswy.eu/pdfs/How_all_Teachers_HRE_EN.pdf (accessed 18 October 2017).

ten Dam, G., Geijsel, F., Reumerman, R., & Ledoux, G. (2010). *Burgerschapscompetenties: de ontwikkeling van een meetinstrument* [Citizenship competences: The development of a measurement instrument]. *Pedagogische Studiën*, 87, 313–333.

ten Dam, G., Geijsel, F., Reumerman, R., & Ledoux, G. (2011). Measuring young people's citizenship competences. *European Journal of Education Research, Development and Policy*, 46(3), 354–372.

8 Comparative studies and teacher education

Wilfried Hartmann

Introduction

Teacher education is the academic field which throughout Europe is considered widely to be a matter of national interest mainly, if not only. This attitude – dating back to the 18th and 19th centuries, when the governments of nation states considered the development of a national school system a guarantee to educate loyal citizens – is still prevalent in most European countries, in spite of the fact that we are no longer living in states sealed off from their neighbours, but in an European Union (EU) with complex interwoven structures.

Thus, when approaching the task to educate European teachers, one of the first steps should be to raise the students' awareness for the net every member of a society is caught in: a system of often unquestioned local traditions, regional behavioural patterns, and national prejudice. One of the unpleasant features of this net is the fact that you will never have a chance to destroy it from the inside; some even never notice it, being surrounded by their fellow captives. The only chance to tear or cut the net is to look at it from the outside to discover its strengths and weaknesses by comparison with other systems.

Today teachers are confronted with deviant expectations and unexpected behaviour when welcoming migrant children of foreigners – enjoying the European right to reside freely – of migrants or of refugees in their classrooms. Unavoidably they start to compare behavioural patterns and manners of pupils and their parents with those they are used to.

In everyday life comparison is a method we use almost without reflecting: we compare prices, distances, and when choosing a seat on the train even travellers, direction, space, and sunshine. The Internet offers tools for many comparative tasks, but superfluous or distracting information often leads to wrong conclusions, as do insufficient data: asked to tell what kind of animal is pictured in a black-and-white photo of stripes, it is almost impossible to tell whether it is a zebra, a fish, a beetle, or a tiger. We observe similar patterns, but they stand for different realities. On the other hand, we may observe different things, which prove to be alike: the winner of an in-school tournament and the loser at a national championship might be the same person.

To compare, to distinguish, to consider similar, to state uniformity, are ways of thinking and reflecting, prevalent in the approach of the mathematician and the physicist as was as in that of the comparing anatomist or linguist – every generalisation is the result of comparison (Dilthey, 1964, p. 303).[1] In order to raise this awareness among those students who want to become European teachers, the task was to convince them of the usefulness of comparative approaches in all academic fields, define the place of comparison in the system of educational subareas, and prove that comparison has a long history in education as well.

Since the Age of Enlightenment, Comparative Studies in a variety of fields have offered sets of instruments for research. Montesquieu (1748) created a method for comparative law analysis. Using data from the vast travel literature and deciding between competing interpretations, he used comparison to show differences and to demonstrate similarities among international laws and legal practices in different periods, and to explain both uniformities and diversities. He devised five distinct modes of comparison, each with a different set of categories, and looked at regime types, modes of subsistence, reliance of systems (law, manners, and tradition), feudalism versus constitutionalism, and causal explanation in terms of national character or general spirit. Other examples for comparative approaches were those by Goethe (1795) for anatomy, Humboldt (1836) for linguistics, and Carus (1886) for comparative psychology. Comparison does not only allow us to construct relations between variables, but also to determine the bandwidth of variation. The question in this chapter is whether this holds true for education and pedagogy as well.

Where? The place of comparative education in pedagogy and educational research

The wide field of General Education, backed up by Educational Philosophy, is embracing a variety of specialised areas looked at from the perspective of pedagogy or education, such as Anthropology, Psychology, Sociology, Technology, and Economy. These overarching fields contribute to the more specific fields of Andragogy, Social and Special Education, School Pedagogy or Business Education, and to the specific characteristics of methods, didactics, and philosophy of methods for the vast array of taught subjects. Research on these fields can make use of hermeneutical and empirical procedures. The system as a whole can be looked at from a historical perspective and/or from a comparative or international perspective. Given this multitude of approaches, what is Comparative Education able to add?

Comparative Education as a whole applies historical, philosophical, and sociological theories and methods to education. Above all it is an academic, interdisciplinary approach. It can be distinguished from International Education (sometimes regarded as a similar field), which, in short, is the use-oriented branch of Comparative Education. If observers look at synchronic similarities and differences, they move into the field of Comparative Education; when asking about diachronic stability or change during the course of time, they enter the field of

Historic Comparative Education; and when trying to anticipate future developments, they move into Extrapolative Comparative Education.

One has to keep in mind that in the course of time not only objects or ways of acting change (the number of pupils per classroom, the types of disciplinary methods) but also the centre of interest. Looking for example at the school setting in Germany in 1854, all seems to be similar to today: 26 hours per week simple and enriching teaching of religion, reading and mother tongue, writing, arithmetic, singing, knowledge of fatherland and nature in the elementary school (Krueger, 1970). A more thorough look shows the differences: if only the class size exceeded 80 pupils would an additional class be opened, and for more than 120 pupils, a third parallel class; necessary equipment included a blackboard with chalk and sponge, and a teacher's desk and cupboard; requested additional teaching aids were wall maps and globe, a violin, a ruler and circle, one copy of the textbooks, and additional pictures (Preußen Ministerium, 1877).

The diachronic view shows us the development of the school's character, changes of thinking patterns of school policy, assumed necessity of schooling time, importance of certain subjects, usual class size, fees and stipends, school types, and mobility. Caution is even more necessary when looking in a synchronic approach at contemporaries, we should not be trapped by our own prejudice and stereotypes. As Boulding put it: 'It is what we think the world is like, not what it is really like that determines our behavior' (Boulding, 1959, n.p.).

A description of the Chinese school system might illustrate our tendency to be preoccupied by prejudice: moral education (i.e., love of the motherland, love of the party, and love of the people, and previously love of Chairman Mao); sports; extra-curricular activities; productive labour for two weeks per semester; and the '9-6-3' rule (nine of ten children began primary school, six completed it, and three graduated with good performance; Hsi-en Chen, 1981, p. 12). Adding more information changes the picture: after the eighth wave of curriculum reform (Cui & Zhu, 2014) all of this makes up 32% of the curriculum; Chinese language and Fundamental Mathematics fill 60% of the schooling time, Natural and Social Science another 8% (OECD, 2016).

When? The development of comparative education

History of comparison in education

Xenophon (430–355 BC) in his *Kyrupedie* – almost a historical educational novel – described the Persians as being educated to become militant and ethical (Xenophon, 2009); Cicero (106–43 BC) in *De Oratore* compared Romans (interested in laws) and Greek (preoccupied with philosophy) and created a synthesis of their education and thinking (Cicero, 1986). Caesar (100–44 BC) praised the Druids for 20 years of education concentrated on memorising, and compared this with Roman and Greek ideals (Caesar, 2010).

In the Middle Ages, this interest in comparison with other systems continued. In China, the I Ching (635–713) extolled the high level of Buddhist scholarship and advised Chinese monks to study in Nalanda, India, at one of the world's first residential universities, 'which between 427 and 1197 attracted pupils and scholars from all Asia' (Deeg, 2017, p. 18). Marco Polo (1254– ~1325) praised the training of civil servants at the Mongolian court (Guignard, 1983). While these reports implicitly compare with the respective situation at home, Ibn Khaldoun (born in Tunisia in 1332, died in Cairo 1406) reflects in almost modern terms the scientific value of comparison as a tool of research, when stating that the historian has to rely

> on knowing the nature of existing things, the difference between nations, areas and epochs with respect to the mentality, customs, religious sects and all circumstances (influencing society). He has to know, which of all these will survive, so that he can compare the presence with the future [. . .], he has to distinguish aspects, in which they coincide or contradict, as well as the reasons for these analogies and differences.
>
> (Lê Thành, 1981, p. 10)

Around 1800 a number of authors emphasised the usefulness of comparison in education: Brinkmann (1788) asked which type of education serves the highest possible advancement of the pupil's nature by maximising the development of all his potency. Hechtius (1795–1798) published his book *De re scholastica Anglica cum Germanica comparata*, and Evers (1806) gave his work the title 'Fragment of the Aristotelian Art of Education as Introduction to a Tentative Comparison of Antique and Modern Pedagogy'.

Epochs and structures of comparative education

Widely acknowledged as the father of comparative education is the French revolutionary and social scientist Marc-Antoine Jullien de Paris (1775–1848), the author of *Esquisse et vues préliminaires d'un ouvrage sur l'éducation comparé* (1817). This work aimed at the renewal and refinement of education, the derivation of rules and principles, education as positive science, a working plan for categorical order, and the creation of an Institute for Comparative Education and Research in the Swiss cantons. He developed methods to standardise questionnaires, collect information, compile tables, recognise differences and transferable elements, and consider national specifics and mentality differences.

In 1900 Sir Michael Sadler took up this approach, especially with *How far can we learn anything of practical value from the study of foreign systems of education?* He stated:

> We cannot wander at pleasure among the educational systems of the world, like a child strolling through a garden, and pick off a flower from one bush and some leaves from another, and then expect that if we stick what we have gathered into the soil at home, we shall have a living plant.
>
> (Bray, Adamson, & Mason, 2007, p. 378)

He considered cross-country comparison inappropriate for the reform of educational systems, but useful to detect relevant traits in a successful system when judging it in a social context.

Where Jullien believes in certain laws, Sadler is describing ideas; while Jullien tries to isolate a restricted number of social factors to explain pedagogical procedures, Sadler states that Comparative Education as such generates comprehension. Thus, in Jullien's view, the testing of hypotheses with reference to social and pedagogical variables generates explanations that allow reform, while Sadler expects that intensive studies of the relation of school and society lead to insights, which culminate in reforms.

In the USA, James E. Russell was the first to give a lecture on Comparative Education, in 1899–1990 at Columbia University, New York. He sketched the development of a number of countries (starting with Germany, France, and England), following a general pattern: starting with its educational history, then describing the present structure of public education, and closing the lecture with a general summary and comparison (Bereday, 1963).

The necessity for a comparative approach was already seen by Dilthey (1888), when stating:

> a comparative look at educational systems will be required, and it will show that just here the individual forms are connected with each other by the progressive development of mankind. In certain limits, it will hereby be possible to determine the tendency of the development of education, and in such a way use our scientific insight for directing the educational system [. . .] for the historical mind it is self-evident that the historical ethos of a people, which generated as well its system of education should not be hurt or dissolved by the interference of a radical theory, which aims at regulating the education of nations on the basis of a universally valid system.
>
> (Dilthey, 1888, n.p.)

A German comparatist, Friedrich Schneider, edited the *Internationale Zeitschrift für Erziehungswissenschaft* in 1931–1932; in 1962 Franz Hilker developed methods to compare different systems of education under quantitative and normative points of view, understanding comparison as a mental process, leading from the observation of actual facts to valid insights by analysis and value assessment. On this basis he called Ibn Kaldoun's work pre-scientific, and Jullien's approach objective-descriptive compared with his analytic-explicative work. According to Hilker (1962), comparison takes place in a four-step procedure (Table 8.1). His epistemological insight that reality is available as awareness of facts is a challenge to identify these and to check if they exist in more than one specification and are playing a relevant role in education worldwide, thus allowing description and comparison.

During the last decades the hope that comparative education could turn into a tool to find solutions to political or social problems contributed considerably to its development. Mitter (1997) identified five stages:

Table 8.1 Hilker's four-step procedure for comparison

Step	This means	Example
1. Phenomenality of Approach	Something you can observe	Achievement is judged
2. Plurality of Object	Existing in more than one form	Different types of measurement
3. Globality of Pedagogical Situation	Prevalent everywhere	Round the world
4. Comparability of Phenomena	Allows comparison	You can compare it

1. the East/West conflict (1950s and 1960s);
2. the phase of important educational reforms (1970s);
3. intercultural education in multicultural societies and gender-oriented questions (late 1970s and 1980s);
4. transformation processes and postmodern 'Revolta' against the hegemony of theories of modernity (late 1980s and 1990s); and
5. universalism versus cultural pluralism (1990s).

Around the turn of the millennium it seemed that the dissolution of the importance of national specifics and the growing importance of internationality and interculturalism would require comparative educationalists to look for new paradigms and define a grounded, consistent theoretical reference (Adick, 2008; Parreira do Amaral & Amos, 2015). The necessity was seen to include comparative approaches into the curricula of teacher education in order to cater for the needs of transmigrants in transnational context (Dirim et al., 2015). However, recent nationalistic tendencies around the globe will most likely ask for another shift of approach.

Who? Organisations involved

Universities, societies, and journals

Learned societies for comparative education, like the SEEC (Sociedad Española de Educación Comparada), the PCES (Polish Comparative Education Society – Polskie Towarzystwo Pedagogiki Porównawczej), the NOCIES (the Nordic Comparative and International Education Society), and the MESCE (Mediterranean Society of Comparative Education), and overarching societies like the CESE (Comparative Education Society in Europe) or the Comparative and International Education Society (CIES), as well as the WCCES (World Council of Comparative Education Societies), publish their own journals, such as the *Comparative Education Review* (published by the CIES since 1957) or *Compare* (published by the British Association for International and Comparative Education since 1975).

Activities of UNESCO, OECD, and the European Commission

The UNESCO set up a system of about a dozen institutes in order to foster the development of education around the world. The International Bureau of Education Genève, established as a private institution in 1925, became an integral part of UNESCO in 1969, and is nowadays responsible for educational contents, methods, and teaching/learning strategies through curriculum development. Another example is the UNESCO Institute for Lifelong Learning Hamburg, founded in 1952, which is responsible for adult education and lifelong learning, literacy, and non-formal education, and publishes the *International Review of Education*, in English, German, and French.

The organisation the general public associates the most with comparative education is the OECD, established in 1961. Its Directorate for Education administers the Programme for International Student Assessment, widely known as PISA studies. Its success might lead one to forget that in previous years the OECD had undertaken a number of projects in the field of comparative education, such as the Indicators of Education Systems Programme, the Teaching and Learning International Survey, the Programme for the International Assessment of Adult Competencies, and the Skills Project. Since 1996, the OECD – in many cases together with national ministries for education – has presented an annual overview under the title *Education at a Glance*, and has published reference books and tools (*Higher Education to 2030* and *Demography and Globalization*, and the *OECD Handbook for Internationally Comparative Education Statistics*, published in 2004). Another valuable tool is the Online Database (accessible at www.oecd.org/edu/database.htm).

PISA tries to give answers to questions concerning the situation in the partaking countries: It is not just trying to find out what students know in science, mathematics, and literacy, but whether they are able to apply this knowledge. Are they prepared to meet the challenges of the future? Are they able to analyse, reason, and communicate their ideas effectively? Do they have the capacity to continue learning throughout life? These findings are of importance for educators and policymakers in the individual countries: comparing the learning outcomes achieved elsewhere, the quality and equity of the results with those from their own country, gives them a unique chance to learn from policies, structures, and practices in other countries. Detailed analyses of the influence of teachers' behaviour, education, and knowledge on the results allow a fresh view on the teaching profession and its image, and might prove to be an incentive to further develop teacher education with an international or at least European perspective in mind.

The Education, Audiovisual, and Culture Executive Agency (EACEA) of the European Commission supplies a set of interesting tools for comparisons at the European level. Being responsible for the management of certain parts of the EU's funding programmes in the field of education, it provides an overview of programmes, and through Eurydice offers information on and analyses of the educational systems of the EU member countries.

Table 8.2 Dimensions of comparative research

Focus of Research	Approach of Research	Method of Research	Type of Research
Interregional	Description of Countries (*Auslandspädagogik*)	Quantitative	Situative Comparison
Intranational	Comparison of Countries	Qualitative	Systematic Comparison
International	Comparison of Systems		Dual Comparison
Intercultural	Comparison of Elements		Multiple Comparison

How? Approach and methods: dimensions of research

Approaching comparative research in education in order to better understand both one's own society and system as well as that of others requires that we position our own research in order not to come to misleading conclusions. An often cited model for positioning is the cube, developed by Bray and Thomas (1995, p. 475). Its 343 elements allow the researcher to aim at very specific traits. In most cases, however, it will be sufficient to choose one's research approach by accounting for only one element out of each of the four columns in Table 8.2, which describes the four main dimensions to be considered.

Focus of research

In countries with a variety of independent school systems, the comparative focus can be laid on the differences, advantages, and disadvantages of regional specifics (Figure 8.1). A closer look into the situation in a given country is the aim of the intranational focus. Dealing with two or more countries is possible under the international focus, whereas the intercultural focus looks at ways of education based on culture, tradition, religion, and history, without caring primarily about national boundaries.

Approach of research

The approach of research aims at descriptions as exhaustive as necessary or just at the comparison of single elements (such as school entrance age, type of transgression between programmes, and grading systems).

Method of research

Two main types are prevalent: the quantitative approach, stating the number of various elements, and the qualitative approach, attributing characteristics to certain elements. Figure 8.2 shows how results may differ when looking at a fact under a quantitative or qualitative viewpoint. The left picture shows a black scaffold

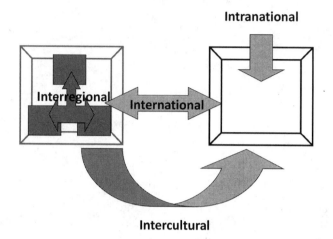

Figure 8.1 Foci of research

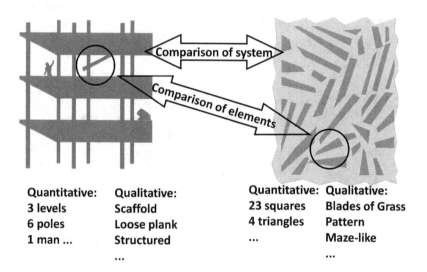

Figure 8.2 Method and approach of research

constructed from a number of different countable elements. The original version of the right picture would show light green elements on a yellow background. Listed below the pictures are elements from quantitative and qualitative descriptions. The double-pointed arrows name two approaches of research, looking at the picture as a whole (comparison of the system) or at individual elements (e.g., form).

Types of research

Situative comparison, usually comparing two (sometimes more) elements without using a *tertium comparationis* is often used for checking the data basis and probing the *tertium comparationis*. For example, would it make more sense to look for difference in colour or in shape when comparing painted geometrical elements, or to concentrate on the number of children in a classroom or the age span? Systematic comparison aims at a comprehensive analysis of two (dual) or more (multiple) systems and therefore often requires the cooperation of a number of researchers who have coordinated their work categorically or methodologically.

From theory to practical use

In the HOWBET Summer School context, the 'Comparative analysis in education' workshop departed from the assumption that looking at the place of Comparative Education in education helps future European teachers get a feeling of the dynamic change of views on educational issues over space and time. The historical view, describing educational processes and elsewhere and else when, stimulated the reflection of one's own actions, but by no means suggested models to imitate without further consideration. The closer look at epochs and structures should help with understanding one's own academic position, not justifying a personal position. Studying comparative approaches of institutions helps to apprehend the capacity of a method and its limitations, but it could be counterproductive just to copy them.

Being a meeting place for students from eight European countries with different traditions, the HOWBET Summer School was a forum suitable to apply comparative tools immediately. As most participants seemed convinced of their ability to look at facts impartially, they greeted with laughter and a sense of superiority a coloured 18th century painting depicting stereotypes about nations. The students were asked to fill in as national groups an 8 × 18 cell table – showing eight columns, one for each of the seven nationalities plus an extra column for England – and 18 rows of categories as completely as possible. Uttermost care was taken not to use the terms 'stereotype' or 'prejudice', but to ask for national character traits.

After some discussion, the groups filled the table with 114 entries. There was a majority of positive qualities attributed to the countries. Often a foreign group's self-perception was more negative than the other groups' hetero-perception. For instance, Germans described Lithuanians as 'proud', whereas Lithuanians described themselves as 'xenophobic'; Austrians considered themselves to be 'rude', whereas the Finns described them as 'more relaxed than the Germans'. Seldom a more positive self-perception was found: Finns regarded themselves as 'shy' or 'silent', while Austrians described them as 'stubborn'. Occasionally, entries pointed in the same direction, namely concerning the Finns, who were perceived as 'reserved'. An intensive discussion led to the insight that we are resistant to see features of reality if we are reluctant to accept them emotionally, and we are more likely to recognise something if it is of importance for our personal vision.

The participants agreed that individual experience, unquestioned modes of behaviour, and traditional ways of thinking may lead to a bias in perception.

Eager to overcome this barrier, the students tried to apply insights from the information on comparative methods to gain a more impartial view on other educational systems. They considered the comparison of numbers to be the easiest and most objective task. Therefore, the country groups listed the marks used in their schools' grading systems. Though this seemed to be an easy task, it required intensive discussions on where to draw the border lines between categories of marks. It became extremely difficult to put the national scales into a common table. The result is shown on Table 8.3.

The advantages and disadvantages of the system were discussed, especially the distinction between 'good' and 'excellent', 'mediocre' and 'failed', and reasons for having multiple marks per category, especially up to five different marks to indicate failure. Suggestions were made to construct a more convincing system to be applied on the European level. The next step was to move from numbers to contents. A table was presented showing the starting age of compulsory schooling, its regular duration, the earliest school-leaving age, the number of class levels (total or by cycle), the number of programmes, and the institution of teacher education in selected European countries not represented in the HOWBET Summer School. After discussing the meaning of the categories in a multiple interpersonal comparative approach, country teams were asked to provide information on their country. Soon it became apparent that the information provided intranationally was not at all consistent. This required more group work in an attempt to compile information backed by all members of a national group. Table 8.4 presents the Portuguese report.

The national texts were discussed in multinational groups in order to clarify misunderstandings and unclear passages. Then the plenary had a chance to react. Only information that was clear to everybody was inserted in the original table. The result is shown in Table 8.5, where information on neighbouring European countries is included.

Although before starting the work all groups had confirmed that the research fields and terms were clear to them (as no further help would be offered), it soon became obvious that dissenting opinions on the meaning of some categories occurred. Some students took 'grades' to be steps on a scale of marks (this was corrected during the multinational group discussion), others as cycles of the programme (as the Lithuanians), the number of grade levels or year cohorts (as the Latvians), or types of examination or tracks (as the Polish). Thus, everybody understood the importance of thorough preparation and discussion of the elements in multiple settings, and the fact that just in one category severe misunderstandings occurred was seen as encouragement. Checking the participants' information against data from Eurydice database caused a discussion on the reliability of information, followed by reflections of the reasons for certain features and their justification. A positive result was the students' refusal to adhere to rules they considered inadequate, such as giving one age as school entry or leaving point.

Table 8.3 Scales used in various countries to measure achievement in secondary schools

A	F	G	LAT	LIT	PL	PT	UK GCSE old	UK GCSE 2017
sehr gut 1	10 kiitettävä		10	10	6 celujacy	18–20 muito bom	A*	9
							A	8
								7
	9	1–1.5 sehr gut	9	9	5 bardzo dobry		B	6
								5
gut 2	8 tyydyttävä	1.6–2.5 gut	7–8	7–8	4 dobry	15–17 bom	C	4
befriedigend 3	7	2.6–3.5 befriedigend	5–6	5–6	3 dostateczny	10–14 suficiente	D	3
							E	2
genügend 4	5–6 välttävä	3.6–4.4 ausreichend	4	4	2 dopuszczajacy	6–9.5 mediocre	F	1
							G	
nicht genügend 5	4 (−1) heikko	4.5–6 mangelhaft ungenügend	1–3	1–4	1 niedostateczny	0–5.5 mau	N/U	U

Austria – A; Finland – F; Germany – G; Latvia – LAT; Lithuania – LIT; Poland – PL; Portugal – PT

Table 8.4 The Portuguese school system as described by students

SCHOOL SYSTEM		PORTUGAL		
Described by: Portugal				
Date: 15/07/2014				
Start of compulsory education: 6 years	**Explanation:** In the first cycle of Basic Education (grades 1 to 4; pupils aged 6–10) there is only one teacher who manages the national curriculum as he/she wants. In the fourth grade there is a national exam of Maths and Portuguese. In the second cycle of Basic Education (grades 5 to 6; pupils aged 10–12) and in the third cycle of Basic Education (grades 7 to 9; pupils aged 12–15) there are many national programmes for each course and there is one teacher for each one. At the end of grade 6 and grade 9 students take national exams (Maths and Portuguese).			
Type of Graduation	**Age**	**Years of Schooling**	**%**	**Entitlement/Qualification to**
Basic education	6–15	9 years	No answer	Scholar/Professional
Secondary	15–18	3 years	No answer	Scholar/Professional
Duration of first school with classroom teacher in years: 4 years				
Transition from . . . to. . . .	**When?**	**Who decides?**	Prerequisites/Procedure? Probation period?	
First to second cycle	9–10 years	Grades of frequency at primary school and the results of national exams	No answer	
Second to third cycle	11–12 years	Grades of frequency at school and the results of national exams	No answer	
Third cycle to secondary	14–15 years	Grades of frequency at school and the results of national exams	No answer	

(*Continued*)

Table 8.4 (Continued)

Structure of Secondary School System:	
At secondary level (grades 10–12; pupils aged 15–18) there are programmes for each course depending on the area that the student has chosen. The areas that students can chose are: Science and Technology, Economics, Social Sciences and Humanities and Professional programmes. At this level, there is one teacher for each course. In the 11th and 12th grades students do exams according to specific areas of their programmes.	
Specific contents/Emphasis on	
In the first, second and third cycles of Basic Education the emphasis is on Portuguese and Maths. At secondary level the contents depend on the programme chosen by the students.	
Financial Aspects	
Tuition fee	Public school is free. Private schools have different fees.
Costs for teaching material	It depends on the financial situation of the students' families. There are two types of social support: the first type pays books, meals, and public transportation; the second type pays half the total of the amount.
Other: transportation/uniform/meals	There are two types of social support: the first type pays books, meals, and public transportation; the second type pays half the total of the amount. A uniform is used in only some private schools.

Table 8.5 Summing up of answers by national groups

	Finn-Scandia				Mediterranean					Eastern Europe				Core-EU				GB/I	
	DK	S	N	FI	PT	E	IT	G	PL	LT	LV	R	AT	D	F	EN	IR
S	7	7		7	6		6	6	6	6/7	7	6	6	6		5	6
D	9	9		9	12		9	9	10	10	9	10	9	9		11	
E	16	16		16	18		15	15	16	16	16	16	15	16–18		16	15
G	8	3			4/2/3/3				3	2	9	5		>3			
#		1		1	4					4	4		8				
Q		U		U	U				U	?	U		TE + U	TE+ U			

Rows: S = starting age of compulsory schooling; D = duration of compulsory schooling; E = end of compulsory schooling at the age of. . .; G = number of grade levels; # = number of programmes; Q = qualification of teachers (U = university; TE = teachers college)

Columns: DK = Denmark; S = Sweden; N = Norway; FI = Finland; PT = Portugal; E = Spain; IT = Italy; G = Greece; PL = Poland; LT = Lithuania; LV = Latvia; R = Russia; AT = Austria; D = Germany; F = France; EN = England; IR = Ireland

Next, multinational groups started drafting an optimal school system for Europe. The opening questions were: 'Given the tradition, experience, discussions in your country, what would you recommend for Europe with respect to...'

1   starting age and duration of primary education and its contents;
2   structure of secondary education, duration, tracks, achievable qualifications;
3   selectivity, retention, based on tests, parents' decisions, school recommendation;
4   best way of teacher education, one, two or three tier-education, number of subjects; and
5   a common curriculum for all European countries or country specific contents?

As the unit on Comparative Education took place on the second day of the HOW-BET Summer School, no immediate answers were expected. The aims were to sharpen the participants' awareness of differences and similarities of the educational systems throughout Europe, to motivate them to question national particularities in order to be open to judge different approaches impartially, and to be interested in developing promising ideas not only during the summer school but throughout their studies and their career.

Summing up

It was a pleasant surprise that the students immediately started discussing solutions. According to written daily feedback and personal communication the students considered the following suggestions for the questions given earlier:

1   Individual starting age based on personal development between 3 and 7 versus same starting age to ensure equal opportunities later in life, at the age of 5 or 7. Specific remarks: 'Some of us went out of the framework of schooling and even questioned the idea of education (schooling) as a whole'; 'I wonder how the two trends in education – individualisation and standardisation – can ever be integrated in one solid and practicable curriculum, at best at a European level.'
2 and 3   No specific recommendation, but emphasis put on the possibility to change tracks, to skip grades, and to concentrate on subjects according to personal interest and development.
4   No detailed suggestions, but general expression of hopes formulated: 'Teachers should necessarily have a similar training and this is a bit difficult to implement'; '(I wonder...) if it will be possible to teach in another European country with the education we will have at the end of our studies'; 'All in all, it would be a good idea to have a curriculum at school and for teacher training that has at least, some common parts (European standards), so that it would include the idea of a European community but also the different cultures of each country.'

5   This was the question causing most reactions. Some typical replies were: 'We finally have to give up our nationalistic perspectives in order to find a common European way'; 'We all agreed that it would be interesting to change to a single European curriculum, however there are some issues to take into account. Firstly, there are problems that could be related to the maintenance of national values of some countries with a more conservative and nationalistic perspective and there are some disciplines that have particular characteristics, such as history, geography and demography. Consequently, it would be necessary to create a part of the curriculum with contents related to the country and the other part with contents related to Europe'; 'In terms of advantages, the only European curriculum could facilitate in reducing bureaucracy and promoting geographical mobility of students in every education levels'; '(We should. . .) find a common European standard (. . . and consider, whether it is. . .) even possible to have ONE curriculum and educational standard for all European countries.'

Note

1 German original: "Der Begriff der vergleichenden Wissenschaften kann nicht durch eine Art Worterklärung daraus abgeleitet werden, daß in demselben das Verfahren der Vergleichung vorherrscht. Denn Vergleichen, Unterscheiden, Ähnlichfinden, Gleichförmigkeiten erkennen, ist das Denkmittel, das ebenso sehr in dem Verfahren des Mathematikers oder dem des Physikers als in dem des vergleichenden Anatomen oder Sprachforschers herrscht. Ist doch jede Generalisation das Ergebnis von Vergleichung" (Dilthey, 1964, p. 303).

References

Adick, C. (2008). *Vergleichende Erziehungswissenschaft: Eine Einführung* [Comparative education. An introduction]. Stuttgart: Kohlhammer.

Bereday, G.Z.F. (1963). James Russell's syllabus of the first academic course in comparative education. *Comparative Education Review*, 7(2), 189–196.

Boulding, K. E. (1959). National images and international systems. *The Journal of Conflict Resolution*, 3(2), 120–131.

Bray, M., Adamson, B., & Mason, M. (2007). Different models, different emphases, different insights. In M. Bray, B. Adamson, & M. Mason (Eds.), *Comparative education research: Approaches and methods* (pp. 363–380). Dordrecht: Springer.

Bray, M., & Thomas, R. M. (1995). Levels of comparison in educational studies: Different insights from different literatures and the value of multilevel analyses. *Harvard Educational Review*, 65(3), 472–491.

Brinkmann, J. P. (1788). *Vergleichung der Erziehung der Alten mit der heutigen, und Untersuchungen welche von beyden mit der Natur am meisten übereinstimme* [Comparison of the education of the old with today's and disquisition which of the two harmonises most with nature] (2nd ed.). Düsseldorf: Danzer.

Caesar. (2010). *De bello Gallico* (Der Gallische Krieg) [Gallic Wars]. Stuttgart: Reclams Universal-Bibliothek.

Carus, C. G. (1886). *Vergleichende psychologie* [Comparative Psychology]. Wien: W. Braumueller.
Cicero. (1986). *De oratore/Über den Redner: Lateinisch/Deutsch* [On the Orator: Latin/German]. Stuttgart: Reclams Universal-Bibliothek.
Cui, Y., & Zhu, Y. (2014). Curriculum reforms in China: History and the present day. In *Revue internationale d'éducation de Sèvres*. Colloque: L'éducation en Asie en 2014: Quels enjeux mondiaux? Retrieved from http://ries.revues.org/3846 (accessed 21 September 2017).
Deeg, M. (2017). Die älteste Universität der Welt. Nalanda [The oldest university of the world. Nalanda]. *Spektrum der Wissenschaft, 5,* 18–22.
Dilthey, W. (1888). Über die Möglichkeiten einer allgemeingültigen Pädagogischen Wissenschaft [On the possibilities of a universally-valid science of education]. In F. Nicolin (Ed.), *Pädagogik als Wissenschaft* [Education as science]. Darmstadt: Wissenschaftliche Buchgesellschaft.
Dilthey, W. (1964). *Gesammelte Schriften* [Collected Papers] (Vol. 5). Stuttgart: Teubner.
Dirim, İ., Gogolin, I., Knorr, D., Krüger-Potratz, M., Lengyel, D., Reich, H. H., & Weiße, W. (Eds.). (2015). *Impulse für die Migrationsgesellschaft: Bildung, Politik und Religion. Bildung in Umbruchsgesellschaften* [Impulses for the migration society. Education, politics and religion in radically changing societies]. Münster: Waxmann-Verlag.
Evers, E. A. (1806). *Fragment der aristotelischen Erziehungskunst als Einleitung zu einer prüfenden Vergleichung der antiken und modernen Pädagogik* [Fragment of the Aristotelian art of education as introduction to a comparison of antique and modern pedagogy]. Aarau: Samuel Flick.
Goethe, J. W. (1795). *Erster Entwurf einer allgemeinen Einleitung in die vergleichende Anatomie ausgehend von der Osteologie* [First sketch of a general introduction to comparative anatomy based on osteology]. Jena: J. G. Cotta.
Guignard, E. (1983). *Marco Polo, Il Milione: Die Wunder der Welt* [Marco Polo's The million. The wonders of the world]. Zürich: Manesse.
Hechtius, F. A. (1795–8). *De re scholastica Anglica cum Germanica comparata* [English and German school education compared]. Freiberg: Gerlach.
Hilker, F. (1962). *Vergleichende Pädagogik. Eine Einführung in ihre Geschichte, Theorie und Praxis* [Comparative education. An introduction to its history, theory, and practice]. München: Hueber.
Hsi-en Chen, Th. (1981). *Chinese education since 1949: Academic and revolutionary models.* Oxford: Pergamon.
Humboldt, W. V. (1836). *Über die Verschiedenheit des menschlichen Sprachbaues und ihren Einfluss auf die geistige Entwicklung des Menschengeschlechts* [On the diversity of human language construction and its influence on the mental development of the human species]. Berlin: Druckerei der königlichen Akademie der Wissenschaften.
Jullien de Paris, M-A. (1817). *Esquisse et vues préliminaires d'un ouvrage sur l'éducation comparé* [Outline and preliminary views of a work on comparative education]. Paris. Société Établie à Paris pour l'Amélioration de l'Enseignement Élémentaire (Reprinted by Bureau international d'éducation, 1962, Genève: Bureau International de l'Éducation).
Krueger, B. (1970). *Stiehl und seine Regulative* [Stiehl and his decree]. Weinheim: Beltz.
Lê Thành, K. (1981). *L'éducation comparée* [Comparative education]. Paris: A. Colin.

Mitter, W. (1997). Challenges to comparative education: Between retrospect and expectation. *International Review of Education, 43*(5), 401–412.

Montesquieu, C. de. (1748). *L'esprit des lois* [The spirit of the laws]. Geneva: Barrillot et Fils.

OECD. (2016). *Education in China – A snapshot.* Paris: OECD.

Parreira do Amaral, M., & Amos, S. K. (Eds.). (2015). *Internationale und Vergleichende Erziehungswissenschaft. Geschichte, Theorie, Methode und Forschungsfelder* [International and comparative education. History, theory and fields of research]. Münster: Waxmann.

Preußen Ministerium der Geistlichen, Unterrichts- und Medizinalangelegenheiten. (1877). *Allgemeine Bestimmungen des Königlich Preußischen Ministers der Geistlichen, Unterrichts-und Medicinal-Angelegenheiten betreffend das Volksschul-, Präparanden- und Seminar-Wesen vom 15. Oktober 1872* [General instructions by the Royal Prussian Ministry of Religious, Teaching and Medical Affairs with respect to elementary school and teacher education matters] (Reprinted from *Die Schule in Staat und Gesellschaft: Dokumente zur deutschen Schulgeschichte im 19. und 20. Jahrhundert* [The School in state and society: Documents of the history of the German school system in the 19th and 20th century], by B. Michael & H. H. Schepp, Eds., 1993, Göttingen: Muster-Schmidt Verlag).

Sadler, M. (1900). How far can we learn anything of practical value from the study of foreign systems of education? (Reprinted in *Selections from Michael Sadler: Studies in world citizenship* by J. A. Higginson, Ed., 1979, Liverpool: Dejalle and Meyorre).

Xenophon. (2009). *Cyropaedia – The education of Cyrus* (H. G. Dakyns, Trans.). Retrieved from www.gutenberg.org/files/2085/2085-h/2085-h.htm (accessed 14 June 2017).

9 The European dimension in practice

Ideas for the classroom

Mónica Lourenço (org.), Eglė Abeciūnaitė, Karin Berger, Gabriela Dobińska, Tamara Gobbo, Filipe Moreira, and Anna Tazbir

Introduction

Ever since the rise of the modern nation states in the 19th century, education has been used a means to foster stronger ties between political institutions and its citizens. The European Union (EU) has been no exception to the rule. After an initial period when economic integration was assumed to ultimately result in socio-political unity, European leaders soon realised that further action would have to be undertaken in the areas of education and training to instil positive attitudes towards European integration and generate popular support and legitimacy for the institution and its endeavours (Keating, 2009; Nóvoa & Lawn, 2002).

In this context, policy documents soon began to take shape. These focused on introducing a European dimension in the school curricula through knowledge of European culture, heritage and civilisation, language learning, and exchange programmes (see, for instance, European Council, 1988, 2011; Commission of the European Communities, 1993). The goal was to make the younger generations conscious of their common European identity without losing sight of their national, regional, and local roots. It was expected that this European dimension, based on the shared values of interdependence, democracy, equality of opportunities, and mutual respect, would constitute an 'added value' that could help foster social integration, extend the opportunities for employment, and contribute to easing pupils' transition to working life.

Despite its laudable purposes, the introduction of this dimension in classrooms throughout Europe proved to be a difficult task for teachers, as it required them not only to learn about the different aspects of Europe, but also (and most importantly) to develop a European perspective alongside national and regional allegiances, overcoming cultural and linguistic barriers. In a seminal study that analysed the introduction of the European dimension by primary teachers in six countries (Denmark, England, Greece, Ireland, Portugal, and Spain), Ritchie (1997) identified several difficulties. These included a multitude of views on what it means to be European and the lack of clear guidance in the country's curriculum, which drove teachers to interpret the European dimension in visibly different ways. More recently, other studies aiming to introduce didactic approaches in the classroom to promote the European dimension have been developed with some success (see for example, Malho, Pombo, & Marques, 2014; Souto et al., 2016). However, they also point out to the need to develop more studies which take this approach into account, namely to help teachers in their classrooms.

Considering these and other research findings that attest the elusive nature and complexity of this topic (see Savvides & Faas, 2016), this chapter aims at shedding more light into the possibilities of integrating the European dimension in education. This is conducted through three lesson proposals that focus on different aspects of this dimension: (a) language learning by children with a migration background, (b) knowledge and awareness of European geography and history through the discovery of European monuments, and (c) encouragement for mobility in a virtual backpacking journey through Central Europe. Each lesson is organised in three sections: the first provides the theoretical background to the lesson; the second gives an overview of the lesson, including its main aims and target audience; finally, the third presents a detailed description of the lesson's stages and activities, including a lesson plan and sample resources designed to give teachers tools that can be used, with necessary adaptation, in their own contexts. All lessons are the product of international collaborative work conducted by student teachers coming from four European universities and based on original lesson plans created during the HOWBET Summer School (see Chapter 3 of this book for a detailed description of this IP).

Lesson 1: 'Where are you from?'

Authors: Tamara Gobbo (University of Vienna, Austria) and Anna Tazbir (University of Łódź, Poland)

Theoretical background

Knowledge is power and the same applies to linguistic knowledge. In fact, it has become more and more important, especially in Europe, to be able to speak more than one language (European Council, 2002). Only if one's linguistic repertoire includes a variety of languages can one compete in the European market and participate as an active citizen in everyday social life. This is also true for children with a migration background. Only when pupils learn the language of their host country are they able to compete and keep up with their peers (European Commission/EACEA/Eurydice, 2009). Languages, therefore, support social integration and embody a chance to keep pace with the surrounding world. Furthermore, the knowledge of diverse languages allows for mutual understanding and fosters intercultural dialogue (Council of Europe, 2016). This means that it is necessary to recognise, support, and value the individual repertoires and cultures that co-exist in our societies in order to preserve the linguistic diversity of Europe, and provide an opportunity to let the different cultures grow and strive together.

Taking this into consideration, it becomes clear that ideally, in every European country, schools should provide pupils with the opportunity to take classes where they can use and learn their heritage language(s) (De Coster, 2009). However, reality shows that it is not always possible to provide these classes for every immigrant pupil, which leads to persistent gaps in their educational attainment *vis-à-vis* their peers (European Commission, 2008). Therefore, it is suggested that there should be at least one class where the main national language is taught to foreign language speakers, and where room is given for pupils to share their own language(s) and cultural traditions. By doing this, pupils will be able to learn the host language and keep their linguistic and cultural origins alive (Faneca, Araújo e Sá, & Melo-Pfeifer, 2016). At the same time, the other pupils in class will profit from the cultural and linguistic insights and resources they will gain and realise that all languages have equal rights.

In the end, it is the linguistic diversity of Europe that is valued and preserved, which is extremely important to maintain historically developed knowledge, individual and group identities, and worldviews (Skutnabb-Kangas, 2002; Van Driel, Darmody, & Kerzil, 2016). The preservation of linguistic diversity is also a catalyst for the promotion of European unity and identity. Indeed, Europe is a 'plurality of languages' and a stronger or weaker sense of belonging is not linked to a particular national language, but to a complex and often contentious history acted and written in several languages. Therefore, it is up to teachers to incorporate and promote this sense of unity and embrace the multilingual gift in their classrooms (see Chapter 5 in this book on how to manage linguistic and cultural diversity in European classrooms). This is the main goal of the lesson 'Where are you from?', which will be described in detail in the following sections.

Overview of the lesson

The lesson is planned to be carried out in the subject Portuguese as a Second Language with pupils with a European migration background aged 7–10, and an A1 language level in the host country's national language. This is one of the first lessons of the year and pupils are expected to learn the adequate phrases and words used to talk about their countries of origin in Portuguese. Additionally, the aim of the lesson is to strengthen the pupils' European identity and to develop plurilingual and intercultural awareness. In particular, pupils are given the chance to share the main linguistic and cultural features of their culture of origin with their peers, and explain what Europe means to them. This lesson is expected to promote pupils' integration and create a sense of unity in the group right from the start, as it becomes clear that all of them share a European identity.

Despite the fact that the focus should always be placed on the Portuguese language, English or another bridge language might function as a helpful communication tool. Therefore, pupils are allowed to use a *lingua franca* in order to facilitate the communication process, particularly in the first lessons of the year.

Description of the lesson

Preparation

The teacher sets up a projector or a multimedia board with a map of Europe where some countries are named in Portuguese and others are not named at all. Those which are not named are the countries where the pupils come from. The teacher has to check earlier on which European countries the pupils come from and prepare different cards with the names of these countries written in Portuguese. The amount of cards must equal the number of countries where the pupils come from, even if the names of the countries are repeated. The teacher should also prepare a box to place smaller cards with the country names of the students, and copy a smaller version of the map of Europe without country names for each pupil to use in the game. Furthermore, the teacher should prepare a laptop, make sure it has Internet access, and install Tagxedo Creator (www.tagxedo.com/app.html), an online tool that creates word clouds.

Motivation

After presenting the goals of the lesson and discussing these with the pupils, the teacher and the pupils design a mind map around the topic of 'Europe' using Tagxedo Creator. The pupils have to call out everything that comes to their mind and is related with the concept of Europe (e.g., the names of the countries, languages, institutions, events, important people, or feelings they associate with the topic). There are no restrictions, not even language wise – meaning that the pupils are allowed to use other languages, as long as they make themselves understood. The main focus does not lie on language, but on motivating the pupils for the topic. After the creation of the mind map, the teacher and the pupils discuss the results. This activity should last up to 15 minutes of the lesson.

Discovery

The teacher projects the question 'De onde vens?' (Where do you come from?) and the corresponding answer 'Eu venho de/da. . . ' (I come from. . .) on the multimedia board. The question is uttered several times and the pupils are asked to repeat it as a whole class. The teacher checks for the right pronunciation and accent. Then, the teacher reads the second sentence completing it with the name of his/her country of origin: 'Eu venho de Portugal' (I come from Portugal). The same repetition drill is followed with this new sentence. Then the teacher sticks the cards with the pupils' country names on the board and asks one child where he/she comes from ('De onde vens?'). The pupil answers the question (e.g., 'Eu venho da Roménia' [I come from Romania]). Then the pupil goes to the board, gets the card corresponding to his/her country name in Portuguese, and sticks it on the correct space in the projected map of Europe. Then the child asks another pupil in class where he/she comes from, and the same drill takes place until nobody is left. At the end, the pupils can see how many pupils there are from the particular countries. This activity should last up to 20 minutes of the lesson.

Practice

The second activity conducted in class is a game with European country names. A game is always a good tool to get pupils involved and to enhance learning while playing. In this way, children can apply their new Portuguese vocabulary in a non-threatening way. The teacher distributes the cards with the map of Europe and explains the task (Figure 9.1). The pupils select six European country names and write them on the correct space of the map in Portuguese. Then the teacher draws the cards previously placed on the box and calls out six countries. The pupil who has the same country names on his/her card is the winner. This activity should last up to 15 minutes of the lesson.

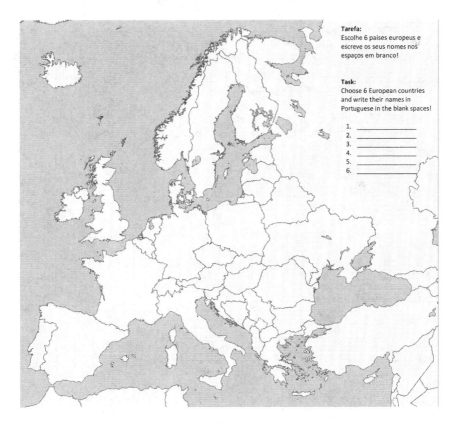

Figure 9.1 Game card with the map of Europe

Practice/Follow-up

The pupils team up in groups of around four people to prepare a presentation about their own countries of origin. In order to do that, they should select a specific topic (e.g., food, monuments, games, festivities, music). For their presentations, pupils can create a word cloud using Tagxedo Creator or use a different support (Microsoft PowerPoint, Prezi, or Canva). Other resources (e.g., pictures, songs, videos) should be included as much as possible. After preparing their presentations, the pupils present their work to the class. Pupils should try to use the Portuguese language, but they are also allowed to use their own language of origin or another bridge language. This activity should last up to 40 minutes and continue in the following lesson. For the follow-up lesson, pupils are encouraged to bring photographs, food, clothes, games, and other items from their own countries of origin to give their peers a taste of their own culture. Table 9.1 provides an overview of this lesson.

Table 9.1 Lesson plan entitled 'Where are you from?'

Subject area	Pupils' age
Portuguese as a Second Language (CEFR level: A1)	7–10 years old

Aims

To help pupils grasp the European geographical dimension
To develop the pupils' linguistic repertoire
To develop the pupils' speaking/writing skills in Portuguese
To become familiar with traits of different cultures and their traditions
To promote respect for linguistic and cultural diversity

Learning outcomes

At the end of the lesson, pupils will be able to. . .
ask someone where they come from and answer the question using the Portuguese language
know the names of some European countries in Portuguese
locate different European countries in a map
identity some cultural traits of European countries
recognise and value the linguistic and cultural diversity of Europe

Activities (pupils' organisation)

Building a 'Europe' mind map (whole class)
Doing a question and answer drill (whole class, pair work)
Filling in a map of Europe with the correct country names (individual work)
Playing a game with country names (individual work, whole class)
Making a presentation about a specific aspect of their own culture (group work)

Resources

Multimedia board or projector
Computer or laptop with Internet connection
Tagxedo Creator

(*Continued*)

Table 9.1 (Continued)

Map of Europe to project
Two sets of cards with the names of European countries
Smaller cards with a map of Europe
Cardboard box
Adhesive strips
Other resources related with the pupils' countries of origin

Assessment

The teacher assesses the pupils' pronunciation and grammatical accuracy in the question and answer drill (formative assessment). In the game, the teacher checks if the pupils have learned the new vocabulary (i.e., country names in Portuguese). For the group work on pupils' countries of origin, the teacher assesses the quality, accuracy and organisation of the information presented, the pupils' confidence and connection with the audience, and the creativity of the resources presented to class.

Steps of the lesson	Time (±90 min.)
1. *Motivation* The teacher and the pupils design a mind map around the topic of Europe using Tagxedo Creator.	15 min.
2. *Discovery* The teacher and the students do a question-and-answer drill (ask someone where they come from and provide an answer in Portuguese), and fill in a map of Europe with the names of their countries of origin.	20 min.
3. *Practice* The pupils play a game with European country names.	15 min.
4. *Practice/Follow-up* The pupils present a specific cultural aspect of their own countries using Tagxedo Creator and/or other resources.	40 min.

Lesson 2: 'Discover Europe'

Authors: Karin Berger (University of Vienna, Austria), Gabriela Dobińska (University of Łódź, Poland) and Filipe Moreira (University of Aveiro, Portugal)

Theoretical background

One of the main aims of the EU is to strengthen the unity of its member states in areas of economy, trade, and the labour market, in an attempt to promote lasting peace, democracy, equality, and the well-being of its people (European Union, 2012). At a cultural level, the EU policy has similar goals. Despite the commitment to preserve the cultural and linguistic diversity of Europe, the cultural policy of the EU looks for underlying common elements which unify the various nations, in an attempt to produce 'an imagined cultural community' (Lähdesmäki, 2012, p. 59). This discourse poses particular challenges, namely for teachers, who are urged to foster a European identity sustained on a common, albeit 'imagined', cultural heritage in increasingly multilingual and multicultural classrooms.

A fundamental starting point when it comes to the concept of 'imagined cultural communities' is precisely the notion of 'imagined communities' proposed by Benedict Anderson (2006), who defines nations not as primordial or natural, but as imagined political communities inasmuch as 'the members of even the smallest nation will never know most of their fellow-members, meet them, or even hear of them, yet in the minds of each lives the image of their communion' (p. 6). Assuming that the EU constitutes a specific type of nation, one whose inhabitants are unable to know each and every one of its members, the identity of the entire confederation must be based on an idea and sustained on a process of consciousness-raising that is constantly updated and reconstructed (European Commission, 2012; Scalise, 2015; Wangler, 2012). Within this process, three crucial dimensions can be pointed out: time-embeddedness, historical context, and location. It is the aspect of location (i.e., place) that is highlighted in this lesson.

Places (landscapes, monuments, and sites) can be defined as material realities to be perceived both visually and tactilely, and to be mapped and located. As Osborne (2001) states, peoples' 'identification with particular places is indispensable for the cultivation of an awareness – an *a-where-ness* – of national identity; that is, nationalising-states occupy imagined terrains that serve as mnemonic devices' (p. 3) that nurture identities. According to Basso (1996), there is a close connection between what people make of their places and what they make of themselves as society members and inhabitants of the world. The relationship between people and the places they live in is of a reciprocal nature. On the one hand, places are produced by people; on the other hand, people work out their identity by repetitive, collective commemoration of/in these places. Therefore, knowledge of place is closely linked to knowledge of oneself and to the capacity of conceiving one's position as a person and as a community member (Basso, 1996). That evidences how important it is to include knowledge about important places in Europe in the school curricula of the EU member states. Particularly meaningful places, where collective memory is strengthened and national identity is constructed, are monuments. Therefore, this lesson focuses on monuments of the different European member states in order to transform them into 'European' instead of merely national.

Overview of the lesson

This lesson is to be carried out in a Geography or History class with a group of 11- to 12-year-old pupils. The main aim of this lesson is to promote pupils' European citizenship and identity by focusing on the topic of famous European monuments (for further discussion on European citizenship, see Chapter 7 in this book). European identity is associated with an awareness of a shared European history, geography, and culture, and sustained on the importance of a spatial dimension in the creation on an imagined community.

The European dimension in practice 131

Taking into account that classrooms are becoming more and more diverse (see Chapter 5 in this book), it is expected that some pupils in class have a migration background. This fact should act as a catalyst to promote intercultural awareness, as the pupils research and share information about the famous monuments that exist in their own countries of origin. It is expected that at the end of the lesson pupils are able to identify and name some basic facts related with European monuments that are not as well-known or popular as the Eiffel Tower.

Description of the lesson

Motivation

After presenting the goals of the lesson and discussing these with the pupils, the teacher gives each pupil a crossword puzzle with a hidden word that is related to the theme of the lesson (Figure 9.2). After the pupils have completed the crossword puzzle, the teacher writes the phrase 'European monuments' on the board and asks the pupils what a monument is and if they can give examples of famous monuments in Europe. Each monument pointed out by the pupils is written on the board by the teacher. Then, the teacher stimulates a dialogue with all the pupils, motivating them to search for more information related with the monuments, namely their inauguration date, functions, and meaning.

Discovery

The pupils get together in groups of around four and select a European monument of their choice to make a brief oral and written presentation to class. The teacher monitors the groups, in order to make sure they have chosen different monuments. In groups where there are pupils with a migration background, the teacher might encourage them to work on a monument of their own country of origin. This will allow pupils to share aspects of their culture and promote positive attitudes towards diversity from the whole group. Pupils have approximately 20 minutes to search for information on the Internet about the chosen monument

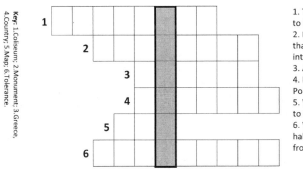

1. The place where gladiators used to fight.
2. Buildings, structures, or sites that are of historical importance or interest.
3. Athens is the capital city of...
4. For example: Germany, Poland, Portugal (singular)
5. When you get lost you can use it to find the way.
6. Willingness to accept feelings, habits, or beliefs that are different from your own.

Key: 1.Coliseum; 2.Monument; 3.Greece; 4.Country; 5.Map; 6.Tolerance.

Figure 9.2 Example of a crossword puzzle

(they can use Google Junior, or websites provided by the teacher). Then, they can prepare a Microsoft PowerPoint, Prezi, or Canva presentation (one to two slides) with the most important dates, facts, and a picture of the monument. The name of the monument must be hidden because later on the other pupils will have to identify it. Each group has five minutes to present the information they have selected for the monument to class. After the presentation, the other pupils can ask questions to the group in order to identify which monument corresponds to the information provided. Once the monument is identified, the group indicates the country and the city it belongs to, and locates it on a map.

Practice

The next activity is related to a central monument in the history of Europe – the Berlin Wall. In order to elicit information about this monument, the teacher asks the pupils some questions: e.g., 'Have you ever heard about the Berlin Wall?', 'In which country was it located?', 'Why was it built?, 'When was it (partially) torn down?' Then, the teacher shows the pupils a short documentary about the history of the Berlin Wall (for a video in English, please see *History Brief: The Berlin Wall Explained*, available at www.youtube.com/watch?v=X3Xe4AdJaFQ). The teacher and the students discuss the video. A possible topic of discussion could be the news of the destruction of parts of the Berlin Wall to make way for a luxury apartment complex (Dempsey, 2013). For this matter a debate can be organised in class with pupils having to select pro and against arguments. The 'pro' group could argue that there is no problem in tearing down parts of the wall, as these can still be visited by tourists in museums; whereas the 'against' group could make the case for the preservation of the wall due to its historical importance and the message that it carries for future generations.

Practice/Follow-up

As a follow-up activity to be conducted in the following lesson or as a homework assignment, the teacher can ask the pupils to write a short text about a monument they would like to visit in another European country. Pupils should justify their choice and highlight five things to have in mind when visiting a European monument (e.g., learning beforehand about the history of the monument, treating the monument and what it represents with respect, etc.). Table 9.2 presents an overview of the lesson.

Table 9.2 Lesson plan entitled 'Discover Europe'

Subject areas	**Pupils' characteristics**
Geography or History	11–12 years old

Aims

To promote the pupils' European citizenship and identity
To promote positive attitudes and respect towards cultural diversity

(*Continued*)

Table 9.2 (Continued)

To develop the pupils' reading skills
To develop the pupils' writing skills
To develop the pupils' speaking and argumentation skills
To develop the pupils' social skills (e.g., collaboration, team work)

Learning outcomes

At the end of the lesson, pupils will be able to. . .
search for information on a specific subject on the Internet
locate different European countries on a map
identify some basic facts about famous European monuments
make an ID card of a famous European monument and present it orally to their colleagues
select pro and against arguments in a debate

Activities (pupils' organisation)

Doing a crossword puzzle (pair work)
Brainstorming on the phrase 'European monuments' (whole class)
Searching for information about a famous European monument on the Internet (group work)
Writing an ID card for a European monument and presenting it to class (group work)
Watching and discussing a video about the Berlin Wall (group work)
Selecting pro and against arguments in a debate (group work)

Resources

Crossword puzzle
Computer or laptop with Internet connection
Map of Europe
Pen
Documentary on the Berlin Wall

Assessment

The teacher provides feedback on the oral presentations and on the debate (accuracy of the information/arguments provided, communication and argumentations skills, collaboration skills, creativity), as well as on the pupils' commitment to the different activities.

Steps of the lesson	Time (±120 min.)
1. *Motivation* The students complete a crossword puzzle whose hidden word is related to the lesson's theme. The teacher and the pupils brainstorm around the topic 'European monuments'.	10 min.
2. *Discovery* In groups, the pupils select a European monument and search for information on the Internet to prepare a class presentation. Once the monument is identified, the group members indicate the country and the city it belongs to, and locate it on a map.	50 min.

(*Continued*)

Table 9.2 (Continued)

3. *Practice* The pupils watch and discuss a documentary about the history of the Berlin Wall. For this matter, a debate is organised in class with pupils having to select pro and against arguments.	60 min.
4. *Practice/Follow-up* The pupils write a short text about a monument they would like to visit in another European country (homework assignment).	

Lesson 3: 'Backpacking through Central Europe'

Author: Eglė Abeciūnaitė (Vytautas Magnus University, Lithuania)

Theoretical background

Wandering and mobility have historically led to the construction and reconstruction of Europe. A land of immigration as well as of migration, Europe evolved through a constant mix and displacement of populations, a permanent ethnic and cultural melting pot (Favell, 2009). Initially, pull and push factors (such as industrialisation and armed conflicts) led citizens to varying degrees of mobility within the European space. Later, with the signing of the Schengen Agreement in 1985 and the subsequent Schengen Convention in 1990, which initiated the abolition of border controls between participating countries, mobility increased exponentially in the European territory. European citizens were then able to freely move to, live, and work in another EU country; among these citizens were international students.

Student mobility in Europe is understood as a short-term stay abroad, usually of six to 12 months duration. This experience is often posited as an instrument of European construction, since the stay abroad induces direct contact with another language and culture, broadening students' horizons and helping them to better understand Europe's most pressing issues (European Council, 2011; Kelo, Teichler, & Wächter, 2006). In the last decades, European institutions have devoted considerable monetary support to student mobility through the launch of programmes such as Comenius, ERASMUS, or Campus Europae. Many governments have also started campaigns which market their countries' higher education institutions worldwide to attract as many students as possible from other countries and regions (Engel, Sandström, van der Aa, & Glass, 2015; Sursock, 2015).

In order to encourage students to study abroad while at university, it is also important that young people are able, while at elementary and secondary school, to have a first experience of mobility. Indeed, so far as cultural customs are concerned, it is necessary for pupils, as young as possible, to have opportunities to encounter different surroundings and meet different people. Such transnational mobility could be based on improved knowledge and recognition of other countries' history and culture, and, most importantly, on creating the necessary dispositions to go outside national borders to meet people that may share different approaches on the world.

The lesson described here aims to fulfil this goal by presenting pupils with a board game that will lead them through a virtual backpacking trip through Central Europe. In this journey, pupils will discover one of the world's richest sources of creative talent between the 17th and 20th centuries, and unravel similarities emanating from historical, social, and cultural characteristics. Although views on which countries belong to Central Europe are vastly varied, this lesson follows what is established in the *Encyclopaedia Britannica*, which defines the region as comprising Austria, Czech Republic, Germany, Hungary, Liechtenstein, Poland, Slovakia, Slovenia, and Switzerland.

Overview of the lesson

The lesson's main goal is to promote the pupils' awareness of European identity by playing a board game consisting of a virtual backpacking trip through Central Europe. In particular, the game aims at familiarising pupils with Central European geography and culture (history, language, music, art, and literature), thus increasing pupils' cultural awareness and plurilingual repertoire. The lesson also aims at fostering European mobility by creating interest in and developing positive dispositions to visit other European destinations and discover our 'common' history. The lesson can be included in Geography or History classes as a review activity for children aged 12–14, and encourage pupils to organise their own backpacking trip to selected countries in Central Europe.

Description of the lesson

Preparation

The teacher should print a large map of Central Europe and draw a path with about 100 squares for pupils to follow across the countries. Each square should be numbered and coloured according to the type of question it represents (e.g., red for questions about language, green for questions about geography, blue for questions about music, etc.). The teacher should also prepare decks of cards containing themed questions (on language, geography, music, history, art, and literature of Central European countries; see examples in Figure 9.3), and procure a dice and a game piece for each group. It is also useful to have the rules of the game printed out or available to display on a projector.

Motivation

The teacher asks the students to recall a previous lesson on Central European countries. He/she may prompt the pupils to recall the country names, city capitals, the languages spoken, and the main historical events and people. Then he/she presents the goals of the lesson, and the concept and rules of the game, and

136 *Mónica Lourenço (org.) et al.*

Figure 9.3 Example of cards with themed questions

discusses these with the pupils. The teacher places the board and the six piles of question cards (one for each theme) face down on a table, and divides the class into groups of around four. The teacher gives each team a game piece and a dice. The pupils choose a team leader to give the final answers to the questions, and another pupil to move the game piece across the board.

Practice

To start playing the game as a whole class the pupils throw the dice. The team with the highest number starts the game. The pupils play the game throwing the dice in turns in a circle going left, and answering the questions from the piles that share the same colour as the squares they land in. The teacher provides immediate feedback to the pupils' answers, stating if they are correct or incorrect. When the team members do not know the answer to a specific question, the team cannot play in the next round. The team that arrives first to the final square and has answered at least one question of each theme wins the game. After the game, the teacher elicits responses to unanswered questions, and gives each team feedback about how they managed the game and where they struggled. Then, a discussion might ensue related with the fact that these different facets of the history and culture of Central European countries are not only specific to those countries but are part of European history and culture, and therefore, part of our common European identity.

Follow-up

The teacher asks the pupils to suggest three destinations they would like to visit in Central Europe and why. Then, he/she suggests that they organise a real trip through some Central European countries, selecting important places to visit or exhibitions to attend. Pupils may also look for sponsors or search for information about exchange programmes with other European schools. Table 9.3 presents an overview of the lesson.

Table 9.3 Lesson plan entitled 'Backpacking through Central Europe'

Subject areas	**Pupils' age**
History, Geography and Foreign Languages (French, German, Czech, Hungarian, Italian, Polish, Romansh, Slovak, and Slovenian)	12–14 years old

Aims
To promote the pupils' awareness of European identity
To identify Central European countries
To build on the pupils' previous knowledge on European geography and culture
To promote the pupils' plurilingual and intercultural competence
To develop the pupils' social skills (e.g., collaboration, team building)

Learning outcomes
At the end of the lesson pupils will be able to. . .
identify Central European countries
name some general facts about Central European countries
say some words in the languages spoken in some Central European countries
become aware of and respect cultural differences

Activities (pupils' organisation)
Playing a board game and answering questions about Central European countries (group work, whole class)
Discussing the common history and culture of Europe (whole class)
Organising a trip to Central Europe (group work)

Resources
Board for the game
Question cards
Game piece (one for each team)
Dice
Computer/projector

(*Continued*)

Table 9.3 (Continued)

Assessment

Assessment is focused on providing feedback for each team during and after the game. During the discussion, the teacher assesses the pupils' communication and argumentations skills and the appropriateness of the arguments provided.

Steps of the lesson	Time (±90 min.)
1. *Motivation* The teacher does a recap of previous lessons, when the pupils explored basic information on Central European countries. Then, the teacher divides the class into groups and explains the concept and the rules of a game aimed at familiarising pupils with Central European culture (history, language, music, art, and literature).	10 min.
2. *Practice* The pupils play the game, throwing the dice in turns and answering the questions from the piles that share the same colour as the squares they land in. Afterwards, the teacher and the students discuss the common history and culture of Europe.	40 min.
3. *Follow-up* The pupils get together to discuss how they can organise a real trip through some Central European countries, selecting important places to visit and sponsors they can get in touch with.	40 min.

Final considerations

The requirement to introduce the topic of Europe in school curricula, integrating it into textbooks, presents itself as a demanding task, particularly for teachers who are often struggling with the concepts of European identity and citizenship, as well as with the means through which they can equip pupils with post-national knowledge, skills, and dispositions. The construction of a coherent and lasting European identity is based not only on growing understanding of our common historical, cultural, and linguistic ties, but also of our different ways of looking at the world and at the problems we are facing today. In education, the aim should be to initiate such teaching processes as soon as possible, so that it can contribute to the development of critical and engaged citizens who understand the difficulties and obstacles that challenge the common development of Europe, and take action to create more equitable, peaceful, and sustainable societies. The implementation of the European idea is, therefore, inconceivable without responsibility, investment, and participation from all people involved, particularly through cross-national collaboration, developing appropriate teaching materials, and experimenting with innovative approaches and teaching methods, as was the case of the activities presented in this chapter. Only when schools and teachers work together, overcoming linguistic and cultural barriers in search of the 'shared layers of identity' (Havel, 2009, n.p.) that connect us all, can we aspire to improve the quality of education.

References

Anderson, B. (2006). *Imagined communities: Reflections on the origin and spread of nationalism* (revised ed.). London: Verso.

Basso, K. H. (1996). *Wisdom sits in places: Landscape and language among the Western Apache*. Albuquerque: University of New Mexico Press.

Commission of the European Communities. (1993). *Green Paper on the European dimension of education*. COM (93) 457 final. Brussels: Commission of the European Communities.

Council of Europe. (2016). *Competences for democratic culture: Living together as equals in culturally diverse democratic societies*. Strasbourg: Council of Europe.

De Coster, I. (2009). *Integrating immigrant children into schools in Europe: Measures to foster communication with immigrant families and heritage language teaching for immigrant children*. Brussels: Eurydice.

Dempsey, J. (2013). Monuments and Europe's identity. *Carnegie Europe*. Retrieved from http://carnegieeurope.eu/strategiceurope/51096 (accessed 13 November 2017).

Engel, L., Sandström, A-M., van der Aa, R., & Glass, A. (2015). *The EAIE barometer: Internationalisation in Europe*. Amsterdam: EAIE.

European Commission. (2008). *Green paper – Migration and mobility: Challenges and opportunities for EU education systems*. Brussels: European Commission.

European Commission. (2012). *The development of European identity/identities: Unfinished business. A policy review*. Brussels: European Commission.

European Commission/EACEA/Eurydice. (2009). *Integrating immigrant children into schools in Europe*. Brussels: EACEA. Retrieved from http://eacea.ec.europa.eu/education/eurydice/documents/thematic_reports/101EN.pdf (accessed 15 November 2017).

European Council. (1988). Resolution of the Council and the Ministers of Education meeting within the Council on the European dimension in education. *Official Journal of the European Communities*, C177(2), 5–7.

European Council. (2002). *Presidency conclusions: Barcelona European Council, 15 and 16 March 2002*. Retrieved from http://ec.europa.eu/invest-in-research/pdf/download_en/barcelona_european_council.pdf (accessed 14 November 2017).

European Council. (2011). "Youth on the move" – Promoting the learning mobility of young people. *Official Journal of the European Communities*, C199(1), 1–5.

European Union. (2012). Consolidated version of the Treaty on European Union. *Official Journal of the European Union*, C326, 13–390. Retrieved from http://eur-lex.europa.eu/legal-content/EN/TXT/?uri=CELEX%3A12012M%2FTXT (accessed 14 November 2017).

Faneca, R. M., Araújo e Sá, M. H., & Melo-Pfeifer, S. (2016). Is there a place for heritage languages in the promotion of an intercultural and multilingual education in the Portuguese schools? *Language and Intercultural Communication*, 16(1), 44–68.

Favell, A. (2009). Immigration, migration, and free movement in the making of Europe. In J. T. Checkel & P. J. Katzenstein (Eds.), *European identity* (pp. 167–190). Cambridge: Cambridge University Press.

Havel, V. (2009, November). *Speech at the European Parliament on the occasion of the twenty years after the fall of the Iron Curtain*. Retrieved from www.scnr.si/sl/ostalo/speech-of-vaclav-havel-in-the-european-parliament/ (accessed 14 November 2017).

Keating, A. (2009). Educating Europe's citizens: Moving from national to post-national models of educating for European citizenship. *Citizenship Studies, 13*(2), 135–151.

Kelo, M., Teichler, U., & Wächter, B. (Eds.). (2006). *EURODATA: Student mobility in European higher education*. Bonn: Lemmens Verlags- & Mediengesellschaft, Academic Cooperation Association.

Lähdesmäki, T. (2012). Rhetoric of unity and cultural diversity in the making of European cultural identity. *International Journal of Cultural Policy, 18*(1), 59–75.

Malho, A., Pombo, L., & Marques, L. (2014). Supervisão colaborativa online de práticas letivas de Biologia em contexto Europeu (Portugal e República Checa) [Collaborative online supervision of Biology teaching practices in the European context (Portugal and Czech Republic)]. *Indagatio Didactica, 6*(2), 93–106.

Nóvoa, A., & Lawn, M. (2002). *Fabricating Europe: The formation of an education space*. New York, NY: Kluwer Academic Publishers.

Osborne, B. S. (2001). *Landscapes, memory, monuments, and commemoration: Putting identity in its place*. Halifax, NS: Department of Canadian Heritage.

Ritchie, J. (1997). Europe and the European dimension in a multicultural context. *European Journal of Intercultural Studies, 8*(3), 291–201.

Savvides, N., & Faas, D. (2016). Does Europe matter? A comparative study of young people's identifications with Europe at a State School and a European School in England. *European Journal of Education Research Development and Practice, 51*(3), 374–390.

Scalise, G. (2015). The narrative construction of European identity: Meanings of Europe "from below". *European Societies, 17*(4), 593–614.

Skutnabb-Kangas, T. (2002). Why should linguistic diversity be maintained and supported in Europe? Some arguments. In *Guide for the development of language education policies in Europe: From linguistic diversity to plurilingual education*. Strasbourg: Council of Europe. Retrieved from www.coe.int/t/dg4/linguistic/Source/Skutnabb-KangasEN.pdf (accessed 14 November 2017).

Souto, L., Tavares, F., Moreira, H., Fidalgo, R., Pinho, R., Mendes, A., & Pombo, L. (2016). Forensic toolbox: proposal of a forensic educational kit. *Indagatio Didactica, 8*(1), 1709–1723.

Sursock, A. (2015). *Trends 2015: Learning and teaching in European universities*. Brussels: European University Association.

Van Driel, B., Darmody, M., & Kerzil, J. (2016). *Education policies and practices to foster tolerance, respect for diversity and civic responsibility in children and young people in the EU*. Luxembourg: Publications Office of the European Union.

Wangler, A. (2012). *Rethinking history, reframing identity – Memory, generations, and the dynamics of national identity in Poland*. Wiesbaden: Springer.

Part 3
Envisioning the future of teacher education

10 Restructuring teacher education in the UK
Insights into the future

Joanna McIntyre

Introduction

The chapter presents a critical analysis of teacher education policy as it is differently conceived in England, Scotland, and Wales. In so doing, it offers a unique lens through which to consider the European models of teacher education outlined in Chapter 2. There are similar pressures and tensions relating to the impact of PISA, the focus on student learning and on raising standards, and the importance of a continuum from pre-service education to early induction into the profession. However, there are distinctive differences not only between what is happening in Europe but also within the UK itself. This chapter therefore offers a case study of the ways in which teacher education[1] is being reshaped within England, Scotland, and Wales through an exploration of the impact of the different national reviews of teacher education in each locality (Carter, 2015 in England; Donaldson, 2011 in Scotland; and Furlong, 2015 in Wales).

Before going any further, it is important to briefly explain the governance of each constituent part of Great Britain in order to understand the ways in which legislation and policy affecting education more generally and teacher education specifically are driven. Great Britain comprises England, Scotland, and Wales, which together with Northern Ireland make up the UK. All parts of the UK were governed centrally by parliament in London until the devolution process began in 1999. This gave more powers to the three smaller countries as power was transferred from the UK parliament to the Welsh and Northern Irish assemblies and the Scottish parliament. Whilst some matters are reserved for governance by the UK parliament in Westminster, education is now a devolved area of administration, meaning that education policy (including that relating to teacher education) is different in England, Scotland and Wales.

The English context

England has a complex school system. Alongside a tradition of independent (fee-paying) schools (sometimes termed 'public schools') there are a range of state-funded schools. Some schools are administered and funded by a local authority. These are usually comprehensive schools, though there are some parts of England that maintain a selective grammar schools system. Academy schools have their running costs met directly by central government (rather than a local authority) and typically had their start-up costs funded by private means. Free schools are newly established schools in England set up by parents, teachers, charities, or businesses, and are not controlled by a local authority. There are also voluntary aided schools which are predominantly faith schools. More freedom is given to academies and free schools; they do not have to teach the national curriculum or employ teachers with Qualified Teacher Status (QTS). All non-fee-paying schools are subject to assessment and inspection by the Office for Standards in Education, Children's Services and Skills (Ofsted). Children attend full-time education from ages 5 to 16 and have to be in employment, training, or education until they are 18. This full-time education does not need to be at a school; a small number of parents choose to home educate. The school system is divided into age-related key stages. Key Stages 1 and 2 are classed as primary schooling, and at age 11 a pupil moves into Key Stages 3 and 4 (usually at a secondary school). Children are assessed at the end of Key Stages 2 and 4 through externally devised assessments and at the age of 16, at the end of Key Stage 4, pupils take their General Certificate of Education (GCSE).

Whilst UK countries rank mid-table in terms of PISA outcomes, England slightly outperforms the other countries within the UK. However, ministers are concerned about stagnating performance in England (Coughlan, 2016). International comparisons of performance alongside a commitment to a schools-led self-improving system have had consequential effects on the preparation of beginning teachers in England.

Pre-service teacher education in England has been subject to a raft of changes over the past half a century. Locally based teacher training colleges, which had been the traditional site of Initial Teacher Training (ITT), were restructured during the 1970s following the James Report (1972), leading to a significant reduction in the number of providers of teacher training, as polytechnics and universities became the site of most pre-service provision. The James Report also placed significant emphasis on practical training led by 'professional tutors' in schools. The 1988 Education Reform Act introduced a National Curriculum for schools and a reduced role for local education authorities. These have had long-lasting implications for teaching and for teacher education through increased prescription in terms of curriculum and the introduction of a marketised approach to education, as localised and national companies step into the space formerly occupied by local authorities. In the early 1990s there was more change, such as a (short-lived) statutory curriculum for teacher education programmes (see Department for Education [DfE] Circular 9/92, DfE Circular 14/93), moves for schools to be involved in the selection and training of new entrants, and a requirement for higher education institutions to transfer funds to schools for this. In the same time period, Ofsted was introduced, with a remit that included teacher training programmes. Finally, and perhaps most significantly, the 1990s saw the introduction of alternative routes into teaching, including the development of School

Centred Initial Teacher Training (SCITT) in 1995, which meant that schools could access government funding directly to become providers of pre-service training and to recommend trainees for QTS. Thus, a long-term government policy has been to involve schools directly in the training of future teachers. Yet, until relatively recently, the majority of teacher preparation remained within Education departments in universities.

This changed dramatically with the publication of 'The importance of teaching', a white paper by the Conservative-led coalition government in 2010, which signalled the 'pendulum swing' (Murray & Mutton, 2016) away from programmes involving university-schools' partnerships to 'school-led' teacher preparation routes with a clearly market-driven approach to teacher training and supply through the introduction of a school-led teacher training route entitled 'School Direct'.

The 2010 white paper outlines the education policy agenda for the Coalition government drawing on 'the best education systems in the world' (in terms of international comparisons through PISA measures) to identify two main tenets for policy directives for teacher education (DfE, 2010, p. 9). The first is that the quality of an education system is dependent upon the quality of its teachers. The second is that the best performing systems provide autonomy to schools, which are positioned in the document as the best training environments for beginning teachers to learn their craft, 'our strongest schools will take the lead and trainees will be able to develop their skills, learning from the best teachers' (DfE, 2010, p. 23). The white paper details how it will achieve raising the quality bar for entrants to the profession through provision of bursaries (financial incentives aimed at attracting graduates with high degree classifications) and by ensuring that numeracy and literacy skills tests are a pre-requisite to entry to an ITT programme. The paper also introduces an extension of possible routes into teaching, especially the expansion of school-based training routes, such as 'Teach First' and School Direct. The white paper formalised the government's promise that 'by 2016 teaching schools and the best schools and academy chains will be leading teacher training' (Taylor, 2014, n.p.). In 2015, the centralised system of allocating teacher training places meant that, if recruitment targets were met, more than half of all trainees would be preparing to teach through the School Direct route. However, it is clear that the complexity of choices of training route and variations in qualifications (school-led routes may lead to recommendation for QTS but need a university partner to award the academic qualification of Postgraduate Certificate in Education [PGCE]) were factors contributing to the House of Commons Public Accounts committee's observation that, '[t]he Government has missed recruitment targets for the last five years, and in 2016/17 the number of graduates starting initial teacher training fell' (House of Commons Education Committee, 2017, p. 10).

The 2010 white paper and the ensuing enactment of policy clearly positioned schools as the preferred providers of teacher training supported by structural changes that favoured new, privileged routes into teaching, and the creation of a market with the perhaps unintended consequences of detriment of university-based routes:

> In many ways, this was a rearticulation of a debate and a set of policy initiatives that had characterised the 'contested space' of teacher education and training since the early 1980s; the main difference on this occasion was that the Government, and in particular key Ministers, were ideologically committed to pushing the changes through.
>
> (Cater, 2017, p. 15)

Key to this ideology was a commitment to the view of teaching as a 'craft . . . best learnt as an apprentice' (Gove, 2010, n.p.). Enactment of this ideology was therefore in the shape of programmes of training (rather than education) for new teachers delivered by current practitioners within the classroom in schools at the forefront of a self-improving school-led system. It is in this context that the Carter Review was undertaken.

The Carter Review of ITT

The Government announced an independent review of ITT in May 2014. The review was chaired by Sir Andrew Carter, an executive primary head teacher and chief executive officer of a SCITT. The representation of university teacher educators on the selected panel of experts assigned to work with him was notably limited. The aims of the review were to define effective ITT practice, assess how far the system delivered effective ITT, recommend where and how improvements could be made and to recommend ways to improve choice by improving the transparency of course content and method (Carter, 2015). The report was published in January 2015 and accompanied by the government's response (DfE, 2015).

The report concluded that the quality of pre-service provision was generally good, supporting Ofsted's findings that 99% of providers were 'good' or 'outstanding' with none rated as 'unsatisfactory' (Ofsted, 2016). There were 18 recommendations and the government response to the report detailed which of these would be taken forward (DfE, 2015). Of particular note was the decision by the government not to proceed with Carter's recommendation that it should be made clearer to applicants that the academic award of PGCE was optional, and that teachers only needed to achieve QTS to enter the profession (and so by implication universities should not be seen as the better option for pre-service programmes). Interestingly, the government response document detailed that this recommendation could not be taken forward because of a lack of consensus by its coalition partners (DfE, 2015).

A feature of policy paradox since 2010 has been that it is not for government to promote a preferred mode of delivery or teaching in a self-improving school system, and so whilst some of Carter's recommendations were supported there was an avoidance of making anything mandatory. However, the recommendation for a framework of core ITT content was supported, and accordingly, the response document stated that the government will 'use the framework as part of the quality criteria for allocations' of teacher training places in the future (DfE, 2015). So, whilst not a mandatory requirement there are compelling reasons for providers of pre-service programmes to engage with the core curriculum. As a result of the review three expert groups were established to develop a new framework of content, specific behaviour management content for that framework, and new standards for school-based mentors. In a similar way to the composition of the Carter Review panel, the expert groups were led by individuals and organisations (an independent working group led by a Chief Executive Officer of an Academy Trust, the Teaching Schools Council, and a yet-to-be-established future College of Teaching), which support the ideological policy direction of a school-led teacher training system described earlier. In addition, the Government agreed to develop and expand the official 'Get into Teaching' website to provide greater clarity of information both for applicants and for schools when deciding which training providers to partner with.

The Scottish context

Scotland's education system is different to that in England. There has not been the same emphasis on parental choice and a self-improving school-led system as in England. Local authorities are responsible for the administration of schools, though there is a small proportion of independent fee-paying schools. The Scottish system has emphasised breadth of curriculum; children do not specialise in particular subjects until they have left compulsory schooling. In comparison with other countries within the UK, there is markedly less emphasis on external testing. The most significant initiative in recent years is the Curriculum for Excellence, which was launched in Scottish schools in 2012 with the aim of providing a wider, more flexible range of courses and subjects. Scotland was a mid-ranking country in terms of PISA measures until 2015, when it dropped in the rankings in all three areas of English, Mathematics, and Science (BBC, 2016).

In Scotland, teaching is an all-graduate profession with two routes into teaching: a four-year undergraduate Bachelors in Education or a one-year Postgraduate Diploma in Education (PGDE). Successful graduates of these pre-service programmes are then offered a paid one-year placement in a mainstream school, where they are supported to achieve the Standard for Full Recognition (SEED, 2002). These Scottish induction arrangements for new teachers were described as world class in a review of Scotland by the OECD in 2007.

ITE was formerly located in local teacher education colleges until concerns about the reduced school population and oversupply of teachers in the late 1970s and 1980s led to structural changes, as smaller teacher education colleges merged. In 1997, following the Sutherland Report, the remaining colleges of education merged with universities. However, concerns about the oversupply of teachers continued into 2007, when the newly elected Scottish National Party became a minority government. This led to a change in the management of local budgets, and education was no longer part of a protected budget line. Part of the newly elected government's manifesto had been to reduce class sizes, but the imposed budget restrictions at a local government level meant that the local authorities were not in a financial position to employ the number of teachers needed to realise this election pledge. Consequently, the Scottish government reduced the number of places for pre-service teachers on ITE programmes. However, other questions about teacher education had been on the agenda for some time. In 2001, there was a First Stage Review of ITE by the Scottish Executive Education Department (SEED, 2001) followed up by the Second Stage in 2005 (SEED, 2005). These reviews identified some concerns relating to the differing roles of schools, universities, and local authorities in the preparation of new teachers, though did little to change practice (O'Brien, 2012).

These concerns along with questions about the oversupply of teachers were the rationale for the Scottish government's commissioning of a review of ITE, which began in 2009 leading to the published report in 2011.

The Donaldson Review: Teaching Scotland's future

The review of teacher education was led by Graham Donaldson, head of the Scottish Inspectorate and Chief Professional Advisor on Education to the Scottish Government. The reference group for the review comprised two practising teachers, three head teachers, two higher education teacher educators, the chief executives of the Law Society of Scotland, and NHS Education, Scotland. The remit for the review was broad-ranging:

> To consider the best arrangements for the full continuum of teacher education in primary and secondary schools in Scotland. The Review should consider initial teacher education, induction and professional development and the interaction between them.
>
> (Donaldson, 2011, p. 106)

The review involved discussions with all of the universities involved in teacher education, along with a selection of local authorities, schools, and other agencies, open consultation and commissioned research. The report presents findings from a review of international research and a thorough literature review, which was presented as a full and separate text (Menter, Hulme, Elliot, & Lewin, 2010). In the overview at the beginning of the report is a recognition of the 'need to challenge the narrow interpretations of the teacher's role which have created unhelpful philosophical and structural divides, and have led to sharp separations of function between teachers, teacher educators and researchers' (Donaldson, 2011, p. 5). The report concludes with 50 recommendations for 21st century teacher preparation with a particular focus on 'extended professionalism' and the importance of conceptualising teacher education as a 'career long' endeavour. So, the focus is on a continuum from ITE through induction to CPD, which is research-led and delivered through a partnership of schools, universities, and local authorities. A simplistic model of teacher preparation focused on prescriptive standards and more time in the classroom is rejected in the early pages of the review.

A model of collaborative partnership is suggested where there is a well-conceived integrated programme with a clear role for school-based mentors and university tutors, and where all teachers involved in supporting pre-service teachers are teacher educators. The report calls for a clear identification of what each role in the partnership has to offer and for more defined input from schools in the process. The emphasis is on a need for more integrated partnerships, and there is a section devoted to the notion of clinical models and school-university partnership hubs (for ITE and for ongoing CPD):

> New and strengthened models of partnership among universities, local authorities, schools and individual teachers need to be developed. These partnerships should be based on jointly agreed principles and involve shared responsibility for key areas of teacher education.
> (Donaldson, 2011, p. 48)

The review argues for the importance of the role of the university and recommends that university teacher educators are engaged in planned CPD, which allows them to support the development of a research-led profession. There is also an argument for universities to offer broader academic programmes for pre-service teachers, allowing them to engage with a range of related academic subjects and to move their university experience away from a narrow focus on training towards a richer education involving intellectual and social development with peers in related disciplines. A planned two-year (five for undergraduates) programme of pre-service and induction development is suggested, drawing on the strengths of universities, schools, local authorities, and other agencies. Whilst the report does not argue for a Masters-level profession, it does identify Masters-level study as a sensible option for those wanting to pursue this goal, and supports programmes of professional development with Masters accreditation.

In the final chapter of the review, there is a clear sense that there will need to be a coordinated response if the recommendations are to be met. Nobody in the sector is assumed to be in a more privileged position to deliver the recommendations, and the report concludes with clear articulation of the roles and responsibilities of teachers, school leaders, local authorities, universities, and the General Teaching Council for Scotland (GTCS) in delivering the 50 recommendations.

The review was well received by professional bodies in the Scottish education sector. Three months after the publication of the Donaldson Review, the Scottish Government produced its response in March 2011. In this response nearly all the recommendations were accepted in full and others in part or principle.

> The effort needed must be genuinely collective – the implications are far-reaching and change cannot happen overnight. All of those involved in the delivery of school education (in local authorities and schools themselves), in

the provision of aspects of teacher education and professional learning (in universities and other organisations) and in supporting those at a national level need to be fully engaged.

(Scottish Government, 2011, p. 2)

In order to address the recommendations, the National Partnership Group was established. This comprised representatives from the Scottish Government, the universities, local authorities, Education Scotland, the GTCS, head teachers, and teachers. There were also subgroups tasked with working on recommendations linked to the early phases of professional learning, career-long professional learning, and professional learning for leadership.

The Welsh context

Like Scotland, Wales has remained committed to community-based local state schools. There is a compulsory requirement to study Welsh until the age of 16 and Welsh medium education is available in all age phases of the Welsh education system.

The Welsh Government has had long-standing concerns about the performance of Wales in PISA tests, where the country regularly is outperformed by the other countries within the UK. This has led to a review of the school curriculum and proposals for a new 'curriculum for life' (Donaldson, 2015).

Poor performance in PISA has also led to a focus on ITE and training in Wales, leading to the Government commissioning a number of reports to address the concerns raised. In 2006, a review of this provision focused on the oversupply of new teachers in Wales pointed out that there was likely to be reduction in demand for teachers over the next decade (Furlong, Hagger, & Butcher, 2006). This report also recommended a reduction in the number of providers of ITE along with suggested reductions in the number of places available on these ITE programmes. This led to some structural reorganisation and rationalisation, resulting in there being three providers of teacher education. However, concerns about quality remained on Government agendas. In 2013, Ralph Tabberrer was asked to review ITT. In his report, he stated that 'the current quality of ITT in Wales is adequate and no better. . . . This assessment is largely shared by providers, officials, and leading stakeholders' (Tabberrer, 2013, para 36). These observations were supported by the Estyn's inspections of ITE provision in Wales.

These official concerns were compounded by demand for the kind of educators that would be required to deliver the new 'curriculum for life' with a view that the *status quo* would prove inadequate in developing the skills required (Furlong, 2015, p. 7). In this context, John Furlong was commissioned to review what would be needed to educate tomorrow's teachers by the Welsh Government.

Currently, there is a high level of university involvement in teacher education in Wales. There are three teacher education centres which draw on the involvement of five universities. These comprise postgraduate one-year programmes (i.e., the PGCE), which account for three-quarters of university-led provision, with the remaining quarter made up of a three-year Bachelors in Education undergraduate provision. In addition, there are two small employment-based programmes: the Graduate Teacher Programme and Teach First (both of which have university involvement). All pre-service programmes of teacher education in Wales provide support for Welsh language development. There is also a fully funded Masters in Educational Practice programme available to all newly qualified teachers in Wales.

The Furlong Report: Teaching tomorrow's teachers

A key recommendation of the Tabberrer Review was that the Welsh Government appoint a senior advisor with specific responsibility for ITE who would play a pivotal role in providing policy advice and raising standards (Tabberrer, 2013). 'Teaching tomorrow's teachers', or the Furlong Report, is a result of that work (Furlong, 2015). John Furlong, an emeritus professor of Oxford University, is an experienced commentator and advisor on teacher education who was involved in the British Educational Research Association–Royal Society for the Encouragement of Arts, Manufactures and Commerce (BERA-RSA) Inquiry into the role of research in teacher education. His focus was on identifying the current situation and to clarify what was needed in Wales in terms of the 'forms of ITE and CPD that will allow and encourage the achievement of a new kind of teacher professionalism of the sort proposed by Donaldson; one that is appropriate for the challenges of 21st century schooling' (Furlong, 2015, p. 7).

Furlong consulted the three teacher education centres, the regional consortium schools, and representatives of key national agencies alongside a review of international evidence of what constitutes high-quality teacher education. His report is presented in two sections: Section A outlines the case for change, and Section B suggests options for change.

In Section A, Furlong argues that teacher education in Wales is not of sufficiently high quality and that there is a need to attract better quality entrants to the profession, who, as the ' "teachers of tomorrow" will have to respond to the changing nature of knowledge in society' (Furlong, 2015, p. 5). His report draws on the findings of the BERA-RSA inquiry (BERA-RSA, 2014) by outlining the five core features of high-quality teacher education:

> This would suggest that in order to be of the highest quality, initial teacher education needs its universities to provide strong, research led courses; it needs a school system that is willing to take responsibility and provide leadership in key parts of all programmes; and it needs to ensure that both university and school components are carefully integrated with each other.
> (Furlong, 2015, p. 8)

Furlong identified weaknesses in provision at the national level, the institutional level, and the programme level. Specifically, he called for more effective national coordination and leadership, possibly through a body such as the General Teaching Council of Scotland. The report drew attention to the fact that Wales, like

England, relied on a standards-based approach to teacher education which was outdated, narrow, and heavily reliant on competencies measuring what new teachers 'must know and do'. In a similar way to the Scottish system, the report called for approaches that 'conceptualise teacher learning in a developmental way' (Furlong, 2015, p. 12), which recognises the role of critical reflection and research linked to teachers' future professional learning. The content of teacher education programmes in Wales were narrowly conceived around the standards, and the report drew attention to this being insufficient to develop teachers able to respond to the demands of the new curriculum and assessment proposed in the Donaldson Review, which would demand 'active professionals' (Donaldson, 2015, p. 13).

At the institutional level, the report raises concerns about the quality of the provision and the organisational structures of the three centres of teacher education. The report also suggests that there is a need for investment in research and teaching underpinning teacher education in university departments of education. At the programme level, the report identified weaknesses in relation to the five principles of high-quality provision outlined in the BERA-RSA Inquiry. 'In the future, Wales will need a different type of teacher professional; one who has significantly more responsibility, one who understands the "why" and the "how" of teaching as well as the "what"' (Furlong, 2015, p. 19).

The report's conclusions in this area can be summarised as follows:

- concerns about the quality of entrants to teacher education programmes;
- need for a higher profile for the role of research in teacher education programmes and in teaching;
- a move to a clinical practice model, with new models of partnership to challenge the current theory-practice divide;
- a need for systematic coordination between universities, schools, and other agencies to establish strong links between ITE and ongoing CPD; and
- a need for a research based approach that builds on professional literature as well as excellent practice.

Section B of the report outlined a number of options for responding to the challenges identified in Section A. There were two main emphases: a call for QTS standards to be redrafted to reflect a broader conceptualisation of professional learning, and a call to revise accreditation procedures for teacher education providers (which would include developing new models of partnership). This would necessitate future further investment in research capacity, if teacher education programmes were to prepare 'student teachers to be both critical consumers *of* as well as participants *in* research' (Furlong, 2015, p. 32). There would also need to be improved links between ITE and further professional development, with university-school partnerships working together to plan and deliver this.

In addition, Furlong suggested a review of entry requirements to teacher education programmes and a consideration of financial incentives for student teachers. The report also debated alternative structures to the undergraduate programme with a suggestion that this be increased from a three to a four-year degree.

In an oral statement to the Welsh Assembly in June 2015, Huw Lewis, The Minister for Education and Skills, 'broadly' welcomed the findings and the nine recommendations of the report. The Welsh Government commissioned an internal reference group 'to engage with the profession, create a vision for the future and build revised professional standards to develop and support practice for the future' (Welsh Government, 2015, n.p.). John Furlong was also asked to chair a task and finish group made up of university teacher educators, regional consortia, and school representatives. Their remit was to review the accreditation criteria for teacher education providers. The other recommendations of the report were to be addressed in a range of other ways, including an independent review of financial incentives, and to explore the option of extending undergraduate provision for primary trainee teachers from three to four years.

Discussion

What this summary of differing key policy texts in the devolved countries has shown is that there are contextual influences on policy development and enactment in relation to education more generally and teacher education specifically. What is clearly prevalent in the three countries is a concern to raise standards and to achieve better performance outcomes in terms of international comparatives, especially given Governments' interest in PISA measures. The way to improve performance in international comparisons and league tables such as PISA is widely believed to relate to quality measures of teaching and teachers: '[t]he quality of an education system cannot exceed the quality of its teachers and principals' (OECD, 2005, p. 235).

As in other jurisdictions across the world, the three countries in this study have focused on pre-service teacher education and training to be a key driver for improved teacher quality. In this way, responses in England, Scotland, and Wales are similar to other international contexts where teacher education is conceived as a 'policy problem'. Thus, there is a shared commitment in post-devolution Great Britain to review and improve systems of teacher education.

On the surface, there is much in the Carter, Donaldson, and Furlong reviews that is similar. Each report focuses on measures to ensure that new entrants to the profession are of a high quality. Commonly this is through raising entry requirements to undergraduate or postgraduate programmes, ensuring high competency in literacy and numeracy (though this is enacted differently in England with the online literacy and skills tests), and in England and Wales providing financial incentives for those with higher qualifications training to teach shortage subjects. Similarly, each review recommends a focus on subject knowledge and a strengthening of the continuum between IT and induction into the profession post-qualification. There is a shared emphasis on the importance of leadership and on the importance of partnerships between schools and teacher education providers.

However, there are significant areas of difference, not least in the role of universities and in the diversification of routes and qualifications in England when compared to Scotland and Wales. Teacher education programmes have 'consistently been a significant site of societal and political debate' (Menter et al., 2010, p. 17) and the post-devolution move to take education away from Westminster has led to greater divergence in teacher education policy in each context. This is partly because there are different push and pull factors driving policy, not least disparities between historical teacher oversupply (in Scotland) and teacher shortages and the academies programme in England. This means that what Cochran-Smith (2005) describes as '*new* teacher education' is enacted differently in the three countries. Cochran-Smith's analysis of teacher education policy in the USA and elsewhere is apt for this present chapter where, despite some obvious similarities, England becomes identifiable as an outlier. Cochran-Smith articulated four tensions as the focus of contestation in this policy arena:

> the conflict between diversification and selectivity of the teacher workforce, the valorization of subject matter at the expense of pedagogy, the competition between university and multiple other locations as the site for teacher preparation, and the contradictions of simultaneous regulation and *de*regulation.
>
> (Cochran-Smith, 2005, p. 12)

In England, the new teacher education project has been intensified with the Coalition government's reforms of teacher training in 2010, which prioritised a 'school-led' policy of teacher preparation (see, for instance, Murray & Mutton, 2016; Mutton, Burn, & Menter, 2017) within the context of a self-improving school system. Mutton et al. (2017) extend Cochran-Smith's (2005) four frameworks by adding two tensions specifically applicable to their analysis of the English teacher education policy context. These are, firstly, the tension between teaching as values based with nuanced moral purpose, rather than teaching as a list of professional behaviours and competencies; and secondly, the requirement for teacher education programmes to deliver 'urgent' content in place of learning about the complexities of education and pedagogy (Mutton et al., 2017).

The latter point by Mutton et al. is especially relevant as it speaks directly to where teacher education could best be located. In Scotland and Wales, there is an acknowledgement of the role of universities as part of a collaborative partnership of teacher education along with schools, local authorities, and other agencies. In England, the role of the university in teacher education, beyond that of award conferring, has been questioned and university teacher educators dismissed as 'enemies of promise' by then Secretary of State for Education, Michael Gove (2013).

In other parts of the UK, universities are still regarded as having an important part to play in teacher education, both initially and for longer-term professional development, and within this the importance of research is highlighted. This is signalled by both the choice of individuals to lead the reviews (Graham

Donaldson and John Furlong have acknowledged expertise and experience of working in universities and schools, and have advised governments and international education bodies); and the ways in which groups established to work on the recommendations have comprised a partnership of university educators, local authorities, and school representatives in Scotland and Wales. This is in marked contrast to those chosen to lead the initial review of ITT and then the proliferation of prominent supporters of the school-led system in the makeup of the subsequent expert groups in England tasked with working on the recommendations.

In Scotland and Wales there have been recent reviews of the curriculum with a focus on the needs of 21st century learners, as manifested in *What is a curriculum for excellence?* (Education Scotland, 2016) and the proposed new *Curriculum for Wales – A curriculum for life* (Welsh Government, 2017). Universities are viewed as important players in ensuring that the teaching profession is equipped to deliver such curricula; for example, Furlong actually makes the point that the current university provision in Wales is not strong enough and that there will be necessary changes in order for the new curriculum to be supported (2015, p. 19). In England there has been a different emphasis, with a curriculum that has been criticised as being too narrow and for drawing extensively on the ideas of E. D. Hirsch, and the concept of 'core knowledge' and of 'traditional teaching methods' (Pollard, 2012). Such approaches have been questioned because of an absence of 'cultural critique' and the loss of a 'conception of Education as an intellectual discipline', based on a limited research base of 'positivist studies to discover "best practice"' (Connoll, 2009, p. 218).

Schools are perceived to be the best place to learn how to teach in the ways required in England, because university providers are positioned as problematically progressive and too abstractly intellectual and, as such, are unsuitable training environments (Gibb, 2014). In this way, England, with an emphasis on teaching as a craft, has sought to move teacher education (now only referred to as 'training') into schools with a 'list of auditable competencies' (Connoll, 2009) to be met:

> Whilst all four parts of the UK draw on a teacher competencies framework in assessing the performance of beginning teachers, an examination of revised standards for Qualified Teacher Status or 'eligibility to teach' reveals differences between dominant conceptions of teaching as a technical craft and broader conceptions of teaching as an ethical profession.
> (Hulme & Menter, 2008, p. 48)

All three reviews emphasise that schools need to have a meaningful role in initial teacher preparation and the 'practicum turn' is an important thread throughout. However, there is a difference in how this is conceived. Within England the focus is on schools becoming lead providers of teacher training, recommending teachers that they have grown in their teaching schools for QTS, and where a relationship with a university can be solely for the purpose of accrediting the now-optional PGCE. And so, partnerships become school to school, often within one alliance of schools, with little or no external involvement. In Scotland and Wales there is a different conceptualisation of partnership, with each partner (school, university, and local authority) having a role to play. This is a step change in both countries, where previously there had been a lack of clarity about the responsibility of schools in the process beyond supporting placements. Wales and Scotland both propose significant structural changes to the *status quo* to ensure collaborative partnerships that will extend ITE through induction to career-long CPD.

> [I]n order to be of the highest quality, initial teacher education needs its universities to provide strong, research-led courses, it needs a school system that is willing to take responsibility and provide leadership in key parts of all programmes; and it needs to ensure that both university and school components are carefully integrated with each other.
>
> (Furlong, 2015, p. 8)

This case study comparison illustrates the different emphases within policy expectations across these three regions of the UK. The comparisons clearly demonstrate the unique prominence in England on school-led teacher training rather than long-term teacher education. In conclusion, it is important to consider what this means for the European teacher education project and the future of UK-based teacher education in a post-Brexit European context.

Conclusion

There have been some significant shifts since the publication of the three reviews. A new Secretary of State in Westminster now oversees a DfE which includes universities. At the time of the Carter Review, universities were in a different Government department. That, and an acknowledgment of the current complexity of routes into teaching (National Audit Office, 2016), and news stories about recruitment and shortage crises, have perhaps contributed to a change in discourse about the contribution of universities. Already some universities have received multiple-years allocation of teacher training places, which has injected a level of stability into the landscape. Conversely, in Scotland there is talk of a new Teach First–type route that would lead to new entrants on that programme spending a significant proportion of their training year in schools rather than university (Seith, 2017).

The case of teacher education in England is at the extreme end of what an ideological and unchallenged policy can produce. Menter (2015) reminds us that teacher education is a mirror of society and that in trying to understand a particular policy epoch it is necessary to examine the economy as well as the history, culture, and politics of that society. The Coalition government which introduced the school-led movement in the 'Importance of teaching' white paper did so at a time of economic austerity in England, which allowed measures to be taken to reduce the autonomy of local authorities and to place central government at the heart of funding and monitoring of schools. This allowed for the creation of a marketised approach to ITT regulated by the government's allocation of training places.

This has led to what might have been unintended but long-reaching consequences, the most acute being the current teacher shortage crisis in England. However, another obvious but important point to note is that the uncoupling of QTS from PGCE means that an English teaching qualification is no longer portable. Indeed, someone training to teach in England without a PGCE would not be able to work in Scotland, let alone other parts of Europe.

Curriculum changes within each country also see demarcations of difference as the European dimension is realised more in curricula in some parts of the UK than others (Schratz, 2010). As political debates about Scotland and Wales' position in relation to Europe intensify, with discussions about possible future referendums about Scottish independence in particular, then one can only imagine that education and teacher education will become more and more diverse across the UK. Whilst this might see Scotland and Wales aligning themselves with their European counterparts, it could have the opposite effect in England, which could become increasingly isolated from Europe. However, the new teacher education project described by Cochran-Smith (2005) is taking hold beyond the USA, and the situation in England might be replicated in other parts of the continent. Time will tell where the pendulum swing will hold.

Note

1 The terms initial teacher 'training' and 'education' are used throughout this chapter. Training has largely replaced education in policy discourse in England, which promotes an apprenticeship model of learning to teach. Initial Teacher Training (ITT) will be used in this way throughout this chapter to indicate an ideological technicist model of learning to teach through a practical skills or craft-based approach. In other places in the text, ITE and/or preparation will be used to indicate an approach which includes a more holistic conception of professional learning, education and training.

References

BBC. (2016, 6 December). Scottish schools drop in world rankings. *BBC News*. Retrieved from www.bbc.co.uk/news/uk-scotland-scotland-politics-38207729 (accessed 25 July 2017).

BERA-RSA. (2014). *Research and the teaching profession: Building the capacity for a self-improving education system*. Retrieved from www.bera.ac.uk/project/research-and-teacher-education (accessed 25 July 2016).

Carter, A. (2015). *Carter Review of initial teacher training*. London: Department for Education. Retrieved from www.gov.uk/government/uploads/system/uploads/attachment_data/file/399957/Carter_Review.pdf (accessed 25 July 2017).

Cater, J. (2017). *Whither teacher education and training?* Higher Education Policy Institute Report 95. Oxford: Oxuniprint.

Cochran-Smith, M. (2005). The new teacher education: For better or for worse. *Educational Researcher*, 34(7), 3–17.

Connoll, R. (2009). Good teachers on dangerous ground: Towards a new view of teacher quality and professionalism. *Critical Studies in Education, 50*(3), 213–229.

Coughlan, S. (2016, 6 December). Pisa tests: UK lags behind in global school rankings. *BBC News*. Retrieved from www.bbc.co.uk/news/education-38157811 (accessed 25 July 2017).

DfE (Department for Education). (1992). *Initial teacher training (secondary phase) (Circular 9/92)*. London: DfE.

DfE (Department for Education). (1993). *The initial training of primary school teachers: New criteria for courses (Circular 14/93)*. London: DfE.

DfE (Department for Education). (2010). *The importance of teaching: The schools white paper 2010*. London: Her Majesty's Stationery Office.

DfE (Department for Education). (2015). *Government response to the Carter Review of initial teacher training*. Retrieved from www.gov.uk/government/uploads/system/uploads/attachment_data/file/396461/Carter_Review_Government_response_20150119.pdf (accessed 25 July 2017).Donaldson, G. (2011). *Teaching Scotland's future: Report of a review of teacher education in Scotland*. Scotland: Education Scotland.

Donaldson, G. (2015). *Successful futures*. Scotland: Education Scotland.

Education Scotland. (2016). *What is a curriculum for excellence?* Retrieved from https://education.gov.scot/scottish-education-system/policy-for-scottish-education/policy-drivers/cfe-(building-from-the-statement-appendix-incl btc1–5)/What%20is%20Curriculum%20for%20Excellence? (accessed 25 July 2017).

Furlong, J. (2015). *Teaching tomorrow's teachers: Options for the future of initial teacher education in Wales*. Retrieved from http://gov.wales/docs/dcells/publications/150309-teaching-tomorrows-teachers-final.pdf (accessed 25 July 2017).

Furlong, J., Hagger, H., & Butcher, C. (2006). *Review of initial teacher training provision in Wales: A report to the Welsh Assembly Government*. Retrieved from www.education.ox.ac.uk/wordpress/wp-content/uploads/2010/07/CE-Report-Annex-A-Review-of-ITT-provision-in-Wales-English.pdf (accessed 25 July 2017).

Gibb, N. (2014, 23 April). Teaching unions aren't the problem – Universities are. *The Guardian*. Retrieved from www.theguardian.com/commentisfree/2014/apr/23/teaching-unions-arent-problem-universities-schools-minister (accessed 25 July 2017).

Gove, M. (2010). *Michael Gove's speech to the National College Annual Conference, Birmingham*. Retrieved from www.gov.uk/government/speeches/michael-gove-to-the-national-college-annual-conference-birmingham (accessed 30 May 2016).

Gove, M. (2013). *Michael Gove's speech to teachers and headteachers at the National College for teaching and leadership*. Retrieved from www.gov.uk/government/speeches/michael-gove-speech-to-teachers-and-headteachers-at-the-national-college-for-teaching-and-leadership (accessed 25 July 2017).

House of Commons Education Committee. (2017). *Recruitment and retention of teachers, fifth report of session 2016–2017*. House of Commons: Her Majesty's Stationary Office.

Hulme, M., & Menter, I. (2008). Learning to teach in post-devolution UK: A technical or an ethical process? *Southern African Review of Education with Education with Production, 14*(1–2), 43–64.

James, E.J.F. (1972). *Teacher education and training: A report by a committee of inquiry appointed by the Secretary of State for Education and Science, under the chairmanship of Lord James of Rusholme*. London: Her Majesty's Stationary Office.

Menter, I. (2015). Making connections: Research, teacher education and educational improvement. In The Peter Underwood Centre for Educational Attainment (Eds.), *Education transforms – Papers and reflections* (pp. 30–40). Tasmania: The Peter Underwood Centre for Educational Attainment.

Menter, I., Hulme, M., Elliot, D., & Lewin, J. (2010). *Literature review on teacher education in the twenty first century*. Edinburgh: The Scottish Government.

Murray, J., & Mutton, T. (2016). Teacher education in England: Change in abundance, continuities in question. In The Teacher Education Group (Eds.), *Teacher education in times of change* (pp. 57–74). Bristol: Policy Press.

Mutton, T., Burn, K., & Menter, I. (2017). Deconstructing the Carter Review: Competing conceptions of quality in England's "school-led" system of initial teacher education. *Journal of Education Policy, 32*(1), 14–33.

National Audit Office. (2016). *Training new teachers*. London: Department for Education.

O'Brien, J. (2012). Teacher education in Scotland: The Donaldson Review and the early phases of teacher learning. *Research in Teacher Education, 2*(2), 42–47.

OECD. (2005). *Teachers matter: Attracting developing and retaining effective teachers*. Paris: OECD.

OECD. (2007). *Reviews of national policies for education: Quality and equity of schooling in Scotland*. Retrieved from www.oecd.org/education/school/40328315.pdf (accessed 1 November 2017).

Ofsted. (2016). *Initial teacher education: Inspections and outcomes as at 30 June 2016*. Retrieved from www.gov.uk/government/publications/initial-teacher-education-inspections-and-outcomes-as-at-30-june-2016/initial-teacher-education-inspections-and-outcomes-as-at-30-june-2016-main-messages (accessed 25 July 2017).

Pollard, A. (2012, 12 June). Proposed primary curriculum: What about the pupils? *IOE London Blog*. Retrieved from https://ioelondonblog.wordpress.com/2012/06/12/proposed-primary-curriculum-what-about-the-pupils/ (accessed 25 July 2017).

Schratz, M. (2010). What is a 'European teacher'? In O. Gassner, L. Kerger, & M. Schratz (Eds.), *The first ten years after Bologna* (pp. 97–102). București: Editura Universității din București.

Scottish Government. (2011). *Continuing to build excellence in teaching – The Scottish Government's response to teaching Scotland's future*. Retrieved from www.scotland.gov.uk/Resource/Doc/920/0114570.pdf (accessed 25 July 2016).

SEED. (2001). *First stage review of initial teacher education: Action plan*. Edinburgh: Scottish Executive.

SEED. (2002). *The standard for full registration*. Edinburgh: SEED.

SEED. (2005). *Review of initial teacher education stage 2*. Edinburgh: SEED. Retrieved from www.gov.scot/Resource/Doc/920/0012210.pdf (accessed 25 July 2017).Seith, E. (2017, 2 June). New route into teaching in Scotland could bypass universities. *Times Educational Supplement*. Retrieved from www.tes.com/news/school-news/breaking-news/new-route-teaching-scotland-could-bypass-universities (accessed 25 July 2017).

Tabberrer, R. (2013). *A review of initial teacher training in Wales*. Cardiff: Welsh Government.

Taylor, C. (2014, January). *Towards a school led teacher education system*. Speech given at the North of England Education Conference, Sheffield Hallam University.

Welsh Government. (2015, 23 June). *Minister endorses "Radical Plan" to transform teacher training in Wales.* Retrieved from http://gov.wales/newsroom/education andskills/2015/10292704/?lang=en (accessed 25 July 2017).

Welsh Government. (2017, 26 September). *New school curriculum.* Retrieved from http://gov.wales/topics/educationandskills/schoolshome/curriculuminwales/curriculum-for-wales-curriculum-for-life/?lang=en (accessed 28 November 2017).

11 Teacher education in Europe in the midst of anti-Europeanism

Implications and recommendations for policy, practice, and research

Mónica Lourenço and Ana Raquel Simões

The European project: promise and reality

For many centuries conflicts marked the history of Europe, leading to the creation of highly conscious nationalist states or, contrastingly, to the rise of empires that imposed political, linguistic, and cultural hegemony on individual states, often through military force. These constant changes to the internal fabric of Europe, together with the devastating effects of war and foreign occupation, promoted a desire to unite all the European peoples under common values of solidarity and peace.

Throughout the years, several attempts have been made to unify the 'old continent', usually arising from the more or less megalomaniac intentions of several key figures: the Roman emperors, between 27 BC and 395 AD; Charlemagne, during the early Middle Ages; Napoleon, in the 19th century; and, more recently, Hitler, who sought unity through subjugation. With different aims, intellectuals and philosophers – such as Kant, Leibniz, Marx, Ortega y Gasset, Rousseau, and Victor Hugo – proposed the idea of a European community as a desirable political project to guarantee sustainable peace between all the European states (Pasture, 2015). However, it was not until after World War II that real steps in that direction were taken by Western European politicians.

Many are the origins for what would come to be known as the 'European Movement': the psychological and perspective changes brought by World War II; the need for economic reconstruction and recovery; the growing weaknesses of a fragmented Europe trapped between an Eastern (Soviet) and a Western (American) bloc in the Cold War climate; the decline of individual power and influence of European states over global issues; and decolonisation (Judt, 2005; Lukacs, 2013). In a very general way, these circumstances favoured aspirations for the unity of Europe, leading some individuals – such as Jean Monnet and Robert Schuman – to draw up concrete steps that would lead to gradual political integration and *de facto* solidarity.

The Marshall Plan and the creation of the North Atlantic Treaty Organization (NATO) would be among the first in a series of milestones to mark the road towards a more cohesive Europe. These would be followed by the creation of a new international structure, the Council of Europe, the oldest European institution in operation, and the signing of the Treaty establishing the European Coal and Steel Community, a body which was intended to ensure the international organisation and administration of two of the major industrial resources in Europe – coal and steel – according to sound principles of economic rationalisation. Still, the most significant impetus for greater unity between European states was the signing of the Treaties of Rome which created the European Atomic Energy Community and, more importantly, the European Economic Community, which would pave the way for the EU. On 25 March 1957, Belgium, France, Italy, Luxembourg, the Netherlands, and West Germany joined forces in an organisation that aimed at:

> establishing a Common Market and progressively approximating the economic policies of Member States, to promote throughout the Community a harmonious development of economic activities, a continuous and balanced expansion, an increased stability, an accelerated raising of the standard of living and closer relations between its Member States.
> (European Economic Community, 1952, p. 4)

Sixty years after the signing of the treaties, strong political, social, and economic tension is threatening the cohesion and stability of the EU (Chopin & Jamet, 2016). International terrorism, the migratory crisis, the eurozone crisis, Brexit, and the rise of anti-European populism and right wing extremist parties, all bring new challenges to the EU and foster increased fragmentation in European societies. While European integration brought about peace, reconciliation, and unprecedented prosperity, this is neither a guarantee for social peace in the face of the economic crisis, nor for domestic security in the face of terrorism. European integration seems, therefore, to be directly threatened: 'as a space without internal borders, it raises fears of contagion of the crises from the periphery (geographic and economic) to the heart of the Union, without being adequately equipped to rise to ensure a collective, Community wide response' (Chopin & Jamet, 2016, n.p.). In the face of these challenges, the link between European integration and its founding narratives is waning. One might then wonder whether we still need a European project or if the collapse of the dreams of the EU's founding fathers is inevitable. The answer might be found in two recent events.

On 10 December 2012 the EU received the Nobel Peace Prize. When announcing its decision, the Norwegian Nobel Committee explained that this was based on the stabilising role the EU had played in transforming most of Europe from a continent of war to a continent of peace, highlighting that the EU's most important achievement had been 'the successful struggle for peace and reconciliation and for democracy and human rights' (Norwegian Nobel Committee, 2012, n.p.). In their joint statement on the award, José Manuel Barroso, President of the European Commission, and Herman van Rompuy, President of the European Council, alluded to the role of the EU in reunifying a continent split by the Cold War around common values of respect for human dignity, freedom, democracy, equality, the rule of law, and respect for human rights, adding that these are also the values that the EU promotes, both internally and in their external policies, in order to make the world a better place for all (European Commission, 2012). This was further reinforced in their acceptance speeches, which stress that the EU is not only about peace among nations, but it also embodies a vision of freedom and justice, placing the person and respect of human dignity at its heart and giving a voice to differences while creating unity (European Union, 2012). Therefore, the EU represents an example in the 'art of compromise', of building up mutual confidence and binding common interests so tightly that war and conflict become materially impossible.

These same characteristics were acknowledged five years later, on 21 October 2017, when the EU received the Princess of Asturias Concord Award, a prize bestowed in Spain to entities or organisations from around the world who make notable achievements in promoting values that form part of the universal heritage of humanity. The EU was recognised for

> a unique model of supranational political integration based on the peaceful, progressive and free association of its members. The sum of various elements such as the common market (free movement of persons, goods, workers and capital), the single currency, regional, agricultural and trade policies, among others, and guarantees of stability, prosperity and respect for human rights evidence this fact.
> (Fundación Princesa de Asturias, 2017)

Although this award did not have the same impact as the Nobel Peace Prize, it was a significant recognition in the year that marked the 60th anniversary of the Treaties of Rome. Furthermore, as highlighted by Jean Claude Juncker, President of the European Commission, in his acceptance speech, the word 'concord' in the title of this award reflects the very nature of European integration – a communion between hearts and minds. As he underlines, despite its weaknesses, shortcomings, and frequent failings, the EU is capable of 'achieving the best results when it comes together and Europeans walk side by side towards the same horizon' (European Council, 2017, n.p.).

Despite the obvious recognition of the role of the EU in promoting long-lasting peace and advancing the causes of democracy and human rights in Europe, these two events have a more symbolic meaning. Both awards were given at uncertain times for the EU amidst the financial crisis, unemployment, terrorist attacks, the refugee waves, and, more recently, Brexit and the referendum in Catalonia (two major threats to the eurozone and catalysts for divisiveness and prejudice). This means that at times of grave economic difficulties and considerable social unrest and uncertainty, the EU, despite its imperfections, remains an inspiration for leaders and citizens all over the world. As Martin Schultz, former President of the European Parliament, emphasised, the EU 'is a magnet for stability, prosperity and democracy [. . .], a beacon for reconciliation' (European

Parliament, 2012, n.p.). Indeed, the quest for unity which characterises the EU is a quest for cosmopolitan order, in which abiding by common norms serves the universal values of human dignity, freedom, equality, respect for others, and for our 'common home', and in which working side by side is a guarantee for peace. These are the values upon which a sustainable society is built; hence, these should also be the values to be engraved in the hearts of every citizen in Europe and abroad.

As rightly noted by Nóvoa and Lawn (2002), to consolidate and reinforce the European project we must turn to education. Provided that it is of good quality and inclusive, education from childhood on lays the foundations for social cohesion, social mobility, and an equitable society. Indeed, education can help learners know better each other across borders, respect cultural differences and human rights, and understand the relevance of preserving our cultural heritage and diversity. Thus, education can form the basis for active citizenship and contribute to preventing populism, xenophobia, and violent radicalisation. Furthermore, education can stimulate creativity, innovation, and entrepreneurship, helping learners develop the skills they need to respond to changing circumstances and structural change or disruption (European Commission, 2017). Teachers are key actors in this process and the idea of a 'European teacher' is a step towards achieving these goals.

Role and challenges of the 'European teacher'

As proposed by Schratz (2010), and explored in Chapter 1 of this book, the European teacher is someone who has roots in a specific country, but simultaneously belongs to a greater European whole; is aware of his/her own culture, but is still open to the cultures of others; is proficient in his/her own mother language, but can also speak two other languages with differing levels of competence; shows solidarity and collaborates with citizens (including teachers) in his/her own country, but also in other European countries. The 'European teacher' inspires learners through his/her own actions and promotes the development of their European identity and citizenship. He/she embodies the shared values of Europe (such as respect for human rights, democracy, and freedom), and contributes to the education of autonomous, responsible, and active citizens for a Europe of tomorrow. Therefore, the 'European teacher' is both a herald and a supporter of a cohesive European space.

To fulfil this role, teachers in Europe must overcome several challenges that are directly connected with changed demographics and to the complexities of the globalised world, and more specifically, to recent developments taking place in the European context. In the preceding chapters some challenges were outlined, namely:

- mobility and migration, which continuously reshape European societies where diversity is the norm;
- the rise of populism and xenophobia, the risk of violent radicalisation, and the need to strengthen the sense of belonging together;

- the unprecedented technological (r)evolution of the globalised societies, continued digitisation, automation, artificial intelligence, and the need to integrate cutting-edge ICT in the teaching practice in order to engage digital students in the learning process and promote their creativity; and
- the future of work, its impact on working conditions, and the uncertainty of future learners' needs.

These challenges place new demands on the national education systems in general, and on schools, teachers, and teacher education programmes in particular. Whereas in the past, teachers were only mediators of knowledge and the teaching process was characterised by some sort of standardisation, norm, and conformity (Schleicher, 2012), nowadays students are placed at the centre of the teaching and learning process. This difference in focus has completely transformed the role teachers play and the responsibilities they face, in order to keep pace with rapidly developing knowledge areas and approaches. According to this redefined focus, every child is seen as unique and different (Heacox, 2002; Tomlinson, 1999), and attention should be paid to each student as an individual with special characteristics and learning styles.

Implications and recommendations for the future of teacher education in Europe

In addition to highlighting some of the challenges that the current European and global contexts place on teachers and teacher education, the chapters in this book present recommendations for the future which open up new possibilities for policy, practice, and research. These will be revisited and discussed in the following sections.

Improve teacher quality and increase teacher status

Teachers are keystones in education, innovation, and quality and have a direct effect upon learners' attainment. For this reason, public authorities, higher education institutions, and other agencies need to continue to undertake reforms of curriculum, instruction, and assessment to improve the quality of the teaching staff and increase teacher status. This is particularly relevant in light of an aging teaching population in Europe, and as a response to the increasing difficulties in recruiting and retaining student teachers, particularly ambitious and high-calibre candidates (European Commission, 2015; European Commission/EACEA/Eurydice, 2015).

However, caution should be taken in conducting these reforms not to fall in the trap of the neoliberal 'culture of accountability' (see Ambrosio, 2013). As the example from the UK shows (see Chapter 10 in this book), an excessive focus on raising standards for better performance outcomes in global assessment surveys such as PISA, or on a school-led competency-driven approach to ITE (as opposed to a university-led values-based approach), might undermine the goals to support teacher quality and long-term career development. Instead, these measures may reduce teaching to a static and unattractive craft, disconnected from the 'real' world.

Strengthen the continuum of teacher education

The education and professional development of every teacher is a lifelong task. Therefore, as highlighted in Chapter 2, education policies should be based on the understanding of the teaching profession and the professional development of teachers as a coherent continuum with several, interconnected perspectives. These include teachers' learning needs, support structures, job and career structures, competence levels, and local school culture (European Commission, 2015). Policymakers need to ensure continuity and coherence for each of these elements, and establish interconnections and a smooth transition between the different phases of teachers' professional development.

In this context, ITE needs to be considered as the first stage of a longer and dynamic process, and not as a stand-alone and complete phase. Its success will also depend on mechanisms allowing for interaction with later stages of teacher development, as these will create the continuity that is important to a teacher's development. Throughout their careers, teachers should recognise the importance of acquiring new knowledge and be given attractive possibilities for professional development and diversification of careers. These could include opportunities for practice-oriented and research-based professional development, as these might strengthen the agency of teachers for learner-oriented teaching and innovation (see Schön, 1983).

Include mobility and/or short-term exchanges in teacher preparation

Mobility is perceived as a central component of initial and continuing teacher education programmes. IPs such as the HOWBET Summer School (described in Chapter 3 of this book), and mobility experiences in the framework of ERASMUS, expose teachers to different educational philosophies and new pedagogical strategies, allowing them to gain self-knowledge, and to develop personal confidence, professional competence, and a greater understanding of both global and domestic diversity (Mahon, 2012). These positive effects transversely impact the five domains of knowledge a quality teacher should develop, according to Goodwin (2012). These are personal knowledge (autobiography and philosophy of teaching), contextual knowledge (understanding learners, schools, and society), pedagogical knowledge (content, theories, methods of teaching, and curriculum development), sociological knowledge (diversity, cultural relevance, and social justice), and social knowledge (cooperative, democratic group process, and conflict resolution). Put in other terms, these programmes may allow pre-service teachers to consider their future possible selves with a deeper understanding of diverse learners' needs and how they might strive to address these needs in their own classrooms.

In spite of this, surprisingly little has been done so far to include a stay abroad as an integral part of ITE curricula. On the contrary, this largely remains a voluntary albeit highly recommended option, even for students studying to become foreign language teachers. Hence, efforts should be made, through partnerships between higher education institutions, for instance, to include physical or virtual (online) mobility and exchange opportunities as a mandatory component of the curricula of future teachers.

Promote collaboration and partnerships

Collaboration is an important and widespread expectation of teachers in Europe. Nevertheless, according to the European Commission (2015), significant numbers of teachers have never experienced collaborative learning. Building good relations and partnerships to support wider introduction of collaboration is a key challenge which often entails changes in practice, mindset, and the development of new work cultures and environments. In order to make collaboration everyday professional practice, policymakers, educational leaders, and all relevant stakeholders – including the social partners – should contribute to the preconditions required for a collaborative work culture. This can be carried out through creating and strengthening mutual trust, and developing positive attitudes towards professional dialogue, sharing, collaborative critical thinking, and peer learning.

Priority should, then, be given to solutions favouring several types of collaboration: (a) collaboration within individual institutions (between teachers and/or between teacher educators, for instance); (b) collaboration between institutions (at the same level or across educational levels, and at both national and international levels); and (c) collaboration between educational institutions and the local community, including municipalities, trade unions, and professional associations. This can create a comprehensive approach to teacher development, which can in turn have a positive impact on the overall attractiveness of the profession.

Educate teachers for the 21st century

As highlighted in Chapter 4 of this book, the new globalised world has brought significant changes to the range of competences learners need to possess in order to live and work in increasingly diverse societies. Due to fast and wide technological progress, the traditional working environment is gradually disappearing. Work today is becoming more intellectual than physical, requiring employees to possess new skills such as digital and social skills, foreign languages, and entrepreneurship. In this increasingly complex world, creativity, innovation, and the ability to continue to learn will count as much as, if not more than, specific areas of knowledge (which are liable to become obsolete). Schools are now facing increasing demands to prepare students for more rapid economic and social change, for jobs that have not yet been created, for technologies that have not yet been invented, and to solve social problems that have not been anticipated in the past (OECD, 2016).

In this context, it is imperative to rethink teacher education programmes from a global perspective in order to help pre-service teachers develop confidence in their ability as well as the knowledge, skills, and attitudes required to understand and address the challenges of the 21st century (Lourenço, 2017). Possibilities for the internationalisation of teacher education curricula (Leask, 2015) can include intentional integration of an international, intercultural, or global perspective in the content, learning objectives, methodologies, activities, and assessment tasks of a programme of study; mobility and short-term exchanges; international online collaboration; or service learning in multicultural environments.

Prepare teachers to deal with diversity

As a result of globalisation, immigration, and refugee waves, many countries in Europe are changing rapidly from comparatively homogeneous monolingual and monocultural societies to linguistically and culturally diverse societies. Integrating immigrant and refugee children, respecting their languages and cultures, and promoting learning of the school language is, therefore, an essential part of the work of the 'European teacher'. This work is not only important from the perspective of the learner, as it affects integration and overall academic success, but also from the perspective of society. Indeed, through recognising, supporting and valuing the individual repertoires and cultures that co-exist in our societies, teachers are contributing to the preservation of linguistic diversity, our common cultural heritage, and to the promotion of social cohesion (Harmon & Loh, 2010).

Teaching in linguistic and culturally diverse environments requires new approaches in both pre-service and in-service teacher education (see Lourenço & Andrade, in press). In Chapter 5, several guidelines for teacher education programmes were put forward, namely the need to familiarise teachers with their own cultural heritage and with different cultures and languages; develop their linguistic skills in more than one foreign language, as well as their intercultural communicative competence (see Byram, 1997); help them become aware of the educational and cultural needs of minority groups; develop their skills to adapt educational contents, methods, and materials to the needs of diverse ethnic and linguistic groups; and promote positive attitudes towards diversity, encouraging teachers to regard diversity as an opportunity rather than a problem.

The UNESCO, the Council of Europe and other European institutions and organisations have developed recommendations and materials to support teachers and teacher educators in teaching in and for diversity. These include the *Common European framework of reference* (2017a), which aims to promote plurilingualism; the *European language portfolio* (2017b), a record of a learner's linguistic and cultural skills; and the *Framework of reference for pluralistic approaches* (FREPA), which provides a tool for teachers of all subjects, teacher trainers, decision makers, or programme designers to introduce pluralist approaches in the curriculum (Candelier et al., 2012). Teachers should, then, be given the opportunity to know, experiment with, and receive training on these resources in ITE and throughout their careers.

Help teachers experience and promote inclusion

Inclusion is not only about people with disabilities. As highlighted in Chapter 6, it is about diversity and dealing with each learner and his/her uniqueness, strengths, and weaknesses. Every child has a fundamental right to education and must be given the opportunity to achieve and maintain acceptable levels of learning. In this sense, inclusion is a human right and an issue of social justice.

An inclusive education system would mean that, when possible, all pupils go to the same school. This involves changes and modifications in content, approaches, structures, and strategies (UNESCO, 2005), but also in teacher education programmes. Teachers, and pre-service teachers in particular, should not only know about inclusion and its current developments, but also experience opportunities to discuss and learn about how to deal with it in the classroom. They should learn how to cooperate and work together with other professionals in their field, but be entitled to state their limits and receive effective and appropriate support. Hence, the introduction of inclusive pedagogy in teacher education curricula should not only be desirable but mandatory. If teachers adopt, integrate, and manage inclusive practices and policies, institutions can become more engaged, innovative, and productive.

Prepare teachers through and for citizenship education

Citizenship education aims to help students, from early childhood onwards, to develop the knowledge, skills, and attitudes to interact effectively and constructively with others, think critically, act in a socially responsible manner, and act democratically. These aims form part of both civic 'virtues' and individual 'virtues', and enable each individual to live as a 'good' citizen. Based on principles of equal dignity and respect for others, citizenship education has the task of combating all forms of negative discrimination, racism, sexism, and religious fanaticism. Therefore, citizenship education should be explained and, above all, experienced in daily life in all schools.

In the past decades, citizenship education has been allocated within the school curriculum of European countries in very different ways: as a stand-alone subject, as part of another subject or learning area, or as a cross-curricular dimension. This often reflects the importance that decision makers attach to this area. According to the report *Citizenship education at school in Europe* (European Commission/EACEA/Eurydice, 2017), most education systems use the integrated and/or the cross-curricular approach at all levels of education. This means that teachers from different subject areas are expected to be involved in citizenship education issues.

In order to prepare teachers to work in the field of citizenship education, work has to be undertaken in terms of teacher preparation. Indeed, as highlighted by the Council of Europe (2010), this subject is different from all others, which means that those who will teach it, must first be taught it themselves. In Chapter 7, several possibilities were presented to educate teachers through and for citizenship, including the creation of discussion fora and international IP that offer teachers opportunities to develop knowledge on the theme, as well as to interact with others and discuss their own and their countries' situation regarding citizenship education. This might be an important step towards the development of this field in the European space.

Raise awareness of comparative education

Comparative education is a field of study that systematically examines the similarities and differences between educational systems in two or more national or cultural contexts and their interactions, applying social scientific theories and methods (see Manzon, 2011). According to Marshall (2014), comparative education can be undertaken to learn about one's education system and that of others; to enhance one's knowledge of education in general; to improve educational institutions (namely, their content, processes, and methods); to understand the relationship between education and society; to promote international understanding; and to find possible solutions to educational issues.

In an era of globalisation, when international student and staff mobility are on the increase, there is a growing need for (future and current) teachers to become aware of the similarities and differences of teacher education across countries, as well as of the (often biased) network every member of a society is caught in. Therefore, they should be allowed to study and use comparative education. As described in Chapter 8 of this book, looking at the place of comparison in education and actively comparing policies, structures, and practices in other countries helps future teachers to get a feeling of the dynamic change of views on educational issues over space and time. Summer schools such as HOWBET, are, therefore, valuable possibilities to sharpen the participants' awareness of differences and similarities of educational systems, motivate them to question national particularities, in order to be open to judge different approaches impartially, and to be interested in developing promising ideas throughout their studies and their careers. This might allow a fresh view on the teaching profession and its image and might prove to be an incentive to further develop teacher education with a European or international perspective in mind.

Conduct research on teacher education

Some ideas for educational research around teacher education were approached in the book. These include, but are not limited to, the analysis of the effects of joint programmes and partnerships in European teacher education; the impact of study-abroad experiences integrated in ITE curricula in future teachers' professional development and identity; the design and assessment of teacher education resources, approaches, and scenarios to deal with linguistic and culturally diverse classrooms and promote inclusive education; the elaboration of recommendations on the competences teachers should develop within the field of citizenship education; the effects of ICT integration in changing teachers' practices and beliefs concerning education in a globalised world; and analysis of the voices of teacher educators about the challenges and opportunities of preparing pre-service teachers for the 21st century. Results of this research can, then, be used to inform the design and structure of teacher education programmes.

A common principle for conducting research on teacher education, defended in most chapters in the book, is the need to work in collaboration with teachers, both in ITE and CPD, as the only way to access teachers' beliefs about the role of education and their own role in multicultural and technological societies, uncover what their reality in the classroom looks like, and understand their needs. It is also important that research on education is a bottom-up and not a top-down endeavour, almost wholly conducted by experts in higher education institutions (Lourenço, Andrade, & Sá, 2017). Teachers need to be equipped to interrogate data and evidence from different sources, rather than being mere consumers of research, as well as to investigate the impact of particular interventions and explore their effects on educational practice. As Doyran (2012) highlights, '[t]he impact of any education system can only be as powerful and effective as the teachers or the educational leaders who actually perform this profession' (p. 1).

Concluding thoughts

Teachers are educational leaders who can create positive change in the lives of their students, shape the contexts they work in, and impact the future of their country. Teachers are responsible for creating opportunities that will allow students to develop knowledge, skills, and attitudes that are fundamental in coping with the challenges of a multicultural world. Hence, teachers should organise teaching around the four pillars of learning: learning to know, learning to do, learning to be, and learning to live together in a globalised world (Delors et al., 1996).

In order to educate teachers for this complex and ambitious role, teacher education programmes need to be redesigned. Conformity to a technocratic paradigm and to its associated values of accountability, efficiency, practically, and productivity – which characterises current education systems – results in marginalising humanistic values. Within this scope, teacher education should be sustained on: (a) education policies that value diversity and democratic citizenship; (b) activities and strategies that help teachers to learn how to address the complex challenges of the globalised world; and (c) opportunities for students to participate in out-of-school experiences (exchange, volunteering, service learning, peer teaching), which promote lifelong learning and the ability to engage in multicultural environments.

Therefore, it is of the utmost importance to incorporate a values-based approach in teacher education as a possibility to fulfil the promise of the European project, and promote inclusion and social cohesion in European societies.

References

Ambrosio, J. (2013). Changing the subject: Neoliberalism and accountability in public education. *Educational Studies*, 49(4), 316–333.

Byram, M. (1997). *Teaching and assessing intercultural communicative competence*. Clevedon: Multilingual Matters.

Candelier, M. (coord.), Camilleri-Grima, A., Castellotti, V., de Pietro, J-F., Lörincz, I., Meißner, F-J., Schröder-Sura, A., Noguerol, A., & Molinié, M. (2012). *FREPA – A framework of reference for pluralistic approaches to languages and cultures: Competences and resources* (revised ed.). Graz: European Centre for Modern Languages. Retrieved from http://carap.ecml.at/Start/tabid/3577/language/en-GB/Default.aspx (accessed 23 November 2017).

Chopin, T., & Jamet, J-F. (2016). The future of the European project. *European Issues*, 393. Retrieved from www.robert-schuman.eu/en/european-issues/0393-the-future-of-the-european-project (accessed 6 December 2017).

Council of Europe. (2010). *Charter on education for democratic citizenship and human rights education*. Retrieved from www.coe.int/t/dg4/education/edc/Source/Charter/Charterpocket_EN.pdf (accessed 10 December 2017).

Council of Europe. (2017a). *Common European framework of reference for languages: Learning, teaching, assessment* (revised ed.). Retrieved from www.coe.int/en/web/common-european-framework-reference-languages/ (accessed 14 December 2017).

Council of Europe. (2017b). *European Language Portfolio*. Retrieved from www.coe.int/en/web/portfolio (accessed 14 December 2017).

Delors, J., Al Mufti, In am, Amagi, I., Carneiro, R., Chung, F., Geremek, B., . . . Nanzhao, Z. (1996). *Learning: The Treasure Within*. Paris: UNESCO.

Doyran, F. (2012). Research on teacher education and training: An introduction. In F. Doyran (Ed.), *Research on teacher education and training* (pp. 1–10). Greece: Athens Institute for Education and Research.

European Commission. (2012). *Joint statement of José Manuel Barroso, President of the European Commission, and Herman van Rompuy, President of the European Council on the Award of the 2012 Nobel Peace Prize to the EU*. Retrieved from http://europa.eu/rapid/press-release_MEMO-12-779_en.htm (accessed 6 December 2017).

European Commission. (2015). *Shaping career-long perspectives on teaching: A guide on policies to improve initial teacher education*. Luxembourg: Publications Office of the European Union.

European Commission. (2017). *Communication from the Commission to the European Parliament, the Council, the European Economic and Social Committee and the Committee of the Regions – Strengthening European identity through education and culture*. Strasbourg: European Commission. Retrieved from https://ec.europa.eu/commission/sites/beta-political/files/communication-strengthening-european-identity-education-culture_en.pdf (accessed 12 December 2017).

European Commission/EACEA/Eurydice. (2015). *The teaching profession in Europe: Practices, perceptions, and policies. Eurydice Report*. Luxembourg: Publications Office of the European Union. Retrieved from https://publications.europa.eu/en/publication-detail/-/publication/36bde79d-6351-489a-9986-d019efb2e72c/language-en (accessed 12 December 2017).

European Commission/EACEA/Eurydice. (2017). *Citizenship education at school in Europe – 2017. Eurydice Report*. Luxembourg: Publications Office of the European Union.

European Council. (2017). *2017 Princess of Asturias Award*. Speech by President Juncker. Retrieved from https://tvnewsroom.consilium.europa.eu/event/2017-princess-of-asturias-award-18875/speech-by-president-juncker-18a60 (accessed 6 December 2017).

European Economic Community. (1952). *Treaty establishing the European Economic Community and connected documents*. Luxembourg: Publishing Services of the European Communities. Retrieved from www.cvce.eu/obj/treaty_establishing_the_european_economic_community_rome_25_march_1957-en-cca6ba28-0bf3-4ce6-8a76-6b0b3252696e.html (accessed 6 December 2017).

European Parliament. (2012). *Schulz on Nobel Peace Prize: This prize is for all EU citizens*. Retrieved from www.europarl.europa.eu/former_ep_presidents/president-schulz-2012-2014/en/press/press_release_speeches/press_release/2012/2012-october/h/schulz-on-nobel-peace-p (accessed 6 December 2017).

European Union. (2012). *From war to peace: A European tale. Acceptance speech of the Nobel Peace Prize Award to the European Union*. Retrieved from https://europa.eu/european-union/sites/europaeu/files/docs/body/npp2013_en.pdf (accessed 6 December 2017).

Fundación Princesa de Asturias. (2017). *European Union: Princess of Asturias Award for Concord 2017*. Retrieved from www.fpa.es/en/princess-of-asturias-awards/laureates/2017-european-union.html?texto=trayectoria&especifica=0 (accessed 7 December 2017).

Goodwin, A. L. (2012). Globalization and the preparation of quality teachers: Rethinking knowledge domains for teaching. In R. L. Quezada (Ed.), *Internationalization of teacher education: Creating globally competent teachers and teacher educators for the 21st century* (pp. 19–32). Abingdon: Routledge.

Harmon, D., & Loh, J. (2010). The index of linguistic diversity: A new quantitative measure of trends in the status of the world's languages. *Language Documentation and Conservation*, *4*, 97–151. Retrieved from www.christensenfund.org/wp-content/uploads/2013/11/harmonloh.pdf (accessed 23 November 2017).

Heacox, D. (2002). *Differentiating instruction in the regular classroom*. Minneapolis, MN: Free Spirit.

Judt, T. (2005). *Postwar: A history of Europe since 1945*. New York, NY: Penguin.

Leask, B. (2015). *Internationalizing the curriculum*. Abingdon: Routledge.

Lourenço, M. (2017). Repensar a formação de professores . . . rumo a uma educação global na aula de línguas [Rethinking teacher training . . . Towards global education in the language classroom]. In A. P. Vilela & A. Moura (Eds.), *Atas das I Jornadas Nacionais de Professores de Línguas: 'Leituras cruzadas para o futuro: movimentos, correntes e diversidades linguísticas e culturais. Construindo pontes para o Entendimento Global'* (pp. 63–92). Braga: Centro de Formação Braga-Sul.

Lourenço, M., & Andrade, A. I. (in press). Embracing diversity in early years' settings: Challenges and opportunities for teacher professional development. In S. Blackman & D. Conrad (Eds.), *Responding to learner diversity and difficulties*. Charlotte, NA: Information Age Publishing.

Lourenço, M., Andrade, A. I., & Sá, S. (2017). Teachers' voices on language awareness in pre-primary and primary school settings: implications for teacher education. *Language, Culture and Curriculum*, 1–15. doi:10.1080/07908318.2017.1415924

Lukacs, J. (2013). *A short history of the twentieth century*. Cambridge, MA: Belknap Press.

Mahon, J. (2012). Fact or fiction? Analyzing institutional barriers and individual responsibility to advance the internationalization of teacher education. In R. L. Quezada (Ed.), *Internationalization of teacher education: Creating global competent teachers and teacher educators for the twenty-first century* (pp. 7–18). Abingdon: Routledge.

Manzon, M. (2011). *Comparing education: The construction of a field*. Hong Kong: Springer.

Marshall, J. (2014). *Introduction to comparative and international education*. London: Sage.

Norwegian Nobel Committee. (2012). *The Nobel Peace Prize for 2012: Statement by the nobel committee*. Retrieved from www.nobelprize.org/nobel_prizes/peace/laureates/2012/press.html (accessed 6 December 2017).

Nóvoa, A., & Lawn, M. (2002). *Fabricating Europe: The formation of an education space*. New York, NY: Kluwer Academic Publishers.

OECD. (2016). *Global competency for an inclusive world*. Paris: OECD. Retrieved from www.oecd.org/education/Global-competency-for-an-inclusive-world.pdf (accessed 12 December 2017).

Pasture, P. (2015). *Imagining European unity since 1000 AD*. New York, NY: Palgrave Macmillan.

Schleicher, A. (2012). *Preparing teachers and developing school leaders for the 21st century: Lessons from around the world*. Paris: OECD.

Schön, D. A. (1983). *The reflective practitioner: How professionals think in action*. New York, NY: Basic Books.

Schratz, M. (2010). What is a 'European Teacher'? In O. Gassner, L. Kerger, & M. Schratz (Eds.), *The first ten years after Bologna* (pp. 97–102). București: Editura Universității din București.

Tomlinson, C. A. (1999). *The differentiated classroom: Responding to the needs of all learners*. Alexandria, VA: ASCD.

UNESCO. (2005). *Guidelines for inclusion: Ensuring access to education for all*. Retrieved from http://unesdoc.unesco.org/images/0014/001402/140224e.pdf (accessed 16 June 2017).

Index

Page numbers in italic indicate a figure and page numbers in bold indicate a table on the corresponding page.

'3Rs' 44
'7Cs' 44
'9-6-3' rule 106
21st century teachers, competences of 47–49
21st century word cloud *51*

Abeciūnaitė, Eglė 123, 134
ability labelling 80–81
academy schools 144
accountability, culture of 5
achievement, measuring in secondary schools **115**
active cooperative learning 46
active learner engagement 13
Agenda 21 42
AHS (*Allgemeinbildende Höhere Schule*) 77
Altaic language family 58
approaches to citizenship education 92–94; cross curricular approach 93–94; as part of another subject or learning area 93; as stand-alone subject 93
assessment: Anderson, Benedict 130; anti-European/ism 5, 9, 161–174; HOWBET Summer School, criteria for **35**; PISA 5, 110
Assessment of key competences in initial education and training: Policy guidance (European Commission, 2012b) 17
Auch-Pädagogik 73
Austria: inclusive education in 76–79; integration of SEN children in 78–79

'Backpacking through Central Europe' lesson **132**, 134–138, **133**, **134**, *136*, **137**, **138**; description of 135–136, *136*; overview 135; practice/follow-up 136–138, **137**, **138**; theoretical background **132**, 134–135, **133**, **134**
'barriers of learning and participation' 81
Barroso, José Manuel 162–163
Basque language 58
BERA-RSA (British Educational Research Association–Royal Society for the Encouragement of Arts, Manufactures and Commerce) 151
Berger, Karin 123, 129
Bologna Declaration 3–4, 48; *The first ten years after Bologna* 4
Bosnia and Herzegovina, inclusive education in 79
Bundesländer 78; Brexit 9, 156, 162–163

Campus Europae: HOWBET 5–6; *see also* HOWBET
Carter, Sir Andrew 146
Carter review of ITT 146–147; discussion on 153–154
Caucasian language family 58
CEFR (*Common European framework of reference for languages: learning, teaching, and assessment*) 65
challenges of the 'European teacher' 164–165
changing role of teachers in the 21st century 11–15
character qualities 44

Index

Charter on education for democratic citizenship and human rights education (Council of Europe, 2017) 92
citizenship: across Europe 95–96; as competence in the European dimension 5; EDC 89; skill requirements 43; and teacher education 94–95; *see also* citizenship education; European citizenship
citizenship education 88–91, *89*; approaches to 92–94; cross curricular approach 93–94; *Declaration and programme of action on education for democratic citizenship* 91; developing 97–100, **98, 99**; dimensions of 88–89, *89*; 'Education for democratic citizenship and human rights' 92; history of 91–92; HOWBET Summer School workshop 98–99, **98, 99**; HOWBET Summer School workshop, students' evaluation of 100–101; 'Learning and living democracy for all' 91; as part of another subject or learning area 93; preparing teachers through 169–170; principles in European democratic citizenship 96–97; as stand-alone subject 93; *see also* HRE (human rights education)
Citizenship education at school in Europe 90–91
'Citizenship education in Europe' workshop 98–100, **98, 99**; students' voices 100–101
classrooms: changing role of teachers in 12; curriculum in integrated classrooms 74; 'European dimension' in higher education 123–124; preparatory classes 61
CLIL (Content and Language Integrated Learning) 61
co-agency 81
collaboration, promoting 167
Committee on the Rights of Persons with Disabilities 72
Common European principles for teacher competences and qualifications (European Commission, 2005) 20–21
'Comparative analysis in education' workshop 113–119, **115, 116, 117, 118**
comparative education 105–106; 'Comparative analysis in education' workshop 113–119, **115, 116,** **117, 118**; epochs and structures of 107–109, **109**; focus of research 111; Hilker's four-step procedure for comparison 108–109; history of 106–107; journals 109; measuring achievement in secondary schools **115**; method of research 111–112, *112*; Portuguese school system 116–117, **116, 117**; raising awareness of 170; types of research 112–113; universities 109
comparative studies in everyday life 104–105
Compass: The manual for human rights education with young people (Council of Europe, 2012) 92
competences 30; '7Cs' 44; of the 21st century teacher 47–49; defining in 'Future needs of learners in a European context' workshop 51–52; for democratic culture 90; developmental tasks 77; in the European dimension 4–5; *European qualifications framework for lifelong learning* (European Parliament and Council, 2008) 41–42; foundational literacies 44; intercultural competence 63; and knowledge 43; learners' needs in the 21st century, theoretical analysis of 41–44; plurilingualism 60; UNESCO 43
Competences for democratic culture: Living together as equals in culturally diverse societies (Council of Europe, 2016) 92
conclusions of Furlong report 152–153
conducting research on teacher education 170–171
consecutive model of teacher education 47–48
Convention of the United Nations on the Rights of Persons with Disabilities 71
Convention on the Rights of the Child 75–76
cooperative group teaching 83
core competences 43
Costa, Nilza 3–10, 29–39
co-teaching 82–83
Council of Europe 60, 162; *Charter on education for democratic citizenship and human rights education* (Council of Europe, 2017) 92; competences for democratic culture 90, 92; ELP 65–66; Second Summit of Heads of State and Government 91

CPD (Continuing Professional Development) 11, 16–17; Donaldson review of teacher education 149
creativity 45
criteria for assessment, HOWBET Summer School 35
cross curricular approach to citizenship education 93–94
cultural awareness 64
cultural dimension of citizenship education 89
cultural diversity 57; CEFR 65; 'draw your own language tree' activity 67; ELP 65–66; FREPA 66; multiculturalism 59; plurilingualism 60
culturally responsive teaching 61–62
'culture of accountability' 5
Curriculum for Wales – A curriculum for life (Welsh Government, 2017) 155
curriculum in integrated classrooms 74

De re scholastica Anglica cum Germanica comparata (Hechtius) 107
Declaration and programme of action on education for democratic citizenship 91
defining 'European teacher' 4–5
developing citizenship education 97–100, **98, 99**
Developing coherent and system-wide induction programmes for beginning teachers: A handbook for policymakers (European Commission, 2010) 17
developmental tasks 77
'digital native' 45–46
dimensions of citizenship education 88–89, *89*
disabilities: 'barriers of learning and participation' 81; Convention of the United Nations on the Rights of Persons with Disabilities 71; developmental tasks 77; HOWBET Summer School workshop on inclusive education 81–84; inclusion as human right and a philosophy 75–76; integration of SEN children in Austria 78–79; National Action Plan for Disability 78; Salamanca Declaration 72–73
'Discover Europe' lesson: description of 131–134, **131**; overview 130–131; practice/follow-up 132; theoretical background 129–130
discussion on teacher education policy in England, Scotland, and Wales 153–156

diversity 22–23, 84; Greenberg's diversity index 58; language diversity 57; languages in European schools 60–61; linguistic diversity 57; multicultural education 61–62; phylogenetic diversity 58; preparing teachers for 168–169; stages of cultural awareness 64–65; structural diversity 58; *see also* cultural diversity; inclusion; linguistic diversity
Dobińska, Gabriela 123, 129
Donaldson, Graham 148
Donaldson review of teacher education 148–150; discussion 153–154
'draw your own language tree' activity 67

EACEA (Education, Audiovisual, and Culture Executive Agency) 110
economic dimension of citizenship education 89; *Standard Eurobarometer 85* survey 95–96
EDC (education for democratic citizenship) 89; principles in 96–97
Education and Training 2010 31
Education and Training 2020 31
Education and training monitor report (European Council, 2017) 38
Education at a Glance 110
'Education for democratic citizenship and human rights' 92
Education Reform Act 144
Effective schools for all (Ainscow, 1991) 72
ELP (European Language Portfolio) 65–66
England: Carter review of ITT 146–147; discussion on teacher education policy in 153–156; '*new* teacher education' 154; teacher education policy in 143–146
ENTEP (European Network on Teacher Education Policies) 4, 19, 29; competences of the 21st century teacher 47–49
epochs and structures of comparative education 107–109, **109**
equity 62
ERASMUS (EuRopean community Action Scheme for the Mobility of University students) 5; *see also* Mobility IPs
Esquisse et vues préliminaires d'un ouvrage sur l'éducation comparé (Jullien de Paris, 1817) 107

Index

ethnocentric stage of cultural awareness 64–65
ETUCE (European Trade Union Committee for Education) 18
eTwinning Conference 43
EU (European Union): citizenship education 90; education policy documents 30–32; 'European dimension' in higher education 123–124; Joined Report 31–32; multilingualism 58; Nobel Peace Prize, conferrence of 162–163
Eurobarometer survey data on European citizenship 95–96
Europe: citizenship and Eurobarometer survey data 95–96; immigrant children in European schools 61–63; languages spoken in schools 60–61; linguistic diversity 58
Europe 2020 strategy 42–43
'Europe for citizens: Remembrance and European citizenship/democratic engagement and participation' programme 92
European Atomic Energy Community 162
European Centre for Modern Languages 58–59
European citizenship: developing 97–100, **98**, **99**; skill requirements 43
European Coal and Steel Community 162
European Commission: activities of 110–111, **111**; *Citizenship education at school in Europe* 90–91; *Common European principles for teacher competences and qualifications* (European Commission, 2005) 20–21; EACEA 110; Joined Report 31–32; role in teacher education 17–18; *Supporting teacher competence development for better learning outcomes* 12
European Council 12
'European dimension' in education 30, 123–124; 'Backpacking through Central Europe' lesson 132, 134–138, **133**, **134**, *136*, **137**, **138**; 'Discover Europe' lesson 129–132, *131*; "Where are you from?" lesson 124–129, *127*, **128**, **129**
European guidelines for teacher education 17–19
'European Movement' 161–162

European qualifications framework for lifelong learning (European Parliament and Council, 2008) 41–42
'European teacher' concept 4, 4–5, 30, 47; changing role of teachers in the 21st century 11–15; competences of the 21st century teacher 47–79; *European qualifications framework for lifelong learning* (European Parliament and Council, 2008) 41–42; HOWBET 5–6; inclusive education 84; and linguistic diversity 63–65; nine key competences 32; profile of European teachers 19–22; qualities of European education 20–21; role and challenges of 164–165; transversal skills 32; *see also* HOWBET
'European Year of Citizens' 92
'Europeanness' 4, 6, 7, 8, 19, 30, 38
evaluation of HOWBET Summer School 36–38
everybody, principle of 81
examples of inclusion 74
exclusion 73
exploratory phase of citizenship education 91

faith schools 144
The first ten years after Bologna 4, 19–20, 47
fluency: language competence of the European teacher 4; *see also* proficiency
focus of research in comparative education 111
formal induction programmes 18
formative assessment, HOWBET Summer School 34
foundational literacies 44
free schools 144
FREPA (Framework of Reference for Pluralistic Approaches) 66
Furlong, John 150–151
Furlong report 151–153; discussion on 153–154
'Future needs of learners in a European context' workshop 49–53, **50**, *51*
The future of learning: European teachers' visions (Ala-Muthka et al., 2010) 43

General Teaching Council of Scotland 151–152
Gilde, Judith 't 8

Global Citizenship Education Model 92
goals: of HOWBET Summer School 6, **33**; of teacher education 22; of UNESCO 61
Gobbo, Tamara 123–124
'good' schools 62–63
Gove, Michael 154
grading system, HOWBET Summer School **35**
grammar schools 144
Greenberg's diversity index 58
GTCS (General Teaching Council for Scotland) 149

Hartmann, Wilfried 8, 104–122
Havighurst, R.J. 77
Hechtius 107
heterogeneous groups 74
Hilker, Franz 108–109
Historic Comparative Education 106
history: of citizenship education 91–92; of comparative education 106–107
HOWBET Summer School 5–6, 71; assessment, criteria for **35**; 'Citizenship education in Europe' workshop 98–100, **98**, **99**; 'Comparative analysis in education' workshop 113–119, **115**, **116**, **117**, **118**; 'draw your own language tree' activity 67; EU guidelines 30–32; 'Future needs of learners in a European context' workshop 49–53, **50**, *51*; goals of **33**; grading system **35**; impact of 36–38; implementation 32–36, **32**, **33**, **34**, **35**, **36**; inclusive education workshop 81–84; language awareness and plurilingualism, promoting in teacher education 66–67; learning outcomes **33**; methodology used **33**; questionnaires for evaluation **36**; rationale behind 29–32; student demographics 32; topics **34**
HRE (human rights education) 88–91, 89–91, *89*; developing 97–100, **98**, **99**; principles in 96–97; *Resolution 23 on the youth policy of the Council of Europe* 92; *White paper on intercultural dialogue: Living together as equals* 92
human rights: inclusion 75–76; *see also* HRE (human rights education)
Human Rights Education Youth Programme 92

I Ching 106–107
ICT (Information and Communication Technology) 6
identifying learners' needs in the 21st century 44–45
Iespejama misija 48
ILD (Index of Language Diversity) 58
'imagined cultural communities' 130
immigrant children in European schools 61–63; intercultural education 63–64; stages of cultural awareness 64–65; underachievement of 62–63
impact of HOWBET Summer School 36–38
implementation: of HOWBET Summer School 32–36, **32**, **33**, **34**, **35**, **36**; of inclusive education 80–81
'The importance of teaching' white paper 145
improving teacher quality 16–17, 165–166
inclusion 8, 80–81, 84; in Austria 76–79; in Bosnia and Herzegovina 79; Convention of the United Nations on the Rights of Persons with Disabilities 71; HOWBET Summer School workshop 81–84; as human right and a philosophy 75–76; versus integration 72–75; National Action Plan for Disability 78; in Nigeria 79; in Pakistan 79; policy recommendations 169; Salamanca Declaration 72–73; teaching strategies 82–83; UNESCO guidelines 73
inclusive pedagogy 82
Index for inclusion (Booth & Ainscow, 2002) 73
individual pedagogy 82
Indo-European language family 58
induction programmes 11, 18–19; European guidelines for teacher education 17–19
informal induction programmes 18
Institute for Lifelong Learning 110
integrated model of immigrant school integration 61–62
integrated model of teacher education 47–48
integration: *Auch-Pädagogik* 73; of immigrant children in European schools 61–62; versus inclusion 72–75; of SEN children in Austria 78–79
intercultural competence 63

intercultural education 63
International Bureau of Education 110
International Conference on Education 64
International Education 105–106
International Review of Education 110
Internationale Zeitschrift für Erziehungswissenschaft 108
Internet, 'digital native' 45–46
IPs (Intensive Programmes) 5; *see also* Mobility IPs
ITE (Initial Teacher Education) 11; and lifelong learning 16–17; quality of 15–17; in Scotland 147–148; in Wales 150–151
ITT (Initial Teacher Training) 144, 157n1; Carter review of 146–147
Ivanova, Ilze 7, 40–56

James Report 144
Jeskanen, Seija 7, 57–70
Joined Report 31–32
journals 109
Jullien de Paris, Marc-Antoine 107
Juncker, Jean Claude 163
'just-in-time learning' 46

Kangro, Ilze 7, 40–56
Key data on teaching languages at school in Europe (European Commission/EACEA/Eurydice, 2017) 60
knowledge 42; '7Cs' 44; of the 21st century teacher 47–49; and competences 43
Kyrupedie 106

labelling, ability labelling 80–81
language competence of the European teacher 4
language diversity 57
language families 58
Latvia case study, competences of the 21st century teacher 47–49
LDI (Linguistic Diversity Index) 58
learners' needs in the 21st century: 'Future needs of learners in a European context' workshop 49–53, **50**, *51*; identifying 44–45; theoretical analysis of 41–44
learning, factors influencing 14–15
'Learning and living democracy for all' 91
Learning Compass 2030 12
learning outcomes: competences as 42; of HOWBET Summer School **33**

lessons from 'European dimension' studies: 'Discover Europe' lesson 129–132, **131**; 'Where are you from?' 124–129, *127*, **128**, **129**
lifelong learning 12, 20; *European qualifications framework for lifelong learning* (European Parliament and Council, 2008) 41–42; Institute for Lifelong Learning 110; of teachers 15–16
Lifelong Learning Programmes 4
linguistic diversity 57; CEFR 65; 'draw your own language tree' activity 67; ELP 65–66; FREPA 66; *Key data on teaching languages at school in Europe* (European Commission/EACEA/Eurydice, 2017) 60; languages in European schools 60–61; mother tongue-based early education 61; and teachers' work 63–65; VALEUR project 58–59
'local and global' 40
Lourenço, Mónica 3–10, 123–140, 161–174

Madalińska-Michalak, Joanna 7, 11–25
Marshall Plan 161
Maslow, Abraham 41
Matura 77
McIntyre, Joanna 9, 143–160
measuring achievement in secondary schools **115**
method of research, comparative education 111–112, *112*
methodology used in HOWBET Summer School **33**
mobility: ENTEP 4; ERASMUS 5; including in teacher preparation 166–167; teaching as mobile profession 20
Mobility IPs 5–6; HOWBET 5–6; *see also* HOWBET
models of teacher education 47–49
Monnet, Jean 161
Montesquieu 105
Moodle learning management system 34
moral education 106
Moreira, Filipe 123, 129
mother tongue-based early education 61
multicultural education 61–62
multiculturalism 59; as competence in the European dimension 4; 'two schools under one roof' 79

Multiculturalism Policy Index 59–60, **59**
multilingualism 58, 60
mutual learning process 63

National Action Plan for Disability 78
national-level provisioning of teacher education 16–17
NATO (North Atlantic Treaty Organization) 161
neoliberalism, 'culture of accountability' 5
'*new* teacher education' 154
New vision for education: Fostering social and emotional learning through technology (World Economic Forum, 2016) 44
Nigeria, inclusive education in 79
nine key competences of European teachers 32
non-formal induction programmes 18
Noored Kooli 48

objectives of ET 2010 and ET 2020 31
OECD (Organisation for Economic Co-Operation and Development): activities of 110–111, **111**; Learning Compass 2030 12; *Teachers matter* (2005) 13
Ofsted (Office for Standards in Education, Children's Services and Skills) 144; Carter review of ITT 146–147
Optional Protocol 75–76

Pakistan, inclusive education in 79
parents, role of teachers in supporting 13
parochial stage of cultural awareness 64–65
participatory stage of cultural awareness 64–65
partnerships: promoting 167; in teaching 21
pedagogical aim of ELP 65–66
pedagogy, comparative education 105–106
peer tutoring 83
PGCE (Postgraduate Certificate in Education) 145
PGDE (Postgraduate Diploma in Education) 147
philosophy of inclusion 75–76
phylogenetic diversity 58

PISA (Programme for International Student Assessment) 5, 110
plurilingualism 60; promoting in teacher education 66–67
policy: Carter review of ITT 146–147; collaboration, promoting 167; educating teachers for the 21st century 167–168; England, teacher education policy in 143–146; ENTEP 4, 29; European Commission documents 17–18; improving teacher quality, recommendations 165–166; inclusion 73; for inclusive education 169; mobility, including in teacher preparation 166–167; multilingualism as EU policy 58; preparing teachers for diversity 168–169; preparing teachers through citizenship education 169–170; raising awareness of comparative education 170; Scotland, teacher education policy in 147–148; strengthening teacher education 166; Wales, teacher education policy in 150–151
political dimension of citizenship education 89; *Standard Eurobarometer 85* survey 95–96
Portuguese school system 116–117, **116**, **117**
'The possible mission' 48
practice/follow-up: 'Backpacking through Central Europe' lesson 136–138, **137**, **138**; 'Discover Europe' lesson 132; 'Where are you from?' lesson **129**
preparatory classes 61
pre-service teacher education in England 144–145
Princess of Asturias Concord Award 163
principal, role of 62–63
principles: in European democratic citizenship and HRE 96–97; of intercultural education 64
professionalism: as competence in the European dimension 4, 21; CPD 11; 'European teacher' concept 30; and lifelong learning 15–16
proficiency: CEFR 65; language competence of the European teacher 4; in the mother tongue, importance of 61
profile of European teachers 19–22
promoting plurilingualism in teacher education 66–67

182 Index

provisioning teacher education at the national level 16–17
'pyramid of needs' 41

QTS (Qualified Teacher Status) 144
qualities of European education 20–21
quality of teacher education 15–17, 165–166
questionnaires for evaluation, HOWBET Summer School 36

raising awareness of comparative education 170
rationale behind HOWBET Summer School 29–32
recommendations: collaboration, promoting 167; conducting research on teacher education 170–171; educating teachers for the 21st century 167–168; of EU education policy documents 30–32; for improving teacher quality 165–166; for inclusive education 169; mobility, including in teacher preparation 166–167; preparing teachers for diversity 168–169; raising awareness of comparative education 170; for strengthening teacher education 166
Renkuosi mokyti 48
research: comparative education 111–113; conducting on teacher education 170–171
Resolution 23 on the youth policy of the Council of Europe 92
reviews of teacher education in Great Britain, discussion on 153–156
Robinson, Ken 45
Russell, James E. 108

Sadler, Sir Michael 107
Salamanca Declaration 72
Schleicher, Andreas 45
Schneider, Friedrich 108
School Direct 145
'school-led' teacher education 145, 154
schools: AHS 77; changing role of teachers in 12; in England 143–144; 'good' schools 62–63; immigrant children in European schools 61–63; languages in European schools 60–61; needs of learners, identifying 44–45; preparatory classes 61; principal, role of 62–63; segregation 62; special needs schools 71; 'two schools under one roof' 79; voluntary aided schools 144
Schratz, Michael 4, 19–20, 30, 47, 164–165
Schultz, Martin 163–164
Schuman, Robert 161
SCITT (School Centred Initial Teacher Training) 145
Scotland: CPD 149; discussion on teacher education policy in 153–156; Donaldson review of teacher education 148–150; teacher education policy in 147–148
Second Summit of Heads of State and Government of the Council of Europe 91
segregation 62
self-actualisation 41
self-transcendence 41
SEN teachers 74; implementing inclusive education 80–81
separated model of immigrant school integration 61–62
short-term impact of HOWBET Summer School 36–38
Simões, Ana Raquel 3–10, 88–103, 161–174
skills 42; '7Cs' 44; of the 21st century teacher 47–49; creativity 45; developmental tasks 77; discovery and interaction 63; foundational literacies 44; requirements for European citizenship 43; 'soft skills' 52; 'survival skills' 44; of teachers 63
social dimension of citizenship education 89; *Standard Eurobarometer 85* survey 95–96
'soft skills' 52
sonderpädagogischer Förderbedarf 78
special needs schools 71
stages of cultural awareness 64–65
Standard Eurobarometer 85 survey 95–96
strategies for inclusive education 82–83
strengthening teacher education 166
structural diversity 58
structure of teacher education in Europe 47
structure of this book 6–9
students: active learner engagement 13; character qualities 44; core competences 43; 'digital native' 45–46; of HOWBET Summer School 32; learners' needs in the 21st

century, theoretical analysis of 41–44; learning, factors influencing 14–15; role of teachers in supporting 12
Supporting teacher competence development for better learning outcomes (European Commission, 2013) 12, 17
Supporting teacher educators for better learning outcomes (European Commission, 2013b) 17
surveys, Eurobarometer survey data on European citizenship 95–96
'survival skills' 44
Sutherland Report 147
synergistic stage of cultural awareness 64–65

Tabberrer Review 150–151
tasks in 'Future needs of learners in a European context' workshop 50
Tazbir, Anna 123–124
Teach First 48, 145
Teach for America 48
teacher education 11; active learner engagement 13; Carter review of ITT 146–147; and citizenship 94–95; *Common European principles for teacher competences and qualifications* (European Commission, 2005) 20–21; conducting research on 170–171; culturally responsive teaching 61–62; Donaldson review of 148–150; England, teacher education policy in 143–146; European Commission, role in 17–18; European guidelines for 17–19; goals of 22; improving the quality of 16–17; induction programs 18–19; Latvia case study 47–49; Learning Compass 2030 12; and lifelong learning 12, 15–16; mobility, including in teacher preparation 166–167; models of 47–49; national-level provisioning 16–17; 'new teacher education' 154; plurilingualism, promoting 66–67; for prospective teachers 18; quality of 15–17; reviews of in Great Britain, discussion on 153–156; 'school-led' 145, 154; Scotland, teacher education policy in 147–148; strengthening 166; structure of in Europe 47; *Supporting teacher competence development for better learning outcomes* (European Commission, 2013) 12; Wales, teacher education policy in 150–151; *see also* teachers
teachers: challenges of the 'European teacher' 164–165; changing role of in the 21st century 11–15; developmental tasks 77; educating for the 21st century 167–168; eTwinning Conference 43; and inclusive education 80–81; intercultural competence 63; learners' needs in the 21st century, theoretical analysis of 41–44; and linguistic diversity 63–65; profile of European teachers 19–22; 'quality' of 15, 165–166; roles of the four major players 15; skills of 63; student learning, influence on 14–15
Teachers matter (OECD, 2005) 13
teaching European democratic citizenship 96–97
technology, 'digital native' 45–46
Terralingua 58
tertium comparationis 112–113
themes in this book 6–9
theoretical analysis of learners' needs in the 21st century 41–44
theoretical background: 'Backpacking through Central Europe' lesson **132**, 134–135, **133**, **134**; 'Discover Europe' lesson 129–130; 'Where are you from?' lesson 124–125
topics of the HOWBET Summer School **34**
Towards inclusive schools (Clark, Dyson, & Millward, 1995) 72
training 157n1; Carter review of ITT 146–147; 'school-led' teacher education 145
transformability 81
transversal skills of European teachers 32
Treaties of Rome 162
trust 81
'two schools under one roof' 79
two-groups-theory 74
types of research in comparative education 112–113

UN (United Nations): 2030 Agenda 42; Agenda 21 42; Convention on the Rights of Persons with Disabilities 71; Convention on the Rights of the Child 75–76; *World population prospects: The 2015 revision* (UN, 2015b) 40

underachievement of immigrant children in European schools 62–63
UNESCO (UN Educational Scientific and Cultural Organization) 43; activities of 110–111, **111**; Global Citizenship Education Model 92; goals of 61; guidelines for inclusion 76; inclusion 73; International Conference on Education 64
universities 109
Uralic language family 58

VALEUR (Valuing All Languages in Europe) project 58–59
values 90; *Standard Eurobarometer 85* survey 95–96
van Rompuy, Herman 162–163
voluntary aided schools 144

Wales: *Curriculum for Wales – A curriculum for life* (Welsh Government, 2017) 155; discussion on teacher education policy in 153–156; Furlong report 151–153; teacher education policy in 150–151
'Where are you from?' lesson: description of 126–127; overview 125; practice/follow-up 128–129, **128**, **129**; theoretical background 124–125
White paper on intercultural dialogue: Living together as equals 92
World Conference on Special Needs Education: Access and Quality 72
World Economic Forum 44, 75–76
World population prospects: The 2015 revision (UN, 2015b) 40

Xenophon 106